LOWERING SUICIDE RISK IN RETURNING TROOPS

NATO Science for Peace and Security Series

This Series presents the results of scientific meetings supported under the NATO Programme: Science for Peace and Security (SPS).

The NATO SPS Programme supports meetings in the following Key Priority areas: (1) Defence Against Terrorism; (2) Countering other Threats to Security and (3) NATO, Partner and Mediterranean Dialogue Country Priorities. The types of meeting supported are generally "Advanced Study Institutes" and "Advanced Research Workshops". The NATO SPS Series collects together the results of these meetings. The meetings are co-organized by scientists from NATO countries and scientists from NATO's "Partner" or "Mediterranean Dialogue" countries. The observations and recommendations made at the meetings, as well as the contents of the volumes in the Series, reflect those of participants and contributors only; they should not necessarily be regarded as reflecting NATO views or policy.

Advanced Study Institutes (ASI) are high-level tutorial courses to convey the latest developments in a subject to an advanced-level audience.

Advanced Research Workshops (ARW) are expert meetings where an intense but informal exchange of views at the frontiers of a subject aims at identifying directions for future action.

Following a transformation of the programme in 2006 the Series has been re-named and re-organised. Recent volumes on topics not related to security, which result from meetings supported under the programme earlier, may be found in the NATO Science Series.

The Series is published by IOS Press, Amsterdam, and Springer Science and Business Media, Dordrecht, in conjunction with the NATO Public Diplomacy Division.

Sub-Series

A.	Chemistry and Biology	Springer Science and Business Media
B.	Physics and Biophysics	Springer Science and Business Media
C.	Environmental Security	Springer Science and Business Media
D.	Information and Communication Security	IOS Press
E.	Human and Societal Dynamics	IOS Press

http://www.nato.int/science
http://www.springer.com
http://www.iospress.nl

Sub-Series E: Human and Societal Dynamics – Vol. 42   ISSN 1874-6276

Lowering Suicide Risk in Returning Troops

Wounds of War

Edited by

Brenda K. Wiederhold

Virtual Reality Medical Center, San Diego, CA, USA
Virtual Reality Medical Institute, Brussels, Belgium

IOS
Press

Amsterdam • Berlin • Oxford • Tokyo • Washington, DC

Published in cooperation with NATO Public Diplomacy Division

Proceedings of the NATO Advanced Research Workshop on Wounds of War: Lowering Suicide
Risk in Returning Troops
Brussels, Belgium
14–18 October 2007

ISBN 978-1-58603-889-2
Library of Congress Control Number: 2008931545

Publisher
IOS Press
Nieuwe Hemweg 6B
1013 BG Amsterdam
Netherlands
fax: +31 20 687 0019
e-mail: order@iospress.nl

Distributor in the UK and Ireland
Gazelle Books Services Ltd.
White Cross Mills
Hightown
Lancaster LA1 4XS
United Kingdom
fax: +44 1524 63232
e-mail: sales@gazellebooks.co.uk

Distributor in the USA and Canada
IOS Press, Inc.
4502 Rachael Manor Drive
Fairfax, VA 22032
USA
fax: +1 703 323 3668
e-mail: iosbooks@iospress.com

Preface

This Advanced Research Workshop (ARW), "Wounds of War: Lowering Suicide Risk in Returning Troops," was convened to discuss the topic of increased suicide risk in service men and women around the world. Research has shown that those who have served in both combat missions and peacekeeping operations are at an increased risk for suicide. Research suggests that this may result from their "wounds of war". Some wounds may be more "invisible"; such as depression, posttraumatic stress disorder, and chronic pain, while others are more visibly apparent; such as physical disabilities. Whatever the wound, however, it seems they may all lead to an increased risk of suicide.

During this workshop, we discussed many aspects of military suicide and how to more effectively deal with this issue. Specifically, some of the questions addressed were:

1. How do we detect those who are vulnerable to increased suicide risk, possibly due to a combination of genetics and past environmental insults?
2. How do we most appropriately assess for increased risk?
3. Once detected, how do we help to decrease that risk?
4. Are there pre-deployment training methods we can employ to help "inoculate" individuals against increased risk?
5. Are there in-theater and post-deployment methods most appropriate for dealing with this risk?

Through this workshop, we have come closer to understanding what programs are already in place in various countries for detection, assessment, prevention, and treatment. We have begun to learn from these existing plans and can start to formulate a more common set of best practices and guidelines which can be implemented throughout organizations in all our countries; having as our common goal to always seek to serve our service members more effectively.

This Advanced Research Workshop has given participants an opportunity to foster essential international collaborative research on military suicide, a common and disabling consequence of war, terrorism, and natural disasters. As a result, it represents an important landmark in efforts to help soldiers and civilians of NATO and partner nations become more resilient in the face of international conflict.

This publication, which contains full papers focused on the key presentations during the workshop, acts as the permanent record of this event; a tangible documentation of the ideas that formed the basis of discussion and collaboration at the workshop. This text is organized to mirror the program from the event so as to provide an overview of the ideas of presenters and participants in the ARW.

Financial support for the workshop was provided by several sponsors. Great thanks to the primary funder, the NATO Security through Science Programme. In addition, we would like to acknowledge the generous contributions of the Telemedicine and Advanced Technology Research Center (TATRC) of the U.S. Army, as well as the Austrian Ministry of Defence (MoD).

The workshop was organized and this accompanying publication was compiled and edited jointly by the Interactive Media Institute, San Diego, California, USA and Interactive Media Institute-Europe (IMI-E), Brussels, Belgium. Professor Brenda K. Wiederhold, program co-chair, conceived the overall design of the workshop and recruited co-chairs Professor Dragica Kozarić Kovačić, of the University Hospital Dubrava in Zagreb, Croatia, and Professor Kresimir Cosic, of University of Zagreb and the Croatian Parliament to help with the event. With the assistance of her co-chairs, Dr. Wiederhold selected and invited the majority of the speakers and participants, and conference coordinators Ruth Kogen, MFA and Magda Horodyska, M.S. organized logistics including registration, travel, lodging and meals, assembling of workshop materials, and other arrangements for the ARW. Professor Dragica Kozarić Kovačić and Professor Cosic extended invitations to several distinguished international speakers, further improving the quality of the workshop. Mag. Christian Marolt uncovered the beautiful Austrian location where the event took place and Astrid Mentzik was responsible for the artistic design of all event-related materials. Sinisa Popovic, Faculty of Electrical Engineering and Computing, University of Zagreb, served as the event's photographer. Ms. Kogen along with McKinley Tolliver reviewed the conference program and full manuscripts, helping with editing and assembly of this and other associated texts.

Editorial

Brenda K. WIEDERHOLD, Ph.D., MBA, BCIA
Interactive Media Institute &
Interactive Media Institute-Europe

Introduction

Thirty-nine scientists and representatives from NATO and Partner countries met in Klopeiner See, Südkärnten, Austria on 14–17 October 2007 for a three-day NATO Advanced Research Workshop entitled *"Wounds of War: Lowering Suicide Risk in Returning Troops."* Formal scientific presentations were delivered by experts from 18 different countries who were invited to take part in the workshop.

The workshop was divided into five scientific sessions:

1. "Vulnerability to Suicidal Behavior" – concentrating on the biological as well as psycho-social determinants of suicidality.
2. "Diagnostic and Assessment Issues" – discussing pre-deployment screening and the integrative diagnostic model for suicidality.
3. "Prevention" – presenting prevention programs from Croatia, Lithuania, the Netherlands, Poland, Italy and the U.S. In addition, an in-depth study of soldiers who committed suicide was discussed.
4. "Treatment" – addressing Pharmacotherapy, Psychotherapy and support issues. During the session the importance of personalized messages and proactive attitudes of psychiatrists and psychologists working with soldiers was underlined.
5. "Increased Suicide with Comorbid Disorders" – looking at Traumatic Brain Injury (TBI) as well as posttraumatic stress disorder (PTSD), aggression, impulsivity and stress events before suicide.

Papers and Presentations

Presenters were invited to submit a full paper for publication in this volume in order to enable those who could not attend the workshop to become educated about the serious issue of suicide in our troops. Their papers, in-depth descriptions of their presentations, are described briefly below.

The first section, "Vulnerability to Suicidal Behavior," discusses the risk factors that make troops susceptible to committing suicide. The opening paper by Professor Nela Pivac of Croatia covers the neurobiology involved in suicidal behavior. Pivac and colleagues point out that since most psychiatric patients never attempt suicide, there are factors other than neurobiology at play in those with suicidal behavior. Though biological and genetic contributions to suicide are still not completely understood, suicidal behavior is assumed to involve changes in neurotransmitter and neuroendocrine systems.

Next, Kostovic, Culjat, and Judas of Croatia present their paper, "Brain Structure and Plasticity: Relation to Suicidality." They assert that three major fronto-limbic circuits must be studied in order to determine the biological correlates of suicidal behavior. Abnormalities have been documented in the neuroimaging studies of those who have attempted suicide, and these abnormalities may involve different levels of circuitry within the brain. Through understanding the neurobiology behind suicidal behavior, the authors hope to succeed in reducing suicides in all populations.

After that, Sareen et al. of Canada and the United States review the literature on the prevalence of mental disorders and the perceived barriers to seeking and receiving care in military samples. They assert that like civilian population samples, the few studies of military samples reveal that the majority of soldiers who meet criteria for a mental disorder do not receive mental health treatment or even feel that they need treatment. Attitudinal barriers appear to be the largest obstacle to receiving and seeking care, while structural barriers are a lesser concern.

The second section continues with diagnostic and assessment issues concerning troops who are at risk of suicidal behavior. First, Col. Castro and colleagues from the United States Army examine the suicides of soldiers who are serving or have served in Iraq. The authors present the Mental Health Advisory Team (MHAT) IV, a group whose mission is to assess Soldier and Marine mental health and well-being, examine the delivery of behavioral health care in Operation Iraqi Freedom (OIF), and provide recommendations for sustainment and improvement to command. Results from large surveys of soldiers and Marines and how these findings might be used to reduce suicidal behavior are discussed.

Subsequently, Professor Dragica Kozarić-Kovačić and colleagues from Croatia present an integrative diagnostic model for PTSD and suicidality in returning troops. Since suicide is one of the top ten causes of death in most countries, creating a negative impact both on families of victims and their environment, the authors assert, it is important to diagnose or prevent suicidal behavior before it occurs. Since the underlying factors of suicide vary, and include both genetic and environmental aspects, this can be a difficult task. The paper reviews actual epidemiological data on suicidal behavior in both Europe overall and then specifically in Croatia, and discusses the authors' experiences in the diagnostic process. Some predictors of suicidality from the group's previous studies in PTSD patients are indicated. They also show preliminary algorithms for predicting suicidal behavior using data mining methods.

The third section of this volume discusses suicide prevention. Professor Krešimir Ćosić et al. from Croatia propose an interdisciplinary joint approach to suicide prevention in the military population. They analyze the impact of stress and untreated mental disorders on this population, and examine the role of military training and leadership in protecting troops from the combat-related stress that can cause mental distress. The authors emphasize the need for an interdisciplinary approach and joint institutional efforts in preventing and alleviating psychological suffering and put forward an integrated strategy for suicidal risk detection and prevention.

Later, a paper by Lapenaite and Vaicaitiene from Lithuania offers a description of the prevention measures against suicide that are established in the Lithuanian Armed Forces. Despite the fact that the suicide rate in Lithuania has recently decreased, it still remains one of the highest in Europe. Though there have been few cases of suicide in the Lithuanian Armed Forces since data began being recorded in 1993, research findings indicate a higher than average prevalence of suicidal behavior among servicemen; their low level of knowledge about suicides, inappropriate attitude toward suicides, but positive view on suicide prevention in the military have become the basis for the Program of Psychological support in the Lithuanian Armed Forces. The Program, which includes a wide spectrum of prevention measures (training, education, psychological support for servicemen and their families, additional care of personnel with psychological problems and/or the risk of suicide, monitoring of servicemen's psychological wellbeing), is currently in progress, and the efficiency of this program is assessed.

MAJ Todd M. Yosick of the United States Army next details a program for suicide prevention in the U.S. Army. The program, named BattleMind, was developed to be a collaborative effort at building Soldier resiliency through all phases of the deployment cycle, life cycle, and support cycle of military service. Yosick states that Battlemind can be defined as a Soldier's inner strength, helping them to face adversity and fear in combat with confidence.

Professor Stanislaw Ilnicki of Poland then discusses suicide prevention in Polish veterans of multinational missions. This paper presents outcomes of research on veterans of multinational missions and military operations within the UN, OSCE, EU and NATO mandate, and discusses suicide risk among soldiers serving both in country and abroad. Ilnicki also presents the combat stress disorders prevention system established in the Polish armed forces, revealing successes and lessons from its implementation.

Finally, Riva et al. from Italy present the innovative idea of using mobile narratives on cell phones as a tool for combating battlefield stress. The idea comes from research that indicates that one of the best strategies for dealing with stress is learning to practice relaxation. These mobile narratives, provided on PDAs or cellular phones, use multimedia to provide advanced coping techniques suitable to the combat context. The authors present the rationale of the approach, a preliminary test of the proposed method, and a protocol for its use on the battlefield.

The fourth section focuses on treatment of patients with suicidal ideation. Henigsberg and colleagues, again from Croatia, discuss pharmacotherapy for suicidal patients with comorbid Posttraumatic Stress Disorder (PTSD). Since the rate of comorbidity in patients with PTSD is incredibly high (especially with major depressive disorder and substance abuse), and there is a dearth of randomized controlled trials for the treatment of suicidal ideation in PTSD, it is not clear if suicidality in PTSD patients is predominantly caused by core PTSD symptoms or by co-morbid disorders. Though selective serotonin reuptake inhibitors are widely used in PTSD treatment, there is some evidence that they can increase the risk of suicidal thoughts and behaviors, most dramatically in younger age groups. In their paper, the authors discuss the use of drugs for treatment of PTSD, and their effect on suicidality.

Next, Dedic, Panic, and Djurdjevic from Serbia talk about suicide in veterans of wars that took place in the territory of former Yugoslavia. The aim of the study was to describe the wounds of war in veterans and professional staff participating in wars, and suggest preventive measures to help improve the Suicide Prevention Program in the modern Army of Serbia. Through psychological autopsy on patients who had committed suicide, the authors found that suicidal veterans have positive psychiatric heredity, more intensively practice bodybuilding, and were more often punished due to problems at work. During pre-suicidal days, these subjects also manifested isolation. Four risk factors were found to be the most influential in suicide in returning troops: the past enviromental factors (taking part in wars), exogenic (punishments at work), endogenic (genetic) and behavioral (early recognition of presuicidal syndrome).

Belgian Senior Captain John Deheegher explains how to organize support for the bereaved service members in the emotional aftermath of suicide. The Centre for Mental

Health (CMH of the Military Hospital Queen Astrid, Brussels) of the Belgian Armed Forces has developed a structured crisis intervention program to help the military unit to better cope with the suicide of one of its members. The program works to prevent further damage following suicide by enhancing emotional support for bereaved colleagues and identifying colleagues at risk for the development of psycho-social difficulties following the suicide of another. Deheegher discusses the various aspects of the "postvention trajectory of care" in his paper.

To round out the section, Ilnicki et al. describe meetings of Polish veterans of the Iraq war. Items discussed in this paper include suicide risk among soldiers serving both in country and abroad, selected legal issues, and the organization of the combat stress disorders prevention system in the Polish armed forces. The authors present detailed information about pre-deployment suicide prevention, treatment and support during deployment and intervention after returning home.

At the end of the meeting several participants presented on the co-morbid disorders that often accompany suicidal ideation or behavior. In the first paper, Pregelj et al. of Slovenia describe the aggression and impulsivity often seen in veterans in the month before they commit or attempt suicide. Despite the training and prevention measures in place to prevent stress-related reactions (including suicide) in troops, evidence is mounting that deployment-related exposure to stress events is associated with mental health problems and suicidal behavior. The aim of the authors' study was to evaluate negative life events, aggression, and impulsivity of suicide victims in the month before a suicide. Findings indicated that suicide victims with previous aggressive behavior have a higher number of negative life events that occur in the month before suicide, and that these subjects also express higher impulsivity than others. This suggests that veterans fitting this profile should be more closely monitored for suicidal ideation.

To finish, Wiederhold and Wiederhold review results from their studies utilizing Virtual Reality (VR) as an adjunct for training and treatment of troops. The authors provide information on VR-enhanced Stress Inoculation Training (SIT), which can be used pre-deployment to provide troops (e.g. combat medics, flight medics, tactical forces) with skill sets to accomplish their tasks, and with coping mechanisms for performing under stress. Post-deployment, VR exposure is a useful tool to enhance traditional cognitive-behavioral therapy protocols for treating PTSD, a disorder that increases suicide risk in troops. In addition, VR is being successfully employed as an adjunct to traditional treatments for those with both acute and chronic pain (due to psychological or physical wounds of war), and for help in rehabilitating those who have sustained physical, cognitive or neurological injuries during combat.

Finally, the volume includes a copy of abstracts from all presentations given at the ARW.

Work Groups

In addition to the presentations, the workshop provided ample opportunities for informal discussions and brainstorming. As part of the meeting, four specialized work groups were convened on the second day to allow participants to examine in greater detail the research presented in the fields of Vulnerability, Diagnosis and Assessment, Prevention, and Treatment Issues. These Work Groups were lead by Professor Dr. Nela Pivac, Dr. Mark Zamorski, Professor Dr. Elbert Geuze, and Captain Dr. Robert Koffman respectively and encouraged informal debate and discussion in the hopes of creating new ideas and solutions for the problem of suicide in returning troops. Work group leaders presented summaries of their discussions to the entire conference on the final day, and time was provided for whole-group discussion concerning the findings.

Summary

The ultimate aim of the ARW was to critically assess the existing knowledge and to identify directions for future actions. Experts who presented their findings seem to indicate that those who have served both in combat missions and peacekeeping operations are at an increased risk for suicide.

Final conclusions reached by participants at the conference indicate that: 1) In-depth research with larger sample sizes is necessary to determine more effective methods of suicide prevention; 2) Countries must work together to pool research on both prevention and treatment strategies for dealing with at risk active duty and veteran populations; 3) Additional workshops must be convened for a more detailed discussion of each "wound of war". Specialized workshop topics recommended were PTSD, traumatic brain injury, chronic pain, physical disability, substance abuse, and impact of combat on military families and relationships.

Co-Chairs

Professor Brenda K. Wiederhold PhD, MBA, BCIA
Interactive Media Institute
Interactive Media Institute-Europe
Rue de la Loi, 28/7
B-1040 Brussels
Belgium
Tel: +32 2 286 8505   Fax: +32 2 286 8508
E-mail: office@imi-europe.eu

Professor Dragica Kozarić Kovačić, MD, PhD
University Hospital Dubrava
Department of Psychiatry
Referral Centre for Stress-related Disorders of the Ministry of Health
Regional Centre for Psychotrauma Zagreb
Avenija Gojka Šuška 6, 10 000 Zagreb, Croatia.
Tel: +385 1 290 26 18   Fax: +385 1 290 37 00
E-mail: dkozaric kovacic@yahoo.com

Professor Kresimir Cosic, PhD
University of Zagreb
Faculty of Electrical Engineering & Computing
Head of the Delegation to the NATO Parliamentary Assembly
Croatian Parliament
E-mail: kcosic@sabor.sabor.hr

Main Lectures/Presentations Given

Session I: Vulnerability to Suicidal Behavior

"Biological Markers in Croatian Veterans with Increased Suicidality"
Professor Dr. Nela Pivac

"Brain Structure and Plasticity: Relation to Suicidality"
Professor Dr. Ivica Kostovic

"Combat and Peacekeeping Operations in Relation to Prevalence of Mental Disorders and Perceived Need for Mental Health Care"
Professor Dr. Jitender Sareen

"Psycho-social determinants of deliberate self-harm in young Ukrainian soldiers"
Professor Dr. Vsevolod Rozanov

Session II: Diagnostic and Assessment Issues

"A Review of the U.S. Army Soldier Suicides in Iraq"
Col. Carl A. Castro

"Integrative Diagnostic Model for PTSD and Suicidality"
Professor Dr. Dragica Kozarić Kovačić

"Findings of an Intensive Pre-deployment Screening Program in the Canadian Forces"
Dr. Mark Zamorski

"Psychological Health and Screening in the UK Armed Forces"
Dr. Neil Greenberg

Session III: Prevention

"Getting the basics right: Lessons from an in-depth study of soldiers who attempt suicide in the British Army"
Dr. Michael Crawford

"Interdisciplinary Joint Approach to Suicide Prevention of Warfighters"
Professor Dr. Kresimir Cosic

"Lowering Suicide Risk: Situation and Prevention Measures in Lithuanian Armed Forces"
Captain Danute Lapenaite

"Lowering the Psychological Impact of Deployment: the importance of prospective research"
Professor Dr. Elbert Geuze

"Prevention of Suicides in the U.S. Army"
Maj. Todd M. Yosick

"Suicide prevention among Polish veterans of the multinational operations"
Professor Dr. Stanislaw Ilnicki

"Mobile narratives for combating battlefield stress: Rationale and preliminary research"
Professor Dr. Alessandra Gorini

"Suicide after deployment in UN peacekeeping missions – a Danish pilot study"
Lt. Col. Dr. Hans O. Jörgensen

Session IV: Treatment

"Pharmacotherapy of Suicidal PTSD Patients"
Professor Dr. Neven Henigsberg

"Importance of Psychotherapeutic Intervention in the Crisis Following Suicide in the Army of Serbia"
Professor Dr. Gordana Dedic

"Suicide of a service member: how to organize support for the bereaved in the emotional aftermath"
Dr. John Deheegher

"Completed suicide and suicidal ideation in Norwegian peacekeepers"
Dr. Siri Thoresen

"Understanding combat trauma - the psychotherapeutic meetings of Iraqi veterans"
Maciej Zbyszewski, M.S.

"Measures of lowering suicide risks in the Austrian armed forces"
Col. MSc. Christian Langer

"Treatment is More Effective with a Patient: Reducing the Stigma of Help-Seeking Behavior through Context and Content"
LCDR Dr. Aaron Werbel

Session V: Increased Suicide with Comorbid Disorders

"Traumatic Brain Injury in the United States Military"
Captain Dr. Robert Koffman

"Family homicide-suicide of a military man: a case analysis"
Dr. Merike Sisask

"Aggression, impulsivity and stress events in the month before suicide"
Assistant Professor Dr. Peter Pregelj

"Virtual Reality as an Adjunct for Training and Treatment"
Professor Dr. Brenda K. Wiederhold

Sponsors

Workshop organizers Interactive Media Institute and Interactive Media Institute-Europe would like to thank the sponsors of this Advanced Research Workshop, listed below. Without their support this event could not have taken place.

North Atlantic Treaty Organization (NATO)

Telemedicine and Advanced Technology Research Center

Austrian Ministry of Defence (MOD)

Contents

Section I. Vulnerability to Suicidal Behavior

Section II. Diagnostic and Assessment Issues

Section III. Prevention

Section IV. Treatment

Section V. Increased Suicide with Co-Morbid Disorders

Section I

Vulnerability to Suicidal Behavior

doi:10.3233/978-1-58603-889-2-3

Neurobiology of Suicidal Behavior

Nela PIVAC[a][1], Dragica KOZARIĆ-KOVAČIĆ[b], Gordana NEDIĆ[a], Maja MUSTAPIĆ[a],
Tamara STIPČEVIĆ[a], Korona NENADIĆ-ŠVIGLIN[c], Mirjana GRUBIŠIĆ-ILIĆ[b],
Dorotea MÜCK-ŠELER[a]

[a]*Division of Molecular Medicine, Rudjer Boskovic Institute, Bijenička cesta 54, HR-
10002 Zagreb, Croatia,*
[b]*Referral Centre of the Ministry of Health and Social Welfare of the Republic of
Croatia for Stress Related Disorders, Department of Psychiatry, Dubrava University
Hospital, Avenija Gojka Šuška 12, HR-10000 Zagreb, Croatia,*
[c]*Centre for Alcoholism and other Addictions, Psychiatric Hospital Vrapče, Bolnička
cesta 12, HR-10000 Zagreb, Croatia*

Abstract: Suicide is a major social and public health problem, one of the leading
causes of death, a major complication of different psychiatric disorders that can
evoke great suffering in patients and their families, and places a financial burden
on society as a whole. Suicidal behavior and suicide are frequently associated with
various psychiatric disorders and personality traits. However, most psychiatric
patients never attempt suicide, indicating that aside from psychiatric diagnoses,
other socio-cultural, environmental, biological and genetic factors are important
risk factors for suicide. The biological and genetic contributions to suicide are still
not completely understood, and the heterogeneity of the underlying neurobiology
makes such investigations particularly difficult. Molecular basis of suicidal
behavior is assumed to involve the changes in different neurotransmitter and
neuroendocrine systems (primarily in the serotonergic and noradrenergic systems,
the activity of the hypothalamic-pituitary-adrenal axis (HPA). Therefore, research
on suicide, which is the major and the most dramatic consequence of suicidal
behavior, should be linked to biological characteristics of suicidal behavior, to find
biomarkers that might predict suicidal behavior, in order to prevent suicide.

Key words: Suicidal behavior, Posttraumatic Stress Disorder, Depression,
Alcoholism, Psychosis, Neurobiology, Hypothalamic-pituitary-adrenal axis, War
veterans, Biological markers, Platelet serotonin, Platelet monoamine oxidase,
Plasma cortisol, Plasma dopamine beta hydroxylase

---

[1] The corresponding author: Nela Pivac, DVM, PhD, senior scientist, Division of Molecular Medicine,
Rudjer Boskovic Institute, PO Box 180, HR-10002 Zagreb, Croatia, Tel: 385 1 4571 207; Fax: 385 1 456
1010; e-mail: npivac@irb.hr

Introduction

Suicidal behavior

Suicide is a major social and public health problem, one of the leading causes of death, which significantly increases the death toll worldwide. According to the WHO, suicide accounts for almost 2% of deaths in the world [1, 2]. Suicide is a major complication of the different psychiatric disorders that can evoke great suffering in patients and their families, and carries a financial burden on society as a whole. However, most psychiatric patients never attempt suicide, indicating the importance of other factors, a diathesis or predisposition to suicidal behavior, proposed by Mann, that are not related to psychiatric illness [3].

Neurobiological factors in suicide

The role of neurobiological factors involved in suicide is far from clear, and therefore the research on the factors that contribute to suicidal behavior and suicide encompasses both biological and psychological aspects of the suicidal individual. It has been suggested that suicidal behavior and suicide are products of a combination of biological factors that are heritable, environmental factors to which the individual is exposed, and psychological and clinical risk factors. The biological and genetic contributions to suicide are still not completely understood, and the heterogeneity of the underlying neurobiology makes such investigations particularly difficult. Suicidal behavior and suicide are frequently associated with divergent psychiatric disorders and personality traits. Psychiatric disorders including major depressive disorder, mood disorders, borderline personality disorder, disruptive behavior disorders, alcohol and drug use disorders, anxiety disorders, anorexia nervosa, and schizophrenia, are well-established risk factors for suicide. In addition, some traits such as hopelessness, social isolation, aggression, and ineffectiveness have also been associated with suicide [2, 4].

Molecular basis of suicidal behavior is assumed to involve the changes in different neurotransmitter and neuroendocrine systems (primarily in the serotonergic, dopaminergic and noradrenergic systems, and in the activity of the hypothalamic-pituitary-adrenal axis (HPA) in basal conditions and after a challenge with the administration of dexamethasone in the dexamethasone suppression test (DST), in the neurotropic factors, such as brain derived neurotropic factor, and in addition, there are a lot of inconsistent data regarding the role of cholesterol in suicidal behavior [3-7].

Therefore, the research on the biological risk factors of suicide, which is a major and the most dramatic consequence of suicidal behavior, should be linked to biological characteristics of suicide, in order to find biomarkers that could be used as a predictors of suicidal behavior.

With the aim of improving our knowledge on the biological basis of suicidal behavior, the goal of the present study was to assess the biological factors which might be used to predict suicidal behavior in different psychiatric patients. The hypothesis was that peripheral markers will help us to identify patients with suicidal behavior to be able to properly treat these suicidal patients in order to prevent suicide.

1. Materials and Methods

1.1. Participants

Participants were male medication-free subjects.

War veterans with combat-related posttraumatic stress disorder (PTSD), had current and chronic PTSD, diagnosed using the Structured Clinical Interview (SCID) for DSM-IV [8] based on DSM-IV Disorders [9], the Clinician Administered PTSD Scale (CAPS) [10], and the Hamilton Rating Scale for Depression-17 (HDRS) [11]. The patients were recruited from October 2001-March 2005 from the Referral Centre for Stress-related Disorders of the University Hospital Dubrava in Zagreb, Croatia. The assessments and ratings (SCID, CAPS, and HDRS) were conducted by psychiatrists with extensive experience in stress-related disorders.

Psychiatric patients with diagnoses other than PTSD (depression, psychosis, acute stress disorder, personality disorders, and other diagnoses), diagnosed using the SCID for DSM-IV, were recruited from October 2001- March 2005 from the Referral Centre for Stress-related Disorders of the University Hospital Dubrava in Zagreb, Croatia.

Alcoholic patients with diagnosis of alcohol dependency were diagnosed using SCID for DSM-IV criteria by the experienced psychiatrists in the Psychiatric Hospital Vrapce, Center for Alcoholism and Other Addictions. Patients were admitted to this hospital due to withdrawal syndrome related to alcohol dependency. Most patients were acutely intoxicated with alcohol. Therefore, the interview and the blood sampling were done when the patients were sober, i.e. 10 hours after admission to the department. All patients were evaluated with the HDRS.

All patients, diagnosed using the SCID, were categorized according to suicidal behavior into suicidal and non-suicidal patients, based on the scores in item 3 (suicide) from the HDRS 17-item scale [12]. Non-suicidal subjects had 0 scores (which indicates absence of any suicidal thoughts or ideation), while suicidal subjects had ≥ 1 scores. Suicidal patients were patients with a score of 1 (a person feels life is not worth living), a score of 2 (a person wishes he/she was dead or has any thoughts of possible death to him/herself), a score of 3 (a person has suicide ideas or gestures), or a score of 4 (a person attempted suicide).

All patients were medication-naïve or medication-free for at least 2 weeks, and had not taken selective serotonin reuptake inhibitors (SSRI) during the previous 6 weeks.

Patients were categorized also according to the results of the DST into suppressors and non-suppressors. Non-suppression to DST (or abnormal DST test result) was defined when plasma cortisol levels exceeded 138 nmol/L after 1 mg of dexamethasone administered at 23.00.

Inclusion criteria for other patients: all participants fulfilled the questionnaire answering the questions about their medical history, drinking and smoking habits. Written informed consent was obtained from all participants, under procedures approved by Ethics Committee of the University Hospital Dubrava, Zagreb, Croatia and Psychiatric Hospital Vrapče, Zagreb. Groups were matched on mean age, education, and drug status.

1.2. Biochemical determinations

Blood (8 ml) was drawn from cubical vein at 8:00 a.m. in a plastic syringe with 2 ml of acid citrate dextrose (ACD) anticoagulant. Platelet-rich-plasma (PRP) was obtained by centrifugation (935 x g) for 70 seconds at room temperature. Platelets were sedimented by further centrifugation of PRP at 10,000 x g for 5 minutes. Platelets were destroyed by sonication (20 kHz, amplitude 8 x 10^{-3} mm for 30 sec). The platelet pellet was washed with saline and centrifuged again.

Platelet serotonin (5-hydroxytryptamine, 5-HT) concentration was determined by the spectrofluorimetric method, as described previously [13]. Platelet protein was determined by the method of Lowry et al. [14]. Platelet monoamine oxidase (MAO-B) activity was determined by the spectrofluorimetric method, using kynuramine as a substrate, by a slight modification of the method of Krajl [15], as previously described [16]. Plasma dopamine-beta-hydroxylase (DBH) activity was determined by a photometric assay, using tyramine as a substrate, by the method of Nagatsu and Udenfriend [18]. Plasma cortisol levels were measured using a radioimmunoassay kit (Diagnostic Products Corporation, USA) with detection limit of 5.5 nmol/l, and with intra- and inter-assay coefficients of variation of 4.7% and 5.2%, respectively, as described previously [13]. Plasma cortisol levels were determined before DST at 8:00 a.m., and 9 or 17 hours later, i.e. at 08:00 a.m. and at 4.00 p.m.

1.3. Statistical analysis

Statistical evaluation of the results, expressed as means ± SD, was performed using one-way analysis of variance (ANOVA), followed by a Tukey's multiple comparison test, using Sigmastat 2.0 (Jandell Scientific Corp. San Raphael, California, USA) and SPSS 10.0 for Windows. The correlations were determined by a Pearson's coefficient of correlation (r). The significance was accepted when p<0.05.

2. Results

Figure 1. Platelet serotonin concentration in male war veterans with combat-related PTSD with or without suicidal behavior.

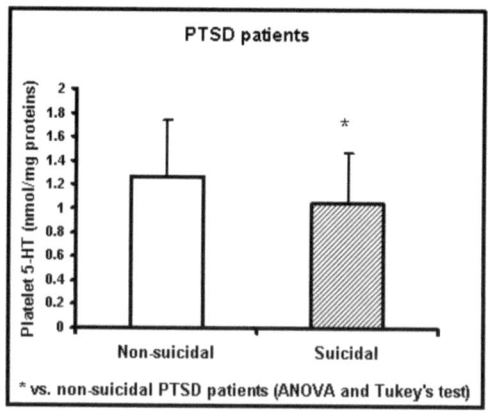

Platelet 5-HT concentration was determined in 265 male war veterans with current combat-related PTSD, who were divided into 101 suicidal and 164 non-suicidal veterans. War veterans with PTSD who were suicidal had significantly ($F=14.29$; $df=1,259$; $p<0.001$, ANOVA) lower platelet 5-HT concentration than non-suicidal war veterans with PTSD, Figure 1.

Figure 2. Platelet serotonin concentration in male patients with diagnoses other than PTSD (depression, psychosis, acute stress disorder, personality disorders and other diagnoses) with or without suicidal behavior

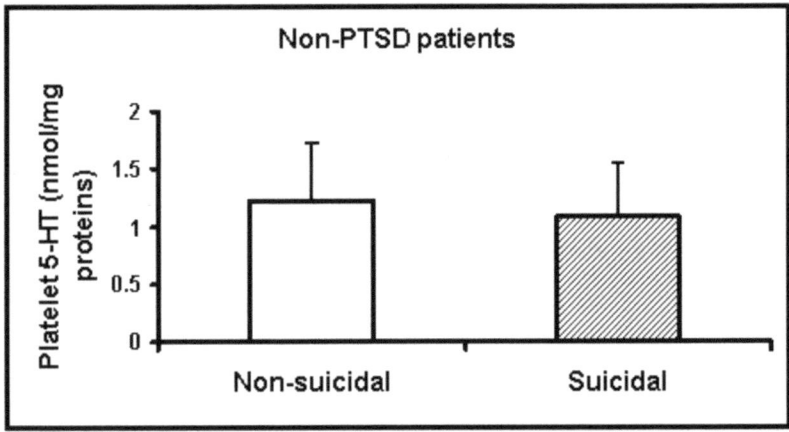

Male patients with diagnoses other than PTSD (depression, psychosis, acute stress disorder, personality disorders and other diagnoses), subdivided into 32 suicidal and 31 non-suicidal patients (Figure 2), had similar platelet 5-HT concentration to non-suicidal psychiatric patients ($F=1.64$; $df=1,71$; $p=0.204$, ANOVA). Suicidal patients had marginally lower platelet 5-HT concentration than non-suicidal patients.

Figure 3. Platelet serotonin concentration in male alcoholic patients with or without suicidal behavior

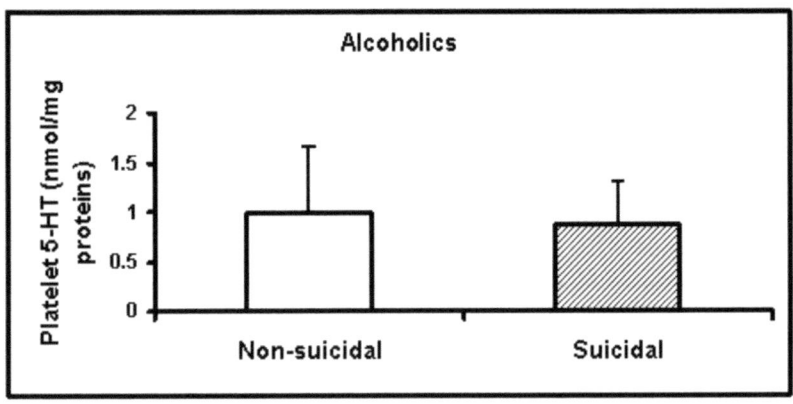

Platelet 5-HT concentration was determined in 63 male suicidal and 39 male non-suicidal alcoholic patients (Figure 3). Platelet 5-HT concentration did not differ significantly between suicidal and non-suicidal alcoholic patients (F=0.837; df=1,100; p=0.363, ANOVA). Namely, suicidal and non-suicidal alcoholic patients had very similar values of platelet 5-HT.

Figure 4. Platelet serotonin concentration in male depressed patients with or without suicidal behavior

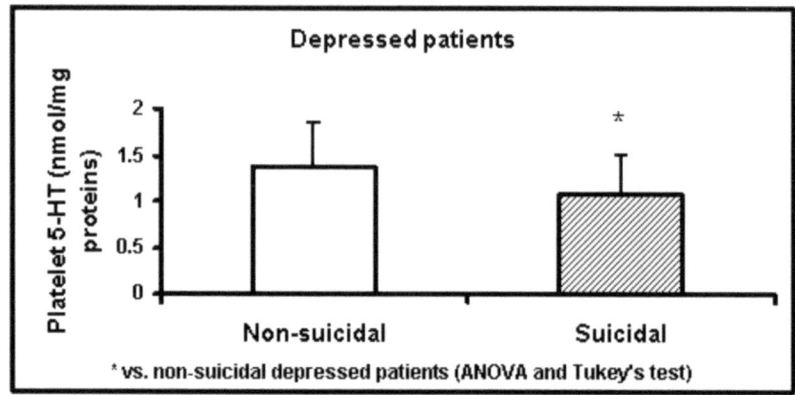

Platelet 5-HT concentration was measured in 74 suicidal and 54 non-suicidal male depressed patients (Figure 4). Depressed patients with suicidal behavior had significantly lower (F=14.28; df=1,126; p<0.001, ANOVA) platelet 5-HT concentration than non-suicidal depressed patients.

Figure 5. Platelet serotonin concentration in male psychotic patients with or without suicidal behavior

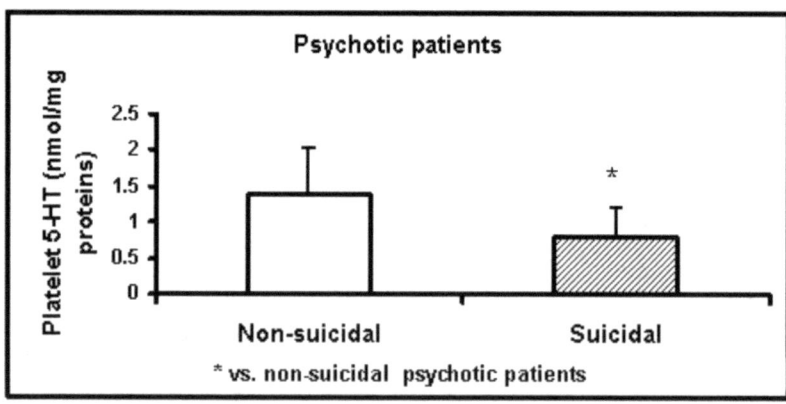

Platelet 5-HT concentration was determined also in 54 psychotic male patients subdivided into suicidal and non-suicidal patients (Figure 5). Psychotic suicidal patients had significantly lower (F=3.78; df=1,52; p<0.001, ANOVA) platelet 5-HT concentration than non-suicidal psychotic patients.

Figure 6. Platelet monoamine oxidase (MAO) activity in war veterans with combat-related PTSD, with or without suicidal behavior, subdivided into smokers and non-smokers

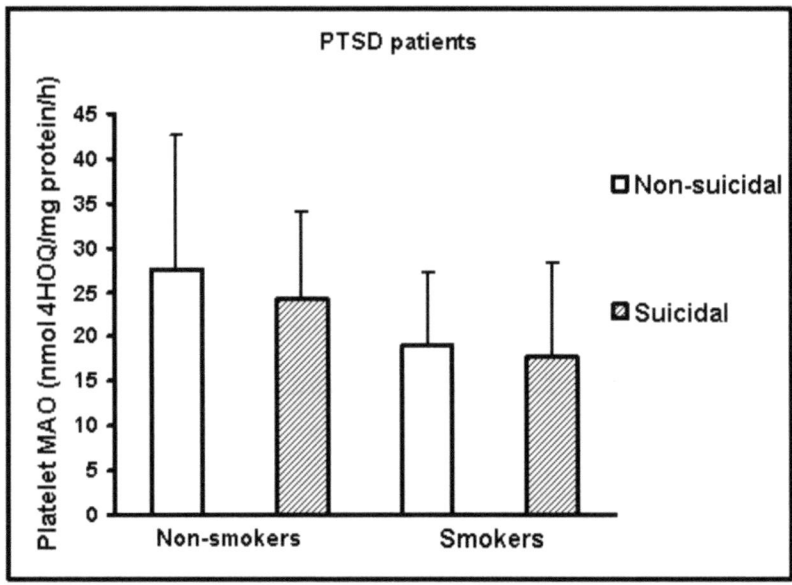

Platelet MAO activity was evaluated in 78 male suicidal and non-suicidal war veterans with combat-related PTSD (Figure 6). Platelet MAO activity was significantly different (F=2.98; df=3,74; p=0.037, ANOVA) between suicidal and non-suicidal war veterans with combat-related PTSD, subdivided according to smoking status into smokers and non-smokers, Fig. 6. However, these differences, detected by ANOVA, were due to the marginally higher platelet MAO activity in non-smokers compared to smokers, while suicidal behavior did not significantly affect platelet MAO activity within smokers (p=0.979, Tukey's test) or within non-smokers (p= 0.879, Tukey's test).

Figure 7. Platelet monoamine oxidase (MAO) activity in patients with diagnoses other than PTSD (depression, psychosis, acute stress disorder, personality disorders and other diagnoses), with or without suicidal behavior, subdivided into smokers and non-smokers

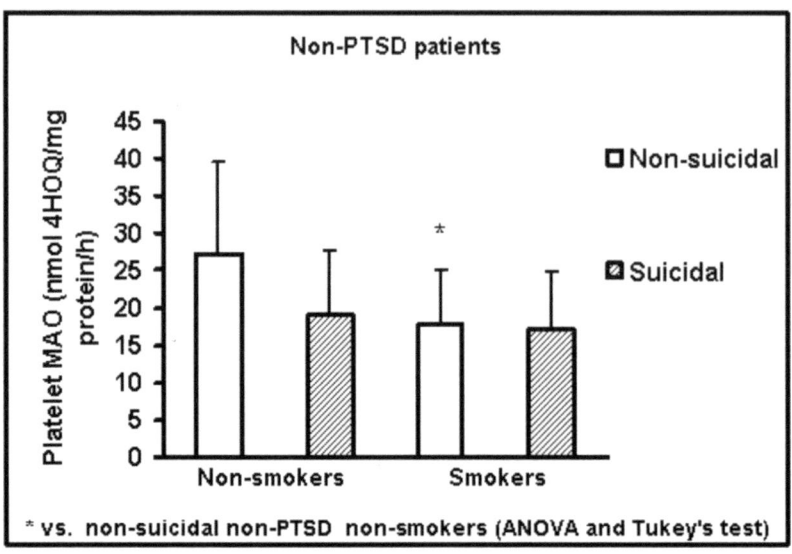

Platelet MAO activity was determined also in 72 male suicidal and non-suicidal psychiatric non-PTSD patients (Figure 7). There were significant differences (F=4.81; df=3,68; p=0.004, ANOVA) in platelet MAO activity between patients with diagnoses other than PTSD (depression, psychosis, acute stress disorder, personality disorders and other diagnoses), with or without suicidal behavior, subdivided into smokers and non-smokers. Non-suicidal smokers had significantly (p=0.003, Tukey's test) lower platelet MAO activity than non-suicidal non-smokers. However, suicidal behavior did not affect significantly platelet MAO activity within smokers (p=0.537, Tukey's test) or non-smokers (p=0.115, Tukey's test).

Platelet MAO activity was measured in 140 male suicidal and non-suicidal alcoholic patients (Figure 8).

Figure 8. Platelet monoamine oxidase (MAO) activity in alcoholic patients, with or without suicidal behavior, subdivided into smokers and nonsmokers

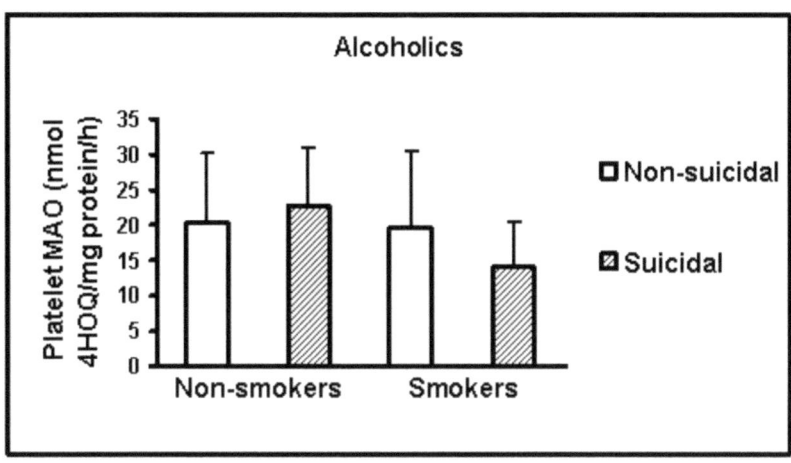

Platelet MAO activity did not differ significantly (F=2.35; df=3,136; p=0.075, ANOVA) between suicidal and non-suicidal alcoholic patients who were subdivided according to the smoking status into smokers and non-smokers. Suicidal alcoholic smokers had marginally lower platelet MAO activity than non-suicidal non-smokers, but in non-smoking alcoholic patients this difference in platelet MAO activity was not visible.

Figure 9. Plasma dopamine-beta-hydroxylase (DBH) activity in war veterans with combat-related PTSD, with or without suicidal behavior

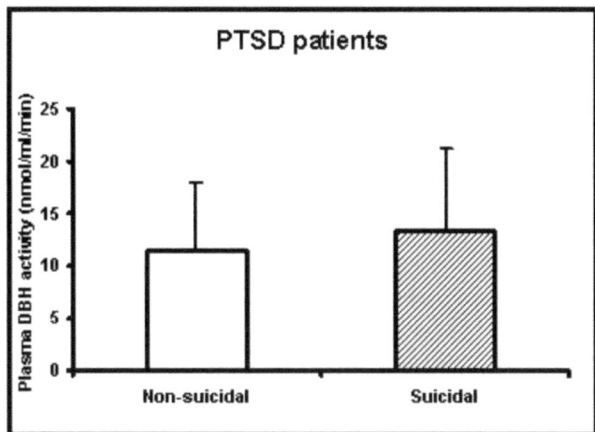

Plasma DBH activity was determined in war veterans with combat-related PTSD, with or without suicidal behavior (Figure 9). There were no significant differences (F=1.35; df=1.87; p=0.249, ANOVA) in plasma DBH activity between suicidal and non-suicidal war veterans with combat-related PTSD.

Figure 10. Plasma cortisol levels at baseline (before dexamethasone suppression test (DST), and 9 and 17 hours after DST, in war veterans with combat-related PTSD, with or without suicidal behavior

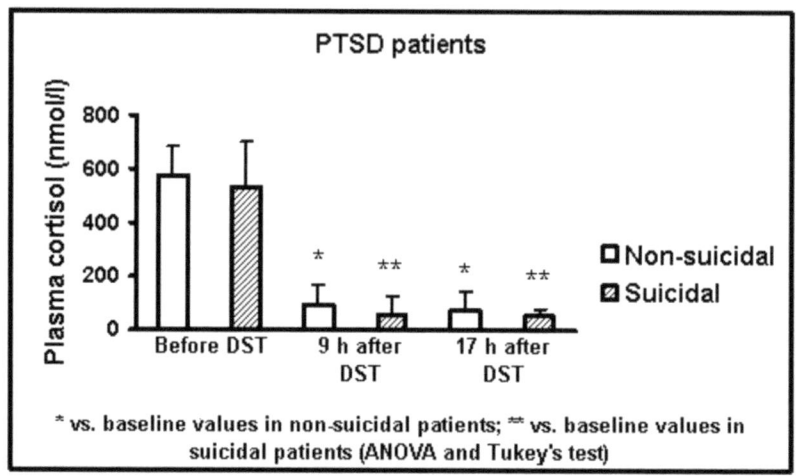

Plasma cortisol levels were determined at baseline (before DST, and 9 and 17 hours after DST in 104 male suicidal and non-suicidal war veterans with chronic combat-related PTSD (Figure 10). Plasma cortisol levels at baseline, and 9 and 17 hours after DST differed significantly (F=109.08; df=5,98; p<0.001, ANOVA) between war veterans with chronic combat-related PTSD who were divided into suicidal and non-suicidal subjects. Plasma cortisol levels were significantly (p<0.001, Tukey's test) lower 9 and 17 hours after DST in both suicidal and non-suicidal war veterans. No significant differences were detected in plasma cortisol levels between suicidal and non-suicidal veterans at baseline (p=0.825, Tukey's test), and in post-DST plasma cortisol levels 9 hours after DST (p=0.961, Tukey's test), and 17 hours after DST (p=0.995, Tukey's test), respectively.

Plasma cortisol levels were also determined at baseline (before DST), and 9 and 17 hours after DST also in 150 male suicidal and non-suicidal depressed patients (Figure 11). In suicidal and non-suicidal depressed patients, plasma cortisol levels differed significantly (F=45.40; df=5,144; p<0.001, ANOVA) at baseline and 9 and 17 hours after DST. Plasma cortisol levels were significantly (p<0.001, Tukey's test) lower 9 and 17 hours after DST in both suicidal and non-suicidal war veterans. Suicidal behavior significantly affected post-DST plasma cortisol levels in the morning, and depressed patients had significantly (p=0.05, Tukey's test) higher plasma cortisol levels 9 hours after DST than non-suicidal depressed patients. Plasma cortisol levels did not differ significantly between suicidal and non-suicidal depressed patients at baseline (p=1.00, Tukey's test), or 17 hours after DST (p=0.069, Tukey's test), respectively (Figure 11).

Figure 11. Plasma cortisol levels at baseline (before dexamethasone suppression test (DST), and 9 and 17 hours after DST, in depressed patients, with or without suicidal behavior

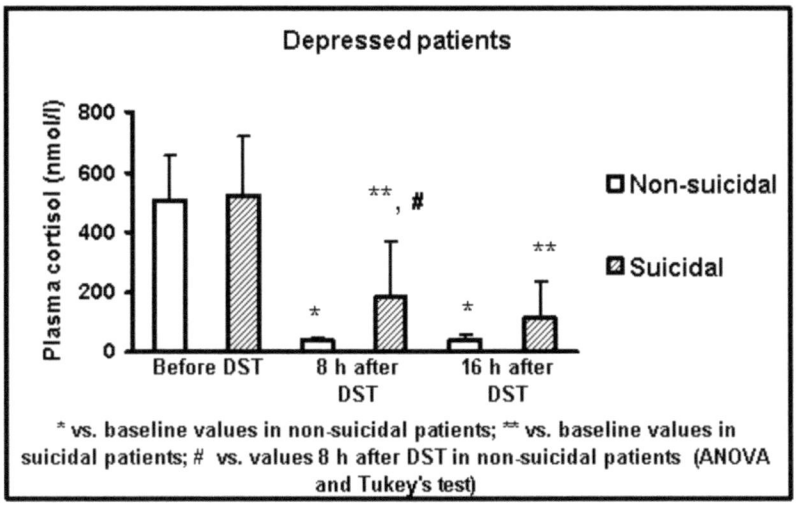

The presented results have shown significantly lower platelet 5-HT concentration in suicidal patients with PTSD, depression and psychosis than in comparison non-suicidal patients. Platelet 5-HT concentration was marginally, but not significantly, lower in suicidal compared to non-suicidal patients with diagnoses other than PTSD and in alcoholic patients. Platelet MAO activity did not differ significantly between suicidal and non-suicidal patients with PTSD, psychiatric diagnoses other than PTSD or alcoholic patients. Plasma DBH activity was similar between suicidal and non-suicidal PTSD patients. At baseline, plasma cortisol levels did not differ significantly between suicidal and non-suicidal patients with PTSD or depression. Post-DST plasma cortisol levels were similar between suicidal and non-suicidal veterans with PTSD, while in depressed suicidal patients post-DST morning plasma cortisol levels were significantly higher than in non-suicidal depressed patients.

Discussion

Suicide is frequently associated with different psychiatric disorders, and in Croatia, the average suicide rate could be divided into three periods between the years 1985-2000: before the Homeland war, during the Homeland war and after the Homeland war. In the pre-war period the suicide rate was 17.83 - 19.57 per 100,000 people; during the war it was 16.59-19.52, and in the post-war period it was 17.78-19.78 [18-20] According to the data from the Register of Suicide of the Ministry of Interior, and Croatian Bureau of Statistics, a higher frequency of suicide was found in younger men during the war, presumably due to the war-induced suffering and development of psychiatric disorders, including PTSD, especially in war veterans who became sick but could not be properly treated during combat [10]. Therefore, an important goal in psychiatry and in the prevention of suicide is to elucidate the association between peripheral biomarkers and suicidal behavior, to identify early the individuals prone to attempt suicide, to treat these individuals properly in order to prevent suicide attempts and suicide.

Biological basis of suicidal behavior

The serotonergic system

The neurobiological findings regarding the alterations in the 5-HT system in suicidal research may be divided into baseline studies, measuring peripheral indices of serotonergic function, pharmacological challenge studies, which assess the biological responses after a challenge (e.g. with fenfluramine), and post-mortem studies in the brains of individuals who have died by suicide. In the central brain 5-HT has a role as a neurotransmitter, neuromodulator, neurotrophic and neuroprotective agent. Serotonin has divergent functions, since it regulates important behaviors such as feeding, sexual functions, hallucinatory behavior, sleep pattern, mood, emotions and sensory pathways including nociception [21, 22]. Serotonin is involved in the processes of learning and memory, i.e. in the cognitive functions [22]. Its neurotrophic functions are achieved during brain development, where it regulates synaptogenesis, neurite outgrowth, and cell survival, as well as during adulthood, where it regulates synaptic plasticity, neurogenesis and neuronal survival and it stimulates the expression of the brain derived neurotrophic factor. In the brain, impairment of the 5-HT neurotransmission induces different behavioral and physiological abnormalities and psychiatric disorders, including depression, autism, eating disorders, schizophrenia, obsessive/compulsive disorder, premenstrual syndrome, anxiety, panic disorder, seasonal affective disorder, extreme violence, hostility and aggression, suicide, migraine, manic depression, addiction, depressed mood, impulsivity and aggression, and more [21, 22].

Serotonin has been associated with suicidal behavior, since a decreased serotonergic function and a reduced serotonin turnover have been found in suicide attempters and suicide victims [3,5,23].

Peripheral 5-HT

The rationale for the use of peripheral, platelet serotonergic measures lies in the similar pharmacodynamics of 5-HT with their central 5-HT synaptosomes [24]. The similarities are in uptake, storage and release of 5-HT, platelet MAO-B, 5-HT transporters [25], 5-HT2 receptors [26], α_2-adrenergic receptors, and binding sites for ^{3}H-imipramine, ^{3}H-paroxetine, and ^{3}H-LSD, and in signaling mechanisms which share identical pharmacologic and kinetic characteristics with the central nervous receptors and binding sites, and resemble the corresponding counterparts and biological processes in the central serotonergic neurons. The differences between platelets and 5-HT neurons are primarily in the fact that platelets do not biosynthesize 5-HT, and in the function [27].

Peripheral 5-HT markers and suicidal behavior

5-HIAA studies and suicidal behavior

Although there are a lot of methodological complexities associated with sampling of the cerebrospinal fluid (CSF), suicidal subjects (suicide attempters or suicide completers) have been found to have a decreased 5-hydroxyindoleacetic acid (5-HIAA) level, a major metabolite of 5-HT [4]. In addition, lower CSF 5-HIAA concentrations in depressed suicide attempters were found [28] and decreased levels of 5-HT and 5-HIAA in blood and CSF of attempted or completed suicide patients [29].

Platelet 5-HT studies and suicidal behavior

Most studies have found lower platelet 5-HT concentration in suicidal than in non-suicidal or comparative control subjects. Reduced platelet 5-HT concentration in suicidal depressed patients [12, 13, 30], in patients with a history of violent suicide attempts [31], in suicidal patients with a first episode of psychosis [32], in suicidal patients with schizophrenia [33], in suicidal patients with schizoaffective disorder [34], in acute suicidal vs. non-suicidal depressed patients [12] was found, when compared to control subjects. Although some particular points in the research of platelet markers, as predictors of the suicidal behavior, have been raised [35], these questions stressed the importance of matching the subjects for age, gender, season, drug status, diagnosis, smoking habits and different comorbid psychiatric diagnoses.

In the present study we have determined platelet 5-HT concentration in male medication-free patients with different psychiatric diagnoses, who were all subdivided into suicidal and non-suicidal patients according to suicidal behavior: non-suicidal subjects (with 0 scores) and suicidal subjects (with scores $\geq$ 1), based on the item 3 (suicide) from the HDRS 17-item scale. All patients were matched on mean age, education, and drug status. In line with our previous data [13, 30, 32], our results from the present study have shown a reduced platelet 5-HT concentration in suicidal male war veterans with combat-related PTSD, in suicidal male depressed patients, and in suicidal male psychotic patients. This finding supports the hypothesis that a decreased platelet 5-HT concentration might be used as a peripheral indicator of suicidal behavior. However, platelet 5-HT concentration was not significantly decreased in male suicidal alcoholic patients, or in male suicidal psychiatric patients with different psychiatric diagnoses, when compared to corresponding non-suicidal patients. The reason for this lack of significant effect of suicidal behavior on platelet 5-HT concentration in alcoholic patients might be explained by the fact that alcoholic patients have reduced platelet 5-HT concentration [36], and therefore suicidal behavior, which is expected to decrease platelet 5-HT concentration, could not additionally reduce platelet 5-HT concentration. In addition, this lack of effect might be also explained by the alcoholism-induced destruction of the enterochromaffine cells from the gastrointestinal mucosa (cells that synthesize 5-HT in the periphery), resulting in lower platelet 5-HT concentration in alcoholics. The other group of patients, male suicidal psychiatric patients with different psychiatric diagnoses, failed to show significantly decreased platelet 5-HT concentration. This could be explained by the smaller number of patients in this group, hence we failed to detect significance even if it was there, or to the different psychiatric diagnoses that might have affected platelet 5-HT concentration [35], or to the presence of psychotic symptoms. If platelet 5-HT concentration is expected to be reduced in suicidal patients, the presence of psychotic symptoms [13, 30, 37, 38, 39], which increase platelet 5-HT concentration, would counteract this effect, and the result would be unaltered platelet 5-HT concentration. Our present and previous data [13, 30, 32] might suggest that decreased platelet 5-HT concentration is a characteristic feature of suicidal behavior across different psychiatric entities.

Platelet serotonin transporter (5-HTT) studies and suicidal behavior

Inconsistent findings have been reported for serotonin transporter (5-HTT) binding in suicidal compared to non-suicidal subjects. Either a decreased 5-HTT binding in the ventral prefrontal cortex of the suicide victims [40], or fewer prefrontal cortex 5-HTT binding sites in suicide attempters [3], or no change in 5-HTT binding between suicide victims and control subjects [41] was found.

Platelet serotonin receptors and suicidal behavior

Serotonin mediates different functions through binding to seven distinct classes of 5-HT receptors which are widely distributed throughout central and peripheral nervous systems, gastrointestinal tract, cardiovascular system and blood. The 5-HT receptors are 5-HT1$_{A,B,D,E,F}$, 5-HT2$_{A,B,C}$, 5-HT3, 5-HT4, 5-HT5$_A$, 5-HT6 and 5-HT7 receptors. An increased binding of the 5-HT1$_A$ and 5-HT2$_A$ receptors has been found in suicide victims compared to controls [42], however, no alterations in raphe nuclei 5-HT1$_A$ binding was also reported between suicidal and control subjects [41]. More 5-HT2A binding and more mRNA in the postmortem prefrontal cortex tissue of suicide victims was reported [43].

Pharmacological challenge studies and suicidal behavior

The administration of a drug that stimulates the release of 5-HT, and inhibits the reuptake of 5-HT, fenfluramine, is frequently used to detect the alterations in prolactin release. A blunted (i.e. a reduced) prolactin response to a fenfluramine challenge in suicide attempters has been detected [44].

Platelet MAO-B activity and suicidal behavior

Monoamine oxidase (MAO) is a flavin-containing oxygen oxidoreductase that catalyzes different monoamine neurotransmitters, such as dopamine, noradrenaline, adrenaline, and 5-HT. Monoamine oxidase exists in two isoenzymes, MAO-A and MAO-B: MAO-A preferentially metabolizes NA, adrenaline and 5-HT, and is inhibited by clorgyline, while MAO-B catalyzes b-phenylethylamine and benzylamine, and is inactivated by a selective inhibitor, deprenyl. Both isoenzymes oxidize dopamine, tyramine, and tryptamine [45]. Monoamine oxidase type B is expressed in platelets, astrocytes and 5-HT neurons, while MAO-A is found in placenta and catecholaminergic neurons in the brain. As platelet MAO-B activity has been found to differ in alcoholism, schizophrenia and suicidality, platelet MAO-B activity has been proposed to be a biomarker for different personality traits such as suicidality [46], aggressive behavior, addiction, sensation seeking, impulsiveness and vulnerability to psychiatric disorders [45, 47-49]. Decreased MAO-B activity was associated with impulsiveness, sensation-seeking and aggressiveness [49], or with various psychopathological conditions, suicidal behavior, hyperactivity, and type II alcoholism [49].

The findings from the literature about MAO activity and suicidal behavior are controversial. No changes in brain MAO-A and MAO-B activity in individuals who committed suicide were found [50]. In addition, regarding platelet MAO-B activity, either no alterations in platelet MAO-B activity in suicidal patients [51], or higher platelet MAO-B activity in suicidal depressed patients [46], or lower platelet MAO-B activity in suicidal women with dysthymia [52] compared to comparison subjects were found.

Platelet MAO-B activity is a biomarker that is affected by sex and smoking [45, 53, 54], hence in our study we used only male patients who were divided into smokers and non-smokers. Our results (present study) have shown that platelet MAO-B activity did not differ significantly between suicidal and non-suicidal male combat exposed veterans with PTSD, male suicidal and non-suicidal psychiatric patients (with depression, psychosis, acute stress disorder, personality disorders and other diagnoses), or male alcoholic patients. Therefore, in line with the results showing no alterations in platelet MAO-B activity between suicidal and non-suicidal patients [51, 55, 56], in our study suicidal behavior did not influence platelet MAO-B activity in psychiatric patients.

The noradrenergic and dopaminergic systems

In post-mortem brain tissue of suicide victims, decreased noradrenalin levels and increased density of the α2-adrenoceptors, presumably upregulated because of the reduction in noradrenalin, were found [57]. There are inconsistent results regarding the role of dopaminergic system in suicidal behavior. In suicide attempters, lower [58] or unchanged [59] levels of a main metabolite of dopamine, homovanilic acid (HVA) in CSF were found. In addition, increased [60] and decreased [61] immunoreactivity of the rate limiting enzyme for the synthesis of noradrenalin and dopamine, tyrosine hydroxylase, were observed. Dopamine beta-hydroxylase (DBH) is an enzyme that converts dopamine to noradrenaline, and is localized in vesicles of central noradrenergic and adrenergic neurons, and in peripheral noradrenergic (sympathetic) neurons and adrenomedullary neurosecretory cells. Activity of DBH can be detected in the serum or plasma because the enzyme is released from vesicles during sympathetic activity. Dopamine beta-hydroxylase is a genetic marker, stable over time, with minimal or no correlation with age, sex, acute stress etc. Its activity is altered in different psychiatric disorders, such as depression, familial paranoid schizophrenia, childhood conduct disorders, bipolar affective disorders [62], and in PTSD [63].

In the present study we have determined plasma DBH in male war veterans with combat-related PTSD, who were categorized into suicidal and non-suicidal groups. Plasma DBH activity did not differ significantly between suicidal and non-suicidal veterans with PTSD. These results suggest that plasma DBH is not associated with suicidal behavior in combat exposed veterans with current and chronic PTSD.

Hypothalamic-pituitary-adrenal axis and suicidal behavior

Alterations in the HPA system have been implicated in the neurobiological basis of suicide. The HPA axis has a major role in stress response: its activation starts with the secretion of corticotropin-releasing factor (or corticotropin-releasing hormone, CRH), triggered by stress. Corticotropin-releasing hormone is released from the nerve terminals of the CRH containing neurons located in the paraventricular nucleus of the hypothalamus, and it controls the release of adrenocorticotropic hormone (ACTH) from the pituitary gland via the CRH-R1 receptor, which mediates anxiety-like behavior. Adrenocorticotropic hormone goes to the adrenal cortex via the bloodstream and controls the release of cortisol. Cortisol acts via a negative feedback mechanism to regulate its own secretion. The HPA axis activation is followed by the activation of the sympathetic axis (locus ceruleus and the release of noradrenalin). Corticotropin-releasing hormone and noradrenalin regulate each other and act synergistically in response to stress. The HPA axis activity is regulated by different neurotransmitters and neuropeptides [64, 65].

The literature data describing the HPA axis activity in suicide are divergent. It has been assumed that a hyperactivity of the HPA axis is a risk factor for suicide, especially in major depressive disorder [6]. These findings were substantiated by the data obtained from the post-mortem studies, since suicide victims had greater adrenal weights [66], increased corticotrophin-releasing factor (CRF) concentrations in CSF [67], increased CRH neurotransmission [68], and more CRH-R2 than CRH-R1 receptors in the pituitary tissue of the suicide completers [69]. Divergent results are presented also for the CRH in CSF. In the CSF, lower [55] or unchanged [67] concentrations of CRH were found in suicide attempters or victims.

In suicidal patients, plasma cortisol response (suppression or non-suppression of cortisol after administration of 1 mg of dexamethasone at 23.00 h) is believed to represent a biological marker that might predict a suicidal risk. In depressed patients, it has been reported that abnormal response to DST (i.e. non-suppression of plasma cortisol to DST) was associated with suicide [70-74], but also that DST non-suppression was not associated with suicide [75, 76], and that suicide attempts were associated with a significantly less dexamethasone suppression [77]. Abnormal plasma cortisol response to DST was related to increased risk of suicide [5]. A recent study [6] suggested that depressed patients with suicide attempts and suicidal ideation had lower ACTH and cortisol response to the administration of the combined dexamethasone-suppression/CRH stimulation test. Another recent study also failed to find a significant relationship between HPA-axis hyperactivity and a risk for suicide, or between DST non-suppression and suicide [78]. The study detected only a significant interaction between suicidality and abnormal DST in depressed inpatients who manifested suicidality in their current episode. These divergent results suggest that HPA-axis hyperactivity is only one additive factor, among many other risk factors for suicide [78].

In the present study we have evaluated the HPA axis activity in basal conditions and after DST in male war veterans with combat-related PTSD and in male depressed patients. Both groups of patients have shown similar baseline plasma cortisol levels when subdivided into suicidal and non-suicidal patients. In addition, within veterans with PTSD, post DST plasma cortisol levels did not differ significantly between suicidal and non-suicidal PTSD patients. Among 20 suicidal patients, only one veteran was a non-suppressor, and among 12 non-suicidal PTSD patients, three were non-suppressors. Hence, our results with combat-related PTSD veterans do not support the hypothesis that suicidal behavior is associated with a hyperactivity of the HPA and with a super-suppression of cortisol to DST, at least not in PTSD. In male depressed patients, plasma cortisol levels were significantly decreased 9 and 17 hours after DST in both suicidal and non-suicidal patients, however suicidal depressed were non-suppressors to DST, i.e. they had significantly higher plasma cortisol levels 9 hours after DST than non-suicidal depressed patients. Among 38 suicidal depressed patients, 18 patients (47%) were DST non-suppressors, while in 12 non-suicidal patients there were no non-suppressors to DST. These results suggest that HPA-axis hyperactivity and abnormal DST was found in depression, but not in PTSD, confirming our previous [13] and other [78] data of the relationship between suicidal behavior and non-suppression to DST in suicidal depressed patients.

In conclusion, we have found significantly lower platelet 5-HT concentration in suicidal patients with PTSD, depression and psychosis, and more non-suppressors to DST in suicidal depressed patients, than in non-suicidal patients, while other peripheral markers, such as plasma DBH activity, platelet MAO activity or plasma cortisol levels before and after DST, did not differ significantly between suicidal and non-suicidal patient groups. The results from our present study, showing significant reductions in platelet 5-HT concentration in suicidal compared to non-suicidal patients, and significant increase in post-DST plasma cortisol levels in suicidal compared to non-suicidal depressed patients, add further support to the role of 5-HT and HPA axis in the pathophysiology of suicidal behavior.

Therefore, further studies are underway to elucidate the association between biological and genetic biomarkers and suicidal behavior, to facilitate the identification of suicidal individuals, to properly treat suicidal patients, and to achieve a main goal, which is prevention of suicide.

Acknowledgements

Thanks are due to the staff of the Department of Psychiatry, Referral Centre of the Ministry of Health for Stress-related Disorders, Regional Centre for Psychotrauma, University Hospital Dubrava, Zagreb, Croatia, and to Martina Dezeljin, BSc (Rudjer Boskovic Institute, Zagreb, Croatia) for the assistance in biochemical analyses. This work was supported by Croatian Ministry of Science, Education and Sport, grants numbers 098-0982522-2455, 098-0982522-2457 and 198-0982522-0075.

References

[1] World Health Organization. World Health Report 2000. Health Systems: Improving Performance. World Health Organization: Geneva, (2000).

[2] B. Bondy, A. Buettner, P. Zill, Genetics of suicide, *Mol Psychiatry* 11 (2006), 336-351.

[3] J. J. Mann, Neurobiology of suicidal behaviour, *Nat Rev Neurosci* 4 (2003), 819-828.

[4] T.E. Joiner, Jr., J.S. Brown, L.R. Wingate, The Psychology and Neurobiology of Suicidal Behavior, *Annu Rev Psychol* 56 (2005), 287–314.

[5] J.J. Mann, A. Apter, J. Bertolote, A. Beautrais, D. Currier, A. Haas et al., Suicide prevention strategies: a systematic review, *JAMA* 294 (2005), 2064–2074.

[6] A. Pfennig, H.E. Kunzel, N. Kern, M. Ising, M. Majer, B. Fuchs, G. Ernst, F. Holsboer, E. B. Binder, Hypothalamus-pituitary-adrenal system regulation and suicidal behavior in depression, *Biol Psychiatry* 57 (2005), 336-342.

[7] Y.K. Kim, H.P. Lee, S.D. Won, E.Y. Park, H.Y. Lee, B.H. Lee, S.W. Lee, D. Yoon, C. Han, D.J. Kim, S.H. Choi, Low plasma BDNF is associated with suicidal behavior in major depression, *Progress Neuro-Psychopharmacol Biol Psychiatry* 31 (2007), 78-85.

[8] M. First, R. Spitzer, J. Williams, M. Gibbon, Structured Clinical Interview for DSM-IV Axis I Disorders (SCID-I). In: Handbook of Psychiatric Measures, Washington, DC: *American Psychiatric Association* (2000), 49-53.

[9] APA, Diagnostic and Statistical Manual of Mental Disorders, 4th ed *American Psychiatric Association*, Washington, DC (1994).

[10] F.W. Weathers, T.M. Keane, J.R.T. Davidson, Clinician-administered PTSD scale: A review of the first ten years of research, *Depress Anxiety*, 13 (2001), 132-156.

[11] M. Hamilton, A rating scale for depression, *J Neurol Neurosurg Psychiatry* 23 (1960), 56-62.

[12] J. Roggenbach, B. Mueller-Oerlinghausen, L. Franke, R. Uebelhack, S. Blank, B. Ahrens, Peripheral serotonergic markers in acutely suicidal patients. 1. Comparison of serotonergic platelet measures between suicidal individuals, non-suicidal patients with major depression and healthy subjects, *J Neural Transm*, 114 (2007), 479–487.

[13] N. Pivac, M. Jakovljevic, D. Muck-Seler, Z. Brzovic, Hypothalamic-pituitary-adrenal axis function and platelet serotonin concentrations in depressed patients, *Psychiatry Res* 73 (1997), 123-132.

[14] O. H. Lowry, N. J. Rosebrough, A. L. Farr, R. J. Randall, Protein measurement with the Folin phenol reagent, *J Biol Chem* 193 (1951), 265-275.

[15] M. Krajl, A rapid microfluorimetric determination of monoamine oxidase, *Biochem Pharmacol* 14 (1965), 1684-1686.

[16] N. Pivac, J. Knezevic, M. Mustapic, M. Dezeljin, D. Muck-Seler, D. Kozaric-Kovacic, M. Balija, T. Matijevic, J. Pavelic, The lack of association between monoamine oxidase (MAO) intron 13 polymorphism and platelet MAO-B activity among men., *Life Sci* 79 (2006), 45-49.

[17] T. Nagatsu, S. Udenfriend, Photometric assay of dopamine-beta-hydroxylase activity in human blood, *Clin Chem* 18 (1972), 980-983.

[18] M. Grubisic-Ilic, D. Kozaric-Kovacic, F. Grubisic, Z. Kovacic, Epidemiological study of suicide in the Republic of Croatia-comparison of war and post-war periods and areas directly and indirectly affected by war, *Eur Psychiatry* 17 (2002), 259-264.

[19] D. Kozaric-Kovacic, M. Grubisic-Ilic, F. Grubisic, Z. Kovacic, Suicide: rates and methods before, during and after the war in Croatia (1985-2000), *Natl Med J India* 15 (2002), 356-357.

[20] D. Kozaric-Kovacic, M. Grubisic-Ilic, F. Grubisic, Z. Kovacic, Epidemiological indicators of suicides in the Republic of Croatia, *Drus Istraz* 57 (2002) 155-170.

[21] I. Lucki, The spectrum of behaviors influenced by serotonin, *Biol Psychiatry* 44 (1998), 151-162.

[22] S. M. Stahl, Mechanism of action of serotonin selective reuptake inhibitors. Serotonin receptors and pathways mediate therapeutic effects and side effects, *J Affect Disord* 51 (1998), 215-235.

[23] A. Roy, M. Linnoila, Suicidal behavior, impulsiveness and serotonin, *Acta Psychiatr Scand* 78 (1988), 529–535.

[24] S.M. Stahl, Platelets as pharmacological models for the receptors and biochemistry of monoaminergic neurons. In: Platelets: Physiology and Pharmacology, Longenecker GL, editor, *Academic Press*, New York (1985), 307-340.

[25] K. P. Lesch, U. Merschdorf, Impulsivity, aggression, and serotonin: a molecular psychobiological perspective, *Behav Sci Law* 18 (2000), 581-604.

[26] A.H. Andres, M.A. Rao, S. Ostrowitzki, W. Enzian, Human brain cortex and platelet serotonin$_2$ receptor binding properties and their regulation by endogenous serotonin, *Life Sci* 52 (1993), 313-321.

[27] P.D. Hrdina, Platelet serotonergic markers in psychiatric disorders: use, abuse and limitations, *J Psychiatry Neurosci* 19 (1994), 87-88.

[28] J.J. Mann, K.M. Malone, Cerebrospinal fluid amines and higher lethality suicide attempts in depressed inpatients, *Biol Psychiatry* 41 (1997), 162–171.

[29] P. Nordstrom, M. Samuelsson, M. Asberg, L. Traskman-Bendz, A. Aberg-Wistedt, C. Nordin, L. Bertilsson, CSF 5-HIAA predicts suicide risk after attempted suicide, *Suic Life Threat Behav* 24 (1994), 1–9.

[30] D. Muck-Seler, M. Jakovljevic, N. Pivac, Platelet 5-HT concentrations and suicidal behaviour in recurrent major depression, *J Affect Disord* 39 (1996), 73-80.

[31] J.C. Alvarez, D. Cremniter, P. Lesieur, A. Gregoire, A. Gilton, I. Macquin-Mavier, C. Jarreau, O. Spreux-Varoquaux, Low blood cholesterol and low platelet serotonin levels in violent suicide attempters, *Biol Psychiatry* 45 (1999), 1066– 1069.

[32] D. Marcinko, N. Pivac, M. Martinac, M. Jakovljevic, A. Mihaljevic-Peles, D. Muck-Seler, Platelet serotonin and serum cholesterol concentrations in suicidal and non-suicidal male patients with first episode of psychosis, *Psychiatry Res* 150 (2007), 105-108.

[33] P. Braunig, M.L. Rao, R. Fimmers, Blood serotonin levels in suicidal schizophrenic patients, *Acta Psychiatr Scand* 79 (1989), 186-189.

[34] M.L. Rao, P. Braunig, A. Papassotiropoulos, Autoaggressive behavior is closely related to serotonin availability in schizoaffective disorder, *Pharmacopsychiatry* 27 (1994), 202-206.

[35] B. Mueller-Oerlinghausen, J. Roggenbach, L. Franke Serotonergic platelet markers of suicidal behavior – do they really exist?, *J Affect Disord* 79 (2004), 13-24.

[36] N. Pivac, D. Mück-Šeler, M. Mustapić, K. Nenadić-Šviglin, D. Kozarić-Kovačić, Platelet serotonin concentration in alcoholic subjects, *Life Sci* 76 (2004), 521-531.

[37] M. Šagud, A. Mihaljević-Peleš, N. Pivac, M. Jakovljević, D. Mück-Šeler, Platelet serotonin and serum lipids in psychotic mania, *J Affect Disord* 97 (2007), 247-251.

[38] N. Pivac, D. Kozaric-Kovacic, M. Mustapic, M. Deželjin, A. Borovecki, M. Grubišic-Ilić, D. Muck-Seler, Platelet serotonin in combat related posttraumatic stress disorder with psychotic symptoms, *J Affect Disord* 93 (2006), 223-227.

[39] N. Pivac, D. Muck-Seler, M. Jakovljevic, Platelet 5-HT levels and hypothalamic-pituitary-adrenal axis activity in schizophrenic patients with positive and negative symptoms, *Neuropsychobiology* 36 (1997), 19-21.

[40] J.J. Mann, J.Y. Huang, M.D. Underwood, S.A. Kassir, S. Oppenheim, T.M. Kelly, A.J. Dwork, V. Arango, A serotonin transporter gene promoter polymorphism (5-HTTLPR) and prefrontal cortical finding in major depression and suicide, *Arch Gen Psychiatry* 57 (2000), 729-738.

[41] V. Arango, M.D. Underwood, M. Boldrini, H. Tamir, S.A. Kassir, S.C. Hsiung, J.J.X. Chen, J.J. Mann, Serotonin 1A receptors, serotonin transporter binding and serotonin transporter mRNA expression in the brainstem of depressed suicide victims, *Neuropsychopharmacology* 25 (2001), 892–903.

[42] C.A. Stockmeier, L.A. Shapiro, G.E. Dilley, T.N. Kolli, L. Friedman, G. Rajkowska, Increase in serotonin-1A autoreceptors in the midbrain of suicide victims with major depression-postmortem evidence for decreased serotonin activity, *J Neurosci* 18 (1998), 7394–7401.

[43] G.N. Pandey, Y. Dwivedi, H.S. Rizavi, X.G. Ren, S.C. Pandey, C. Pesold, R.C. Roberts, R.R. Conley, C.A. Tamminga, Higher expression of serotonin 5-HT2A receptors in the postmortem brains of teenage suicide victims, *Am J Psychiatry* 159 (2002), 419-429.

[44] E.F. Coccaro, R.J. Kavoussi, R.L. Hauger, T.B. Cooper, C.F. Ferris, Cerebrospinal fluid vasopressin levels correlates with aggression and serotonin function in personality-disordered subjects, *Arch Gen Psychiatry* 55 (1998), 708–714.

[45] L. Oreland, Platelet monoamine oxidase, personality and alcoholism: the rise, fall and resurrection, *Neurotoxicology* 25 (2004), 79-89.

[46] G.M.J. Van Kempen, P. Notten, M.W. Hengeveld, Repeated measures of platelet MAO activity and 5-HT in a group of suicidal women, *Biol Psychiatry* 31 (1992), 529–530.

[47] H. Garpenstrand, J. Ekblom, K. Forslund, G. Rylander, L. Oreland,. Platelet monoamine oxidase activity is related to MAOB intron 13 genotype, *J Neural Transm* 107 (2000), 523-530.

[48] M. Paaver, D. Eensoo, A. Pulver, J. Harro, Adaptive and maladaptive impulsivity, platelet monoamine oxidase (MAO) activity and risk-admitting in different types of risky drivers, *Psychopharmacology* 186 (2006), 32–40.

[49] D. Schalling, M. Asberg, G. Edman, L. Oreland, Markers for vulnerability to psychopathology: temperament traits associated with platelet MAO activity, *Acta Psychiatr Scand* 76 (1987), 172-182.

[50] J.J. Mann, M. Stanley, Postmortem monoamine oxidase enzyme kinetics in the frontal cortex of suicide victims and controls, *Acta Psychiatr Scand* 69 (1984), 135– 139.

[51] R. J. Verkes, R. C. Van der Mast, A. J. Kerkhof, D. Fekkes, M. W. Hengeveld, J. P. Tuyl, and G. M. Van Kempen, Platelet serotonin, monoamine oxidase activity, and [3H]paroxetine binding related to impulsive suicide attempts and borderline personality disorder, *Biol Psychiatry* 43 (1998), 740-746.

[52] J. Tripodianakis, M. Markianos, D. Sarantidis, V. Spyropoulou, V. Taktikou, E. Bistolaki, Platelet MAO activity in patients with dysthymic disorder, *Psychiatry Res* 78 (1998), 173– 178.

[53] J.S. Fowler, J. Logan, G.J. Wang, N.D. Volkow, Monoamine oxidase and cigarette smoking, *Neurotoxicology* 24 (2003), 75-82.

[54] N. Pivac, D. Muck-Seler, D. Kozarić-Kovačić, M. Mustapić, K. Nenadić-Šviglin, M. Deželjin, Platelet monoamine oxidase in alcoholism, *Psychopharmacology* Letter to the Editors, 182 (2005), 194-196.

[55] L. Traskman-Bendz, C. Alling, L. Oreland, G. Regnell, E. Vinge, R. Ohman, Prediction of suicidal behavior from biologic tests, *J Clin Psychopharmacol* 12 (1992), 21S– 26S.

[56] H. Meltzer, A. Arora, Platelet markers of suicidality, *Ann NY Acad Sci* 487 (1986), 271–280.

[57] A.G. Ordway, P.S. Widdowson, K.S. Smith, A. Halaris, Agonist Binding to α_2-Adrenoceptors Is Elevated in the Locus Coeruleus from Victims of Suicide, *J Neurochem* 63 (1994), 617–624.

[58] L. Sher, J.J. Carballo, M.F. Grunebaum, A.K. Burke, G. Zalsman, Y. Huang, J.J. Mann, M.A. Oquendo, A prospective study of the association of cerebrospinal fluid monoamine metabolite levels with lethality of suicide attempts in patients with bipolar disorder, *Bipolar Disord* 8 (2006), 543–550.

[59] G.P.A. Placidi, M.A. Oquendo, K.M. Malone, B. Brodsky, S.P. Ellis, J.J. Mann, Anxiety in major depression: relationship to suicide attempts, *Am J Psychiatry* 157 (2000), 1614–1618.

[60] G.A. Ordway, K.S. Smith, J.W. Haycock, Elevated tyrosine hydroxylase in the locus coeruleus of suicide victims, *J Neurochem* 62 (1994), 680-685.

[61] V. Arango, M.D. Underwood, J.J.Mann, Biologic alterations in the brainstem of suicides, *Psychiatr Clin North America* 20 (1997), 581 ff.

[62] C.P. Zabetian, G.M. Anderson, S.G. Buxbaum, R.C. Elston, H. Ichinose, T. Nagatsu, K. Kim, C. Kim, R.T. Malison, J. Gelertner, J.F. Cubells, A quantitative-trait analysis of human plasma-dopamine beta-hydroxylase activity: Evidence for a major functional polymorphism at the DBH locus, *Am J Hum Genet* 68 (2001), 515-522.

[63] M. Mustapic, N. Pivac, D. Kozaric-Kovacic, M. Dezeljin, J.F. Cubells, D. Muck-SelerDopamine beta-hydroxylase (DBH) activity and -1021C/T polymorphism of *DBH* gene in combat-related posttraumatic stress disorder, *Am J Med Genetics Part B Neuropsychiatry Genetics*, (2007) doi: 10.1002/ajmg.b.30526.

[64] J. Kim, J. Gorman, The psychobiology of anxiety, *Clin Neurosci Res* 4 (2005), 335-347.

[65] C. Tsigos, G.P. Chrousos, Hypothalamic-pituitary-adrenal axis, neuroendocine factors and stress, *J Psychosom Res* 53 (2002), 865-871.

[66] T. Dumser, A. Barocka, E. Schubert, Weight of adrenal glands may be increased in persons who commit suicide, *Am J Forensic Med Pathology* 19 (1998), 72–76.

[67] M. Arato, C.M. Banki, G. Bissette, C.B. Nemeroff, Elevated CSF CRF in suicide victims, *Biol Psychiatry* 25 (1989), 355–359.

[68] C.B. Nemeroff, M.J. Owens, G. Bissette, A.C. Andorn, M. Stanley, Reduced corticotropin releasing factor binding sites in the frontal cortex of suicide victims, *Arch Gen Psychiatry* 45 (1988), 577–579.

[69] N. Hiroi, M.L. Wong, J. Licinio, C. Park, M. Young, P.W. Gold, G.P. Chrousos, S.R. Bornstein, Expression of corticotropin releasing hormone receptors type I and type II mRNA in suicide victims and controls, *Mol Psychiatry* 6 (2001), 540–546.

[70] B.J. Carroll, J.F. Greden, M. Feinberg, Suicide, neuroendocrine dysfunction and CSF 5-HIAA concentrations in depression. In: B. Angrist, Editor, *Recent Advances in Neuropsychopharmacology Proceedings of the 12th CINP Congress*, Pergamon Press, Oxford, UK (1980), 307–313.

[71] W. Coryell, M.A. Schlesser, Suicide and the dexamethasone suppression test in unipolar depression, *Am J Psychiatry* 138 (1981), 1120–1121.

[72] W. Coryell, M. Schlesser, The dexamethasone suppression test and suicide prediction, *Am J Psychiatry* 158 (2001), 748–753.

[73] W.H. Norman, W.A. Brown, I.W. Miller, G.I. Keitner, J.C. Overholser, The dexamethasone suppression test and completed suicide, *Acta Psychiatr Scand* 81 (1990), 120–125.

[74] B.I. Yerevanian, J.D. Feusner, R.J. Koek, J. Mintz, The dexamethasone suppression test as a predictor of suicidal behavior in unipolar depression, *J Affect Disord* 83 (2004), 103–108.

[75] S.K. Secunda, C.K. Cross, S. Koslow, M.M. Katz, J. Kocsis, J.W. Maas, H. Landis, Biochemistry and suicidal behavior in depressed patients, *Biol Psychiatry* 21 (1986), 756–767.

[76] D. Lester, The dexamethasone suppression test as an indicator of suicide A meta-analysis, *Pharmacopsychiatry* 25 (1992), 265–270.

[77] S.D. Targum, L. Rosen, A.E. Capodanno, The dexamethasone suppression test in suicidal patients with unipolar depression, *Am J Psychiatry* 140 (1983), 877–879.

[78] W. Coryell, E. Young, B. Carroll, Hyperactivity of the hypothalamic–pituitary–adrenal axis and mortality in major depressive disorder, *Psychiatry Res* 30 (2006), 99-104.

Lowering Suicide Risk in Returning Troops
B.K. Wiederhold (Ed.)
IOS Press, 2008
© 2008 IOS Press. All rights reserved.
doi:10.3233/978-1-58603-889-2-23

Brain Structure and Plasticity: Relation to Suicidality

Ivica KOSTOVIC, Marko CULJAT, and Milos JUDAS
Croatian Institute for Brain Research, School of Medicine, Zagreb, Croatia

Abstract. In order to reveal biological correlates of suicidal behavior, we have to study three major fronto-limbic circuits: 1) orbitomedial prefrontal-limbic (OM PFC-L), 2) precingulate prefrontal-limbic (PC PFC-L), and 3) dorsomedial-dorsoanterolateral (DL PFC-L) limbic circuit. Limbic structures form the limbic lobe, which includes the limbic cortex (cingulate cortex and hippocampal formation) and subcortical structures (amygdala, nucleus accumbens septi, septal nuclei, hypothalamus and limbic midbrain area). The nuclei with identified neurotransmitter systems in the limbic midbrain area (LMA) project directly on three frontal cortical circuits and serve as major modulatory systems: serotoninergic (5-HT), noradrenergic (NA), and dopaminergic (DA) system.

The neural pathways (structural wiring) of fronto-limbic (FC-L) cortical systems connect amygdala - orbitofrontal cortex, dorsomedial thalamic nucleus - dorsolateral prefrontal cortex, prefrontal cortex - nucleus accumbens, precingulate cortex - subcortical limbic nuclei, and numerous cortico-cortical pathways, which interconnect OM, PC and DL prefrontal cortices and establish bilateral connections with limbic cingulate and hippocampal formation cortices.

For each of the fronto-limbic circuits, certain prominent functions have been proposed; OM PFC-L is essential for decision-making and impulse control. Consecutively, fine abnormalities of function of this system are one of the neural substrates for suicidal "diathesis." These abnormalities were documented in neuroimaging studies in individuals who attempted suicide and in postmortem studies in people who committed suicide. The abnormalities may involve different levels of circuitry: principal neurons, interneurons, afferent pathways, synapses, and receptors. It is generally accepted that a decrease in serotonin transporter binding is one of the most prominent and most constant findings in people who have committed suicide. However, the principal abnormality lies in the fronto-limbic circuit, which is under the influence of the 5-HT system. The abnormalities of DL PFC-L are less well documented, but we believe that this circuit plays a role in suicidal behavior because it is necessary for conscious representation of suicidal ideation. For proper diagnostic assessment of underlying psychiatric disorders and suicidal behavior, it is necessary to obtain the following "neurobiologically"-relevant data: imaging on a high-resolution device with 3D morphometry and volumetry, tractography, MR spectroscopy, SPECT, and, in advanced clinical centers, functional MRI and pharmacogenomic screening. The plasticity of fronto-limbic circuits is present throughout life. The structural plasticity of pathways is present only during prenatal and early postnatal life; the plasticity of synapses lasts at least until the third decade of life, while plasticity of the receptors lasts throughout life. The MR imaging and pharmacogenomic parameters may serve as useful indicators for detection of vulnerable individuals who have an increased risk of suicide in addition to principal mental disorder.

Using this neurobiologically-based approach we hope to succeed in lowering suicide risk.

Keywords. Fronto-limbic circuitry, suicidal behavior, magnetic resonance imaging, neurobiology of suicide

Introduction

The association prefrontal cortex is the largest, rostrally situated portion of the human frontal lobe. The frontal lobe is one of the cortical regions that undergoes the greatest expansion in the course of both evolution and individual maturation [1]. The prefrontal cortex is composed of numerous cytoarchitectonic areas corresponding to Brodmann's areas 9, 10, 11, 12, 32, 46, and 47. The main cytoarchitectonic feature of the prefrontal cortex is the presence of large pyramidal neurons in layer IIIC, and, with some variations, in the clearly developed granular layer IV. The prefrontal cortex is functionally rather heterogeneous and is involved in different behavioral, cognitive, and linguistic functions that are characteristic of human beings.

In general, orbital and medial portions of the prefrontal cortex perform a critical role in decision-making and impulse control, and, together with the limbic structures, play a role in emotional and social behavior.

The dorsolateral prefrontal cortex is essential for higher executive functions, which incorporate actions of working and representational memory [2, 3]. The complex neuronal circuitry of prefrontal cortex develops throughout prenatal and postnatal life and sensitive periods of childhood, puberty, and adolescence [4]. The complex organization and development of prefrontal circuitry is obviously one of the major factors of vulnerability of this characteristically human cortical system. Thus, the frontal cortex shows structural and functional abnormalities in different disorders that are characteristic of humans such as schizophrenia, Alzheimer's disease, fronto-temporal dementia, autism spectrum, and other cognitive disorders. In major depressive disorder and suicidal patients, the orbitomedial prefrontal cortex, together with the precingulate area and associated limbic structures, shows structural and functional abnormalities. These findings led to the concept of neurobiological basis of suicidal behavior [5]. Some of these abnormalities, such as a localized decrease in serotonin transporters, seem to be characteristic for suicidal behavior. The mechanism of serotoninergic-frontal innervation reflects the unique role of the prefrontal cortex. The evolutionary "old," ontogenetically early maturing neurotransmitter system modulates synaptic functions of "high" order cortical circuitry, which is evolutionary "new" and late maturing. The abnormalities of the frontal cortex and associated limbic structures should be analyzed at different levels: 1) individual, 2) regional, 3) circuitry level (intrinsic and extrinsic), 4) cellular, and 5) synaptic and receptor level.

The only way to explain the pathogenetic mechanisms is to understand the organization and plasticity of abnormal circuitry. The aim of this paper is to give an overview of basic fronto-limbic connectivity. The knowledge of fronto-limbic connectivity is essential for study of abnormal circuitry in major depression disorder and suicidal behavior and for early detection of prospective abnormalities with modern neuroimaging techniques.

1. Fronto-Limbic Structures and Circuits

On the basis of cytoarchitectonical, connectivity, and neuroimaging studies [2, 6-26], it is accepted that there are at least three major prefrontal networks within the prefrontal cortex that display distinct organization and functions.

The orbital networks can be divided in medial, visceromotor, and lateral sensory network [24]. In this review, we consider medial orbital cortex together with basal medial areas 11 and 12 as orbitomedial prefrontal circuitry (OM PFC).

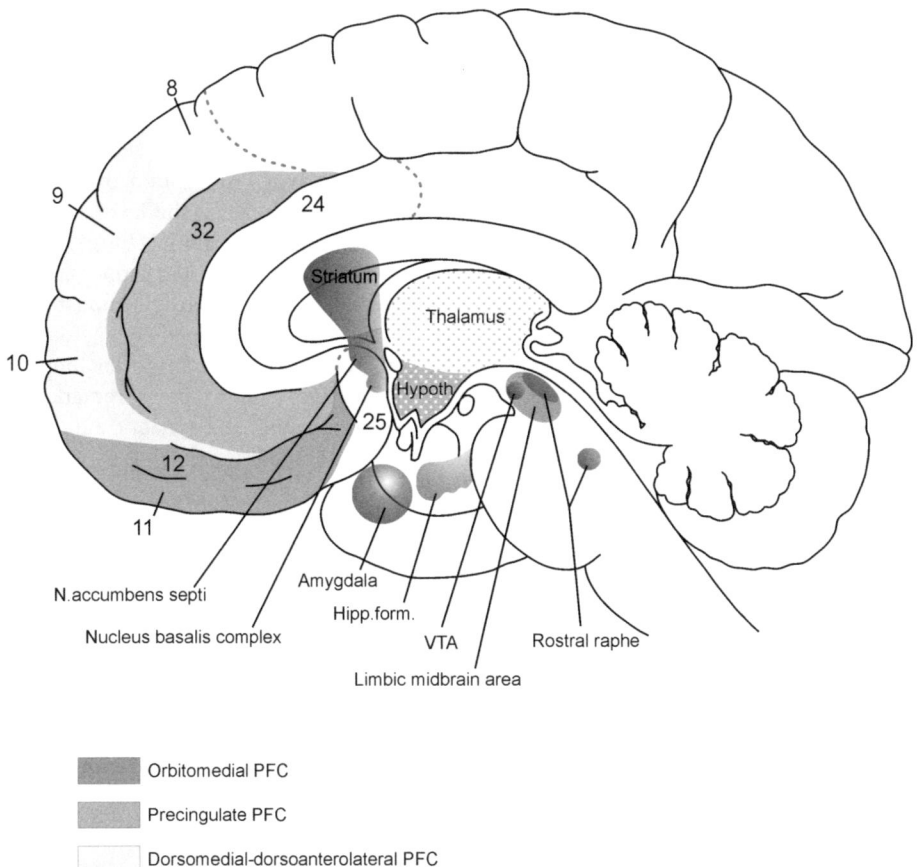

Figure 1. Cortical and subcortical structures which form fronto-limbic circuits. Brodmann areas are marked with Arabic numerals.

The medial portions of areas 9 and 10 are part of the dorsomedial-dorsoanterolateral prefrontal cortex (DL PFC) and are included in fronto-limbic circuitry. The third cortical region occupies the largest aspect of the medial prefrontal cortex and is here described as the precingulate prefrontal cortex (PC PFC) (Figure 1).

This classification is somewhat artificial because all three circuits are strongly interconnected, but we found it useful for systematic analysis of neuropathological, neuroimaging, and developmental data.

The connections of these three regions of prefrontal cortex with limbic cortical and subcortical structures are here defined as fronto-limbic circuitries.

Each part of this fronto-limbic circuitry includes strong cortico-cortical connections and connections with subcortical nuclei in: 1) telencephalon (amygdala, nucleus accumbens septi etc.); 2) diencephalon (hypothalamus, thalamus); 3) modulatory systems of the limbic midbrain area (projections of 5-HT, NA, and DA neurons). These different levels of circuitry are illustrated in Figure 2.

1.1. Serotoninergic pathways to fronto-limbic structures

Serotoninergic projections to fronto-limbic structures originate from rostral raphe nuclei located along the midline of the mesencephalic tegmentum, i.e., the so-called limbic midbrain area (LMA). Ascending serotoninergic axons run within the medial forebrain bundle of the lateral hypothalamus, innervate and divide at the level of basal forebrain and septal-preoptic area, and densely innervate OM, PC, and DL PFC (Figure 2). Serotoninergic fibers also innervate the limbic cortex (cingulate and hippocampal) and limbic subcortical structures; the dense serotoninergic innervation is demonstrated in postmortem studies by visualization of axons immunoreactive for serotonin transporter and visualization of serotonin binding sites. Serotonin transporter binding sites are present in all cortical layers. Theserotoninergic system shows remarkable plasticity and exhibits a number of neurotrophic, neurogenetic, and synaptic functions [27] as revealed by recent genetic studies in experimental models.

1.2. Dopaminergic pathways to fronto-limbic structures

Dopaminergic innervation of fronto-limbic structures originates from the ventral tegmental area, which is also a part of limbic midbrain area (Figure 1). The ascending fibers run through the medial forebrain bundle, innervate the hypothalamus, and spread at the level of basal telencephalon and septal-preoptic area. These fibers heavily innervate nucleus accumbens septi situated (at septal levels) at the junction of caudate nucleus and putamen. Fibers for innervation of the prefrontal cortex proceed to OM, PC and DL PFC. Terminals of dopaminergic fibers innervate principal, pyramidal neurons of the prefrontal cortex and are engaged in synaptic triades [3].

1.3. Limbic cortex- diencephalon/mesencephalon connections

The most robust subcortical connections with the diencephalon are thalamocortical and corticothalamic pathways. The anterior group of thalamic nuclei projects to the anterior cingulate (limbic) area and medial areas of the prefrontal cortex. The dorsomedial thalamic nucleus [3, 7, 8] is the main source of thalamic projections to DL PFC. The projection from dorsomedial nucleus to precingulate and medial cortex is part of the fronto-limbic circuit. The lateral hypothalamus is a key structure for fronto-limbic and limbic connections [28]. Through the hypothalamus, the prefrontal cortex can control emotional behavior and visceromotor functions. More direct influence on visceromotor function may be conveyed through the medial orbital network which projects directly or indirectly (via the hypothalamus) to periaqueductal grey (PAG) in the limbic midbrain area and other parts of the brain stem tegmentum.

1.4. Fronto-limbic connections with basal ganglia

The key structure for emotional behavior and related decision-making is the amygdala (corpus amygdaloideum). This very complex basal ganglion is composed of different groups of nuclei (basolateral, corticomedial, central) and projects predominantly to the orbitomedial cortex (Figure 2). The amygdala is situated at a strategic point between the temporal and the frontal lobes. It receives massive projections from sensory cortices, which are essential for function of the orbital cortex. These sensory inputs terminate in the lateral nucleus of the amygdala. The nucleus accumbens septi [24] is another major point of interaction between neuromodulatory systems, OM and PC PFC. Namely, the nucleus accumbens septi receives robust dopaminergic projections from the ventral tegmental area and has bilateral connections with OM, PC and DL PFC. Very little is known about the influence of cholinergic innervation on functions of fronto-limbic circuitry, but there is a recognizable neural substrate for such interactions: the main cholinergic nucleus, Meynert's basal nucleus, is bilaterally connected with OM PFC. Another structure, which may be involved in motor aspects of emotional behavior, is the caudate nucleus. The caudate nucleus is predominantly connected with DL PFC, but its medial portions receive input from OM PFC [24].

1.5. Cortico-cortical fronto-limbic connections

Medial prefrontal cortical areas represent a typical association cortex with extensively elaborated cortico-cortical connections. Each of these PFC areas is bilaterally interconnected [7, 10, 11, 12, 13, 24]. The real function of these connections is largely unknown. If the main deficit in major depressive disorder and suicidal behavior lies in abnormalities of these cortico-cortical connections and their modulation by serotonin, it would be quite a challenge to reveal the neurobiological basis. Superimposed on cortico-cortical connectivity are intrinsic cortico-cortical connections, which are even more difficult to assess. For the purpose of this review, we defined the main connectivity framework (Figure 2).

DL PFC (areas 9 and 10 of Brodmann) is bilaterally connected with adjacent orbital and precingulate cortex. OM PFC (areas 11 and 12) is interconnected with PC PFC (area 32). PC PFC seems to have a central position because it is bilaterally connected with the cingulate (limbic) cortex on one side, and orbitomedial and dorsomedial cortex on the other side. The connection with the limbic cortex of the hippocampal formation is dual [17], with a long route via the cingulum, and the shorter basal route.

All axons in cortico-cortical pathways originate from layer III pyramidal neurons and are glutamatergic. These excitatory impulses are modified by intrinsic inhibitory GABA-ergic neurons.

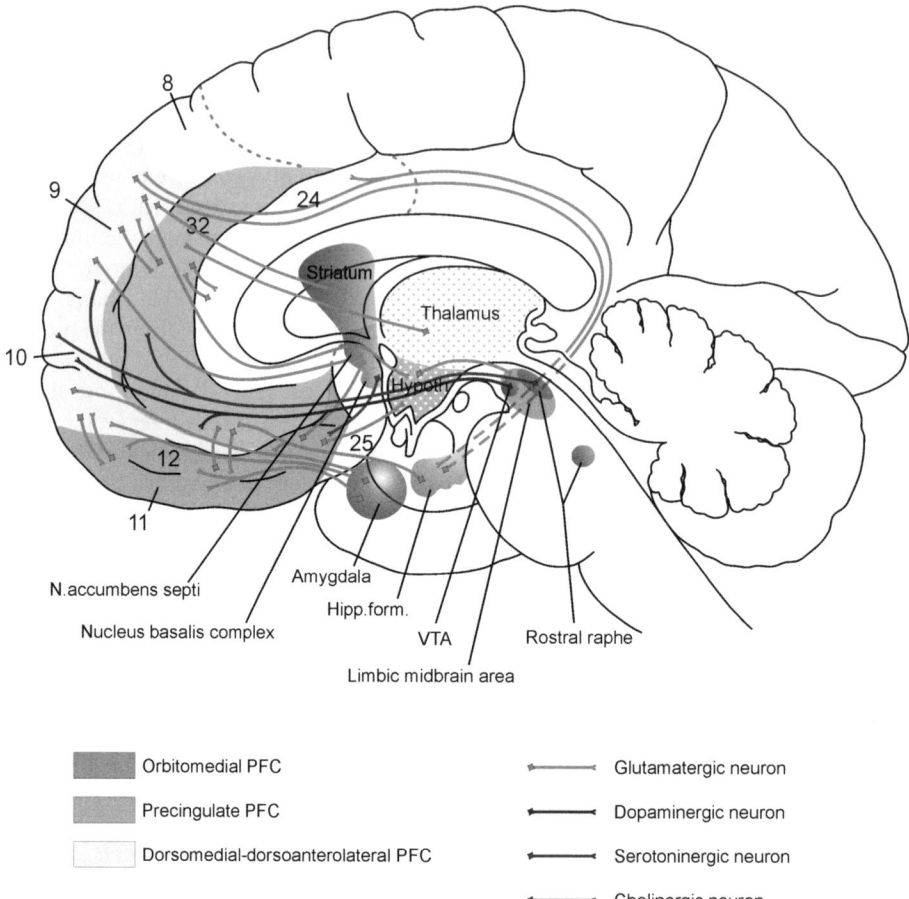

Figure 2. Cortico-cortical and cortico-subcortical fronto-limbic circuits. Note that each of the prefrontal cortices (OM, PC, and DL) receives modulatory input from the midbrain, and has robust projections to subcortical nuclei (amygdala, nucleus accumbens septi, and thalamus).

2. Neurobiological Correlates of Suicidal Behavior

The prefrontal cortex is one of those cortical regions that display pronounced inter-individual variability. Classical studies [29] described prefrontal areas as variable, and this was confirmed in later cytoarchitectonic studies [30]. Cytoarchitectonic variability implies the variability of neurons that send and receive projections. In other words, this variability implies variability in cortical circuitry. Therefore, it is logical to assume that suicide diathesis is a strictly individual feature with respect to the prefrontal cortex. There may be a pronounced variability of serotoninergic innervation. In fact, the main evidence for a neurobiological basis of suicidal behavior relies on classical findings of serotonin system abnormalities [5, 31] and recent findings of neuroimaging abnormalities in cortical structure and function [5, 14, 15, 32, 33, 34]. In addition, there is evidence for various cellular substrates in neuropathological studies of depression [30]. A characteristic feature of serotonin system abnormality is a decrease in the number of presynaptic sites for serotonin transporters in the prefrontal cortex. Decreased serotonin transporter binding was found across all cortical layers. The length of serotonin transporter-positive axons was reduced in layer IV of Brodmann's area 46 [5, 35]. The functional significance of differences between serotoninergic abnormalities in the orbitomedial as compared with the dorsolateral (area 46) cortex is poorly understood. We suggest that differential serotoninergic modulation of two major prefrontal circuits (orbitomedial vs. dorsolateral) may represent one of the key pathogenetic mechanisms in suicidal behavior. The differential modulation of two major prefrontal cortical networks may generate a profound "gap" between decision-making of the orbitomedial cortex and the representation of reality in the dorsolateral cortex. The differences in serotoninergic innervation may be enhanced or potentiated by intrinsic circuits of inhibitory GABA-ergic neurons. Modern neuroimaging techniques have shed a new light on structural-functional deficits in major depressive disorder and suicidal behavior. Areas of increased cerebral blood flow measured by voxel-by-voxel computation show increased cerebral blood flow in the amygdala and medial orbital cortex in comparison to control cases [14, 15]. These results were confirmed with glucose-metabolic measurements. Quantitative studies in suicidal patients [33] using image analysis have shown that grey matter volumes in the orbitofrontal cortex are smaller than in control subjects. Suicidal patients had larger amygdala volumes than non-suicidal patients [33]. Profound quantitative changes in neuronal populations of OM PFC and the amygdala eventually lead to impairment of decision-making. As stated by Strakowski [36], relatively diminished prefrontal modulation of an anterior limbic network may result in mood dysregulation. In accordance with the above-mentioned prediction, the decrease of serotoninergic innervations across all cortical layers may also lead to mood dysregulation.

While searching for a neurobiological basis of suicidal behavior, one should also analyze other components of fronto-limbic circuitry (Figures 2 and 3). Recent studies have demonstrated that changes in blood flow exist also in the nucleus accumbens septi, striatum, thalamus, hypothalamus, cingulate cortex, and hippocampus [32]. An important pathogenetic component may be a dysregulation of the hypothalamic-pituitary-adrenal axis, which is frequently present in depression [32]. The cellular substrate of major depression and suicidal behavior can be assessed by neuropathological analysis. It was shown in cell-counting studies that there are significant alterations in the density and size of neuronal and glial cells in fronto-limbic brain regions. Some of these changes may represent neurodevelopmental abnormalities [30]. Further studies are needed to elucidate whether these changes are specific for depression or suicide victims.

The final proof for the biological basis of suicidal behavior would be a finding of a clear-cut genetic background. Previous studies have shown that the genetic factors play a role in suicidal behavior [14, 31]. However, because suicidal behavior involves several major neuronal circuits, the mechanisms remain unclear. Most fruitful are studies of the serotonergic system [27, 31].

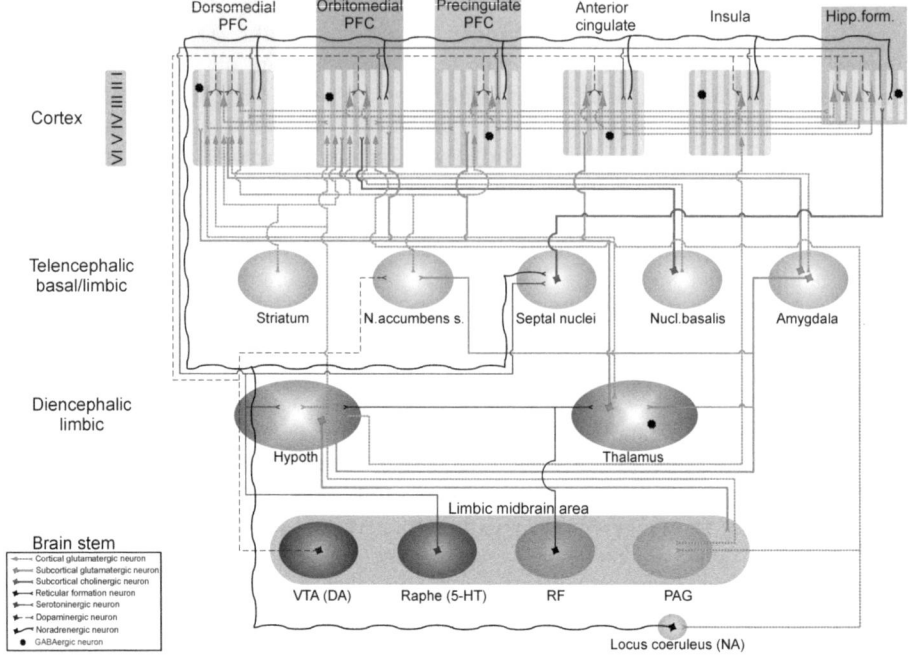

Figure 3. Graphical representation of connections within the three main fronto-limbic circuitries. Note the complexity of cortico-cortical connections and important projections from the midbrain, amygdala, and thalamus.

3. Structural Plasticity

Dynamic changes in regional, areal, laminar, and columnar organization and related changes in spine density, number of synapses, and neurotransmitter systems were observed throughout prenatal and postnatal life [4, 37, 38]. Some of these changes result from interaction with external influences and may be considered as instances of structural plasticity.

It is a frequent fallacy to claim that the prefrontal cortex develops late in comparison to other cortical areas [4]. On the contrary, the prefrontal cortex begins to differentiate very early during fetal life, parallel with other cortical areas. During postnatal development, the prefrontal cortex shows prolonged maturation and protracted plasticity, which last until young adulthood. The major modulatory neurotransmitter system - the serotonin system - shows continuous influence on cortical development and may modulate different developmental processes such as neurogenesis, apoptosis, axon branching, and dendritogesis [27]. It is interesting that the destruction of the serotonin system does not lead to major permanent developmental disturbances. However, modulatory function was shown in numerous models with a sophisticated molecular genetic approach. For example, mutant mice with a targeted $5\text{-HT}_{1/A}$ receptor show increased anxiety and reduced effects of antidepressants [27].

The plasticity of these modulation systems and selective vulnerability of the fronto-limbic system remains one of the most attractive areas of research.

In searching for a neurobiological basis for suicidal behavior, one should take into account prolonged, lifelong reorganization and plasticity of the prefrontal cortex. One of the most interesting developmental and plastic changes is spinogenesis and synaptogenesis [37]. Changes in synaptic number may occur in parallel with changes in receptors. Synapses are sites of major interaction between neurons and transmit external influences on cortical function. Traumatic events may cause changes in synapses in the fronto-limbic cortex and increase vulnerability of the fronto-limbic structures and circuitry.

Synapses differ in their plastic response to external inputs, and certain neurotransmitter systems seem to be particularly prone to plastic changes. This was demonstrated for monoamines, of which serotonin is a prominent member.

4. Conclusions

I.   Suicidal behavior may be a consequence of differential modulation, vulnerability, and plasticity of the orbitomedial-precingulate and dorsolateral fronto-limbic networks.
II. A circuitry-based approach is essential for detection of biological abnormalities revealed by neuroimaging in vivo.

5. Practical Points

1. Detection of structural abnormalities and correlates by *in vivo* structural (quantitative) neuroimaging - regional approach.
2. Detection of functional abnormalities and correlates by *in vivo* functional magnetic resonance – circuitry approach.
3. Detection of individual variability and phase of development – individual approach.

References

[1]   Fuster JM (2002) Frontal lobe and cognitive development. J Neurocytol 31:373-385.
[2]   Goldman-Rakic PS (1997) Space and time in the mental universe. Nature. 386: 559-560.
[3]   Goldman-Rakic PS (1987) Circuitry of primate prefrontal cortex and regulation of behavior by representational memory. In: Handbook of physiology; the nervous system (Plum F, ed.), pp. 373-401. Bethesda, MD: American Physiological Society.
[4]   Kostović I (1990) Structural and histochemical reorganization of the human prefrontal cortex during perinatal and postnatal life. Progr Brain Res 85:223-240.
[5]   Mann JJ (2003) Neurobiology of suicidal behaviour. Nat Rev Neurosci 4:819-828.
[6]   Bachevalier J, Loveland KA (2006) The orbitofrontal-amygdala circuit and self-regulation of social-emotional behavior in autism. Neurosci Biobehav Rev 30:97-117.
[7]   Barbas H, Pandya DN (1989) Architecture and intrinsic connections of the prefrontal cortex in the rhesus monkey. J Comp Neurol 286:353-375.
[8]   Barbas H (1995) Anatomic basis of cognitive-emotional interactions in the primate prefrontal cortex. Neurosci Biobehav Rev 19(3):499-510.
[9]   Bechara A, Damasio H, Damasio AR (2000) Emotion, decision making and the orbitofrontal cortex. Cereb Cortex 10:295-307.

[10] Carmichael ST, Price JL (1995) Limbic connections of the orbital and medial prefrontal cortex in macaque monkeys. J Comp Neurol 363:615-641.

[11] Carmichael ST, Price JL (1996) Connectional networks within the orbital and medial prefrontal cortex of macaque monkeys. J Comp Neurol 371:179-207.

[12] Cavada C (1998) What anatomical connections reveal about primate orbitofrontal functions. Eur J Neurosci 10(Suppl):321.

[13] Cavada C, Company T, Tejedor J, Cruz-Rizzolo RJ, Reinoso-Suárez F (2000) The anatomical connections of the macaque monkey orbitofrontal cortex. A review. Cereb Cortex 10:220-242.

[14] Drevets WC, Videen TO, Price JL, Preskorn SH, Carmichael ST, Raichle ME (1992) A functional anatomical study of unipolar depression. J Neurosci 12:3628-3641.

[15] Drevets WC (2001) Neuroimaging and neuropathological studies of depression: implications for the cognitive-emotional features of mood disorders. Curr Opin Neurobiol 11:240-249.

[16] Frith CD, Friston KJ, Liddle PF, Frackowiak RSJ (1991) Willed action and the prefrontal cortex in man: a study with PET. Proc R Soc Lond B 244:241-246.

[17] Goldman-Rakic PS, Selemon LD, Schwartz ML (1984) Dual pathways connecting the dorsolateral prefrontal cortex with the hippocampal formation and parahippocampal cortex in the rhesus monkey. Neurosciencd 12(3):719-743.

[18] Ingvar DH (1994) The will of the brain: cerebral correlates of willful acts. J Theor Biol 171:7-12.

[19] Kringelbach ML, Rolls ET (2004) The functional neuroanatomy of the human orbitofrontal cortex: evidence from neuroimaging and neuropsychology. Prog Neurobiol 72:341-372.

[20] LeDoux JE (2000) Emotion circuits in the brain. Annu Rev Neurosci 23:155-184.

[21] Mayberg HS (2003) Positron emission tomography imaging in depression: a neural systems perspective. Neuroimaging Clin N Am 13:805-815.

[22] Morecraft RJ, Geula C, Mesulam MM (1992) Cytoarchitecture and neural afferents of orbitofrontal cortex in the brain of the monkey. J Comp Neurol 323:341-358.

[23] O'Doherty J, Kringelbach ML, Rolls ET, Hornak J, Andrews C (2001) Abstract reward and punishment representations in the human orbitofrontal cortex. Nat Neurosci 4:95-102.

[24] Oengür D, Price JL (2000) The organization of networks within the orbital and medial prefrontal cortex of rats, monkeys and humans. Cereb Cortex 10:206-219.

[25] Paus T (2001) Primate anterior cingulate cortex: where motor control, drive and cognition interface. Neuroscience 2:417-424.

[26] Wood JN, Grafman J (2003) Human prefrontal cortex: processing and representational perspectives. Nat Rev Neuroscie 4:139-147.

[27] Gaspar P, Cases O, Maroteaux L (2003) The developmental role of serotonin: news from mouse molecular genetics. Nature 4:1002-1012.

[28] Nauta WJH (1979) Expanding borders of the limbic system concept. In: Functional Neurosurgery, ed. T Rasmussen, R Marino, pp. 7-23. New York: Raven.

[29] Brodmann K (1909) Vergleichende Lokalisationslehre der Grosshirnrinde in ihren Prinzipien dargestellt auf Grund des Zellenbaues. Leipzig: Johann Ambrosius Barth.

[30] Rajkowska G (2003) Depression: what we can learn from postmortem studies. The Neuroscientist 9(4):273-284.

[31] Hranilovic D, Stefulj J, Furac I, Kubat M, Balija M, Jernej B (2003) Serotonin transporter gene promoter (5-HTTLPR) and intron 2 (VNTR) polymorphisms in Croatian suicide victims. Biol Psychiatry 54:884-889.

[32] Nestler EJ, Barrot M, DiLeone RJ, Eisch AJ, Gold SJ, Monteggia LM (2002) Neurobiology of depression. Neuron 34:13-25.

[33] Monkul ES, Hatch JP, Nicoletti MA, Spence S, Brambilla P, Lacerda ALT, Sassi RB,

[34] Joiner TE Jr, Brown JS, Wingate LaRicka R (2005) The psychology and neurobiology of suicidal behavior. Annu Rev Psychol 56:287-314.

[35] Austin MC, Whitehead RE, Edgar CL, Janosky JE, Lewis DA (2002) Localized decrease in serotonin transporter-immunoreactive axons in the prefrontal cortex of depressed subjects committing suicide. Neuroscience 114(3):807-815.

[36] Strakowski SM, Adler CM, DelBello MP (2002) Volumetric MRI studies of mood disorders: do they distinguish unipolar and bipolar disorder? Bipolar Disord 4: 80-88.

[37] Petanjek Z, Judas M, Kostovic I, Uylings HB (2007) Lifespan Alterations of Basal Dendritic Trees of Pyramidal Neurons in the Human Prefrontal Cortex: A Layer-Specific Pattern. Cereb Cortex Jul 25

[38] Giedd JN, Blumenthal J, Jeffries NO, Castellanos FX, Liu H, Zijdenbos A, Paus T, Evans AC, Rapoport JL (1999) Brain development during childhood and adolescence: a longitudinal MRI study. Nature Neuroscience 2(10):861-863.

doi:10.3233/978-1-58603-889-2-33

Mental Disorders, Perceived Need and Perceived Barriers to Care in Military Samples

Jitender Sareen MD, FRCPC [a,b,1], Murray B Stein MD, FRCPC, MPH [c], Shay-Lee Belik BSc (Hons) [a,b], Tracie O Afifi MSc [a,b], and Gordon JG Asmundson PhD [d]

[a] *Department of Psychiatry, University of Manitoba*
[b] *Department of Community Health Sciences, University of Manitoba*
[c] *Departments of Psychiatry and Family & Preventive Medicine, University of California San Diego*
[d] *Anxiety and Illness Behaviours Laboratory, University of Regina*

Abstract. Untreated mental illness is an enormous problem in civilian and military populations. This paper reviews the literature on 1) methods and controversy related to defining the need for mental health treatment at a population level, 2) studies examining the relationship between mental disorder diagnoses and self-perceived need for mental health treatment, and 3) studies examining attitudes and barriers toward mental health care. Similar to civilian populations, the few studies in military samples have found that the majority of soldiers meeting criteria for a mental disorder do not receive mental health treatment or perceive a need for treatment. Attitudinal barriers (e.g., I would be seen as weak; a wish to solve the problem on their own) are more commonly endorsed than structural barriers (e.g., cost of services) toward seeking mental health care. Implications for future research and interventions are discussed.

Keywords. Perceived need, military, mental disorders, barriers to care

Introduction

Soldiers face numerous challenges during deployment. These can include exposure to life-threatening traumatic events (e.g., combat, witnessing death, being injured), as well as non life-threatening but nonetheless traumatic stressors (e.g., separation from friends and family, harsh environments, foreign cultures) [1-5]. Although the majority of deployed soldiers do well upon return from a mission, a significant minority will suffer serious deployment-related mental health problems.

[1] Corresponding Author: J. Sareen MD, PZ430 – 771 Bannatyne Ave, Winnipeg MB Canada R3E 3N4; Email: sareen@cc.umanitoba.ca

Preparation of this article was supported by 1) New Emerging Team Grant PTS—63186 from the Canadian Institutes of Health Research (CIHR) Institute of Neurosciences, Mental Health and Addiction, 2) a CIHR operating grant to Dr. Sareen, 3) a CIHR New Investigator grant awarded to Dr. Sareen, 4) a Career Development (K24) Award from the National Institutes of Health (MH64122) to Dr. Stein, 5) a CIHR Canada Graduate Scholarship – Master's Award awarded to Ms. Belik, 6) a Western Regional Training Centre studentship funded by Canadian Health Services Research Foundation, Alberta Heritage Foundation for Medical Research and Canadian Institutes of Health Research awarded to Ms. Belik, and 7) a Social Sciences and Humanities Research Council Canada Graduate Scholarship to Ms. Afifi.

Soldiers can develop a range of emotional and physical health problems in relation to combat and peacekeeping operations [1, 6, 7]. These include depression, anxiety, alcohol and drug-related problems, and physical complaints. Such problems can lead to long-term dysfunction that can result in poor work performance, prolonged sick leave, medical releases, and poor readiness for future operations [4, 8].

Policymakers require information on the number of people in need of mental health services. Such information is vital in allocating appropriate resources for mental health services and determining the disability associated with mental disorders [9]. Although this goal is well accepted, the optimal method to estimate the number of people who need mental health treatment has been controversial in psychiatric epidemiology.

1. Diagnosis does not equate with need for treatment

In the last 25 years, the main approach for estimating the number of people in the community who "need" care for mental illness has been to provide prevalence estimates of mental disorders based on explicit criteria of an accepted diagnostic system [10]. A recently published study by the World Health Organization International Consortium examined the prevalence of DSM mental disorders, impairment, and unmet need in 14 countries across the world. A wide range of prevalence rates of mental disorders was found across countries [11, 12]. However, consistent with previous surveys from Canada [13, 14], the U.S. [15], Australia [16] and The Netherlands [17], the majority of individuals with a mental disorder diagnosis did not receive treatment. In addition, a substantial proportion of individuals who perceive a need for mental health care do not meet full criteria for a mental health disorder.

In the face of such overwhelming data from international epidemiologic studies suggesting a huge discrepancy between "need" and "care" for mental illness, many leaders in psychiatric epidemiology have persuasively argued that the current DSM-based diagnosis may not be a good measure of "need" for care in the community [18, 19]. Based on low rates of self-perceived need for care and low levels of mental health service utilization, some have suggested that a large proportion of individuals diagnosed with mental disorders may be suffering from transient or mild symptoms that do not require treatment [18, 20, 21]. These authors have argued that defining need for treatment in community samples will require additional severity criteria beyond those in the DSM to adequately estimate the need for care of mental disorders.

Recently, increasing attention has been paid toward self-perceived need for mental health treatment in the community. This concept takes into account a theoretical model of help-seeking proposed by Goldberg and Huxley (1980). They suggest that individuals suffering with emotional problems undergo a number of stages prior to help-seeking for emotional symptoms [22, 23]: *1) experience symptoms, 2) evaluate the severity and consequences of the symptoms, 3) assess whether treatment is required, 4) assess feasibility and options for treatment, and 5) seek treatment or not.*

In considering these stages of help-seeking, it becomes apparent that defining how many people in the community need mental health treatment depends on which stage of the process of help-seeking is used as the threshold to determine "need." Some have argued that in addition to using the presence of meeting criteria for a diagnosis, it may be useful to additionally examine self-perceived need for mental health treatment [21, 24-26].

2. Perceived need for mental health treatment in general population samples

A wide range of prevalence estimates for perceived need for mental health treatment have been noted in the general population studies of several countries (8.0%-19%) [24, 25, 27-31]. These differences in prevalence estimates of perceived need in the different surveys may reflect true differences in level of need of treatment or may be due to differences in methodology of assessment of perceived need. The relationship between perceived need for treatment, meeting criteria for a common mental disorder, and disability has been examined in three separate community samples in Ontario [25], the United States [26], and Australia [21, 32]. There are a number of important findings that are consistent across these surveys. First, the prevalence of perceived need for mental health treatment is much lower than the prevalence of meeting criteria for a mental disorder diagnosis [21, 25, 26]. Second, a significant number of individuals perceive a need for treatment or seek treatment without meeting criteria for any of the DSM disorders assessed in the survey [21, 25, 33]. These individuals could either have subthreshold DSM symptoms or have a DSM disorder that was not assessed in the community survey. Third, self-perceived need for treatment, independent of meeting criteria for a mental disorder assessed in the survey, is an indicator of poorer quality of life and higher levels of disability [25, 32]. Fourth, a range of sociodemographic factors, type of mental disorder, childhood adversity [34] and comorbidity with other mental disorders and presence of physical health conditions influence perceived need for mental health treatment [25, 26]. Based on these studies, our group and others have suggested that determining self-perceived need for mental health treatment is a useful approach in determining the number of people who need help for emotional symptoms.

3. Perceived need and DSM diagnosis in military samples

To the best of our knowledge, only two studies have examined the relationship between diagnosis and perceived need for treatment among military personnel. Hoge et al.[1] studied members of four U.S. combat infantry units. Individuals were assessed before deployment (N=2,530) to Iraq and after deployment (N=3,671) to Iraq and Afghanistan using self-report screening instruments for PTSD, major depression (MDD) and generalized anxiety disorder (GAD) [1]. This study demonstrated that there was a significantly higher prevalence of the three mental disorders (MDD, GAD and PTSD) among military personnel post-deployment (15.6% to 17.1%) compared to pre-deployment (9.3%). Among respondents who met screening criteria for one or more of the three mental disorders assessed in this study, only 38-45% perceived a need for mental health treatment and 23-40% received treatment from any professional. Overall, findings by Hoge et al. [1] suggest that untreated mental illness in the U.S. military is high, and negative attitudes toward mental health treatment-seeking behavior are also prevalent. This study also demonstrates the emerging interest in examining perceived need for mental health treatment in military samples. However, this study did not examine the prevalence of perceived need in the whole sample.

Our group recently published data on the relationship between perceived need, diagnosis, and help-seeking in a large representative sample of Canadian military personnel (n=8441) [6]. A validated measure of perceived need was utilized in this study, called the Perceived Need for Care Questionnaire (PNCQ). The PNCQ assessed if a respondent perceived a need or received help for problems with emotions, mental health, or use of alcohol or drugs in the past year. Five categories were covered: 1) information about mental health problems, its treatments, or available services, 2) medication, 3) therapy or counseling, 4) social intervention (i.e., help for financial or housing problems), and 5) skills training (i.e., help for employment status, work situation or personal relationships). Respondents were also asked if they received as much care as they felt they needed in each of the above domains. All respondents were also asked if they had seen or talked to a professional about their emotions, mental health, or use of alcohol or drugs in the past year. Professionals included psychiatrist, family doctor, general practitioner or medical officer, other medical doctor, psychologist, nurse, nurse practitioner, physician's assistant or medic, social worker/counselor or psychotherapist, religious or spiritual advisor, or other professional (e.g., acupuncturist, chiropractor, herbalist, and massage therapist). In addition, the following DSM diagnoses were assessed using the World Health Organization Consortium Composite International Diagnostic Interview: major depressive disorder, posttraumatic stress disorder, dysthymia, generalized anxiety disorder, panic disorder, and alcohol dependence.

The past-year prevalence rates of at least one DSM disorder, perceived need for care, and mental health service use were 14.9%, 23.2%, and 12.8%, respectively. Overall, 31% of the sample had perceived a need, met diagnosis of a mental disorder, or sought care in the past year. As demonstrated in Figure 1, there was significant overlap between self-perceived need for treatment, meeting criteria for an assessed mental disorder, and seeking care.

- Diagnosis, Perceived Need, Help Seeking = 5.8%
- Diagnosis, Help Seeking = 0.3%
  Diagnosis only = 5.6%
- Diagnosis, Perceived Need = 3.1%
- Help Seeking only = 1.9%
- Perceived Need, Help Seeking = 4.6%
- Perceived Need only = 9.7%
- None = 69%

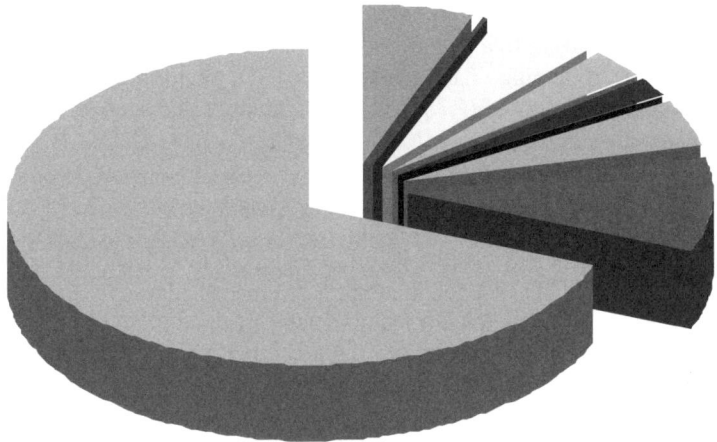

Figure 1. Prevalence of Perceived Need and Help-Seeking in the Canadian Military. Adapted from Sareen et al. 2007 [6].

Figure 2 shows the prevalence of perceived need in the whole sample. Overall, 23.2% of the sample reported a perceived need for mental health care. The prevalence of each type of perceived need was as follows: therapy or counseling - 12.5%, skills training - 12.4%, information - 11.4%, medication - 6.0%, and social intervention - 4.1%. Follow-up questions also examined whether the respondents felt that they received as much treatment as they felt they needed. Figure 2 demonstrates that a perceived need for medication was the most likely to be fully met. However, other types of perceived need were less likely to be fully met. For example, among the 12.5% of the sample that reported a perceived need for therapy, approximately 50% felt that they did not receive as much treatment as they needed.

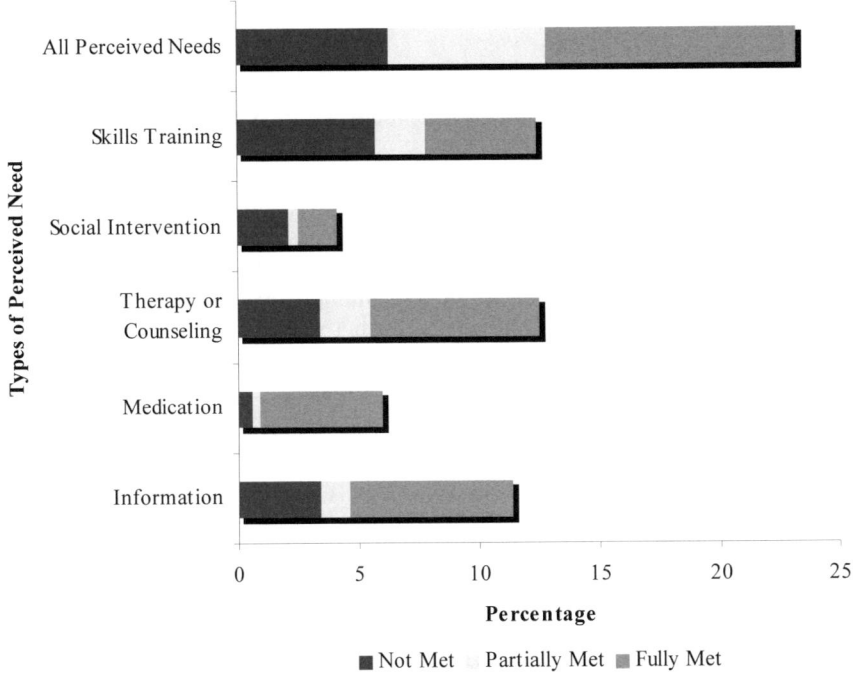

Figure 2. Prevalence of Perceived Need for Care in the Canadian Military. Adapted from Sareen et al. 2007 [6].

4. Combat and peacekeeping in relation to perceived need

Sareen et al. [6] also examined the relationship between exposure to combat, exposure to peacekeeping operations, and witnessing atrocities (e.g., human massacres) in relation to self-perceived need for treatment. Since there was significant overlap between these three deployment-related variables, multivariate models were conducted that adjusted for the effects of sociodemographic factors, combat, peacekeeping, and witnessing atrocities simultaneously. Among the three deployment-related variables, lifetime exposure to witnessing atrocities had the highest likelihood of association with each of the self-perceived need variables [(adjusted odds ratios ranging between 1.62 and 2.01)], with the exception of social intervention. Combat exposure was associated with self-perceived need for medication, information, and counseling (AORs ranging from 1.28 to 1.50). However, exposure to peacekeeping operations was not associated with any of the perceived need variables. These findings suggest that soldiers who are exposed to combat and who witness atrocities while deployed have an increased likelihood of reporting a self-perceived need for treatment. These findings also imply that soldiers deployed to peacekeeping operations without exposure to combat or atrocities are at no greater risk of self-perceived need for treatment. However, it remains unknown whether the association between these deployment-related variables and perceived need is indirectly mediated through the presence of a mental disorder or a direct effect of trauma exposure.

5. Self-reported barriers to care

There has been emerging interest in understanding perceived barriers toward mental health service use. These barriers have been broadly divided into individual attitudinal factors (e.g., fear of stigmatization) and system-level structural factors (e.g., financial cost of services) [35-39]. Previous work has demonstrated that emotionally distressed individuals most commonly identify attitudinal barriers (e.g., respondent's wish to solve the problem on their own, thoughts that the emotional problem would go away) for not seeking mental health treatment [38, 39]. Although fear of stigmatization [35] is commonly thought to be an important reason for not seeking mental health treatment, the limited number of studies to date [38, 39] have not found fear of stigmatization as a commonly reported barrier toward mental health service use. Also, structural barriers, such as the financial cost associated with mental health treatment, may impact significantly upon mental health service utilization.

Table 1. Self-reported barriers to care in a U.S. military sample of respondents meeting probable criteria for a mental disorder (PTSD, alcohol abuse, or depression). Adapted from Hoge et al. 2004

Barrier (n=731)	%
I would be seen as weak.	65
My unit leadership might treat me differently.	63
Members of my unit might have less confidence in me.	59
There would be difficulty getting time off work for treatment.	55
It would harm my career.	50
My leaders would blame me for the problem.	51
It is difficult to schedule an appointment.	45
It would be too embarrassing.	41
I don't trust mental health professionals.	38
Mental health care costs too much money.	25
Mental health care doesn't work.	25
I don't know where to get help.	22
I don't have adequate transportation.	18

To date, only two studies have examined self-perceived barriers to care among soldiers. First, Hoge et al. [1] examined barriers to care among all respondents in a large U.S. military survey. Respondents were asked to rate "each of the possible concerns that might affect your decision to receive mental health counseling or services if you ever had a problem." Thirteen perceived barriers were listed. Respondents had five possible responses to each barrier from strongly agree to strongly disagree. "I would be seen as weak" and "my unit leadership might treat me differently" were the two most commonly endorsed barriers to mental health care. Table 1 shows the prevalence of perceived barriers among soldiers that had a probable mental disorder (at least one of major depression, posttraumatic stress disorder, or alcohol abuse).

Second, Sareen et al. [6] also examined perceived barriers to care among soldiers that reported a need for mental health treatment. Unlike the U.S. study by Hoge et al. [1] that asked about attitudes and barriers towards mental health treatment seeking for all respondents, the Canadian survey only asked questions related to barriers to care among those who perceived a need for treatment and did not receive as much treatment as they felt they needed. Table 2 shows the results of this study. The response "other" reason and "didn't have confidence in the military health, administration or social services" were the two most commonly endorsed barriers to care. The high endorsement of the "other" category as a barrier to care indicates that important reasons for not seeking treatment in the military sample were excluded among the list of possible barriers.

Table 2. Self-reported barriers to care among Canadian soldiers who perceived a need for mental health treatment. Adapted from Sareen et al. 2007

Barriers to Care	Partially Met Need (n=376) %	Unmet need (n=872) %
Other	50.4	32.2
Didn't have confidence in military health, administrative, or social services	30.1	38.1
Have not gotten around to it	13.6	24.3
Didn't know where to go	12.5	22.0
Job interfered (e.g., workload, hours of work or no cooperation supervisor)	20.0	16.9
Afraid of what others would think	11.6	19.5
Help not readily available	19.9	16.6
Couldn't afford to pay	5.5	4.8
Language problems	2.3	1.8

Since different barriers to care were included in the U.S. and Canadian study, it is difficult to compare the findings in these two large samples. However, an overall conclusion that can be drawn from these studies is that attitudinal barriers are more commonly endorsed in military samples than structural barriers. These findings are also consistent with general population samples. However, as shown by Hoge et al.'s [1] study, fear of stigmatization, especially by military comrades, may be very important in military samples. Further research on the barriers to care specific to military personnel is warranted. Efforts to reduce stigma around mental health issues in the military and outreach programs that provide mental health service in primary care settings may be needed.

Limitations and future directions

There are a number of limitations of the present literature. First, to the best of our knowledge, only the two studies (by Hoge et al. [1] and Sareen et al. [6]) have examined the relationship between perceived need for treatment, DSM diagnosis, and barriers to care in military samples. The generalizability of these findings to military samples in other countries remains unknown. Further studies using a systematic assessment of mental disorders and perceived need for treatment in other countries are required. Second, only a limited number of Axis I mental disorders were assessed in these two studies. Axis II disorders might also affect levels of perceived need. Most epidemiologic surveys utilize lay interviews to make DSM-IV diagnoses or use self-report instruments. Although these methods are reliable, they may not match the accuracy of clinician-based assessment of mental disorders or need for treatment. Furthermore, the assessment of barriers to care for mental health services have been assessed based on asking respondents to endorse barriers from a pre-determined list. It would be useful to utilize qualitative methods to further understand in detail the barriers faced by soldiers in receiving mental health care.

Conclusions

In summary, there is an enormous burden of untreated mental illness in military populations. Irrespective of whether need for treatment is defined based on standardized measures, such as meeting criteria for mental disorder, or based on direct respondent appraisal of need for treatment, the majority of people did not receive treatment for their mental health problems. Stigma and negative attitudes toward mental health service use are important barriers to care in the military. Substantial systematic efforts are needed to better understand and address the needs of soldiers suffering with emotional problems.

Reference List

[1] C. W. Hoge, C. A. Castro, S. C. Messer, D. McGurk, D. I. Cotting, and R. L. Koffman, Combat duty in Iraq and Afghanistan, mental health problems, and barriers to care, *N Engl J Med* **351** (2004), 13-22.
[2] C. W. Hoge, J. L. Auchterlonie, and C. S. Milliken, Mental health problems, use of mental health services, and attrition from military service after returning from deployment to Iraq or Afghanistan, *JAMA* **295** (2006), 1023-1032.
[3] M. Hotopf, L. Hull, N. T. Fear, T. Browne, O. Horn, A. Iversen, M. Jones, D. Murphy, D. Bland, M. Earnshaw, N. Greenberg, J. H. Hughes, A. R. Tate, C. Dandeker, R. Rona, and S. Wessely, The health of UK military personnel who deployed to the 2003 Iraq war: A cohort study, *Lancet* **367** (2006), 1731-1741.

[4] C. W. Hoge, A. Terhakopian, C. A. Castro, S. C. Messer, and C. C. Engle, Association of posttraumatic stress disorder with somatic symptoms, health care visits, and absenteeism among Iraq war veterans, *Am J Psychiatry* **164** (2007), 150-153.

[5] R. J. Rona, N. T. Fear, L. Hull, N. Greenberg, M. Earnshaw, M. Hotopf, and S. Wessely, Mental health consequences of overstretch in the UK armed forces: first phase of a cohort study, *Br Med J* **335** (2007), 603-604.

[6] J. Sareen, B. J. Cox, T. O. Afifi, M. B. Stein, S. L. Belik, G. Meadows, and G. J. G. Asmundson, Combat and peacekeeping operations in relation to prevalence of mental disorders and perceived need for mental health care: Findings from a large representative sample of military personnel, *Arch Gen Psychiatry* **64** (2007), 843-852.

[7] B. P. Dohrenwend, J. B. Turner, N. A. Turse, B. G. Adams, K. C. Koenen, and R. Marshall, The psychological risks of Vietnam for U.S. veterans: A revisit with new data and methods, *Science* **313** (2006), 979-982.

[8] H. G. Prigerson, P. K. Maciejewski, and R. A. Rosenheck, Combat trauma: Trauma with highest risk of delayed onset and unresolved posttraumatic stress disorder symptoms, unemployment, and abuse among men, *J Nerv Ment Dis* **189** (2001), 99-108.

[9] S. C. Messer, X. Liu, C. W. Hoge, D. N. Cowan, and C. C. Jr. Engel, Projecting mental disorder prevalence from national surveys to populations-of-interest: An illustration using ECA data and the U.S. Army, *Social psychiatry and psychiatric epidemiology* **39** (2004), 419-426.

[10] R. L. Spitzer, J. Endicott, and E. Robins, Research diagnostic criteria: rationale and reliability, *Archives of General Psychiatry* **35** (1978), 773-782.

[11] The WHO World Mental Health Survey Consortium, Prevalence, Severity, and Unmet Need for Treatment of Mental Disorders in the World Health Organization World Mental Health Surveys, *JAMA* **291** (2004), 2590.

[12] P. S. Wang, S. Aguilar-Gaxiola, J. Alonso, M. C. Angermeyer, G. Borges, E. J. Bromet, R. Bruffaerts, G. de Girolamo, R. de Graaf, O. Gureje, J. M. Haro, E. G. Karam, R. C. Kessler, V. Kovess, M. C. Lane, S. Lee, D. Levinson, Y. Ono, M. Petukhova, J. Posada-Villa, S. Seedat, and J. E. Wells, Use of mental health services for anxiety, mood, and substance disorders in 17 countries in the WHO world mental health surveys, *Lancet* **370** (2007), 841-850.

[13] R. C. Kessler, R. G. Frank, M. Edlund, S. J. Katz, E. Lin, and P. Leaf, Differences in the use of psychiatric outpatient services between the United States and Ontario, *N Engl J Med* **336** (1997), 551-557.

[14] E. Lin, P. Goering, D. R. Offord, D. Campbell, and M. H. Boyle, The Use of Mental Health Services in Ontario: Epidemiologic Findings, *Can J Psychiatry* **41** (1996), 572-577.

[15] R. C. Kessler, S. Zhao, S. J. Katz, A. C. Kouzis, R. G. Frank, M. Edlund, and P. Leaf, Past-Year use of outpatient services for psychiatric problems in the National Comorbidity Survey, *Am J Psychiatry* **156** (1999), 115-122.

[16] G. Andrews, S. Henderson, and W. Hall, Prevalence, comorbidity, disability and service utilization. Overview of the Australian National Mental Health Survey, *Br J Psychiatry* **178** (2001), 145-153.

[17] R. V. Bijl, R. de Graaf, E. Hiripi, R. C. Kessler, R. Kohn, D. R. Offord, T. B. Ustun, B. Vicente, W. A. Vollebergh, E. E. Walters, and H. U. Wittchen, The prevalence of treated and untreated mental disorders in five countries, *Health Aff* **22** (2003), 122-133.

[18] D. A. Regier, C. T. Kaelber, D. S. Rae, M. E. Farmer, B. Knauper, R. C. Kessler, and G. S. Norquist, Limitations of Diagnostic Criteria and Assessment Instruments for Mental Disorders: Implications for Research and Policy, *Arch Gen Psychiatry* **55** (1998), 109-115.

[19] R. L. Spitzer, Diagnosis and Need for treatment are not the same, *Arch Gen Psychiatry* **55** (1998), 120.

[20] C. Issakidis and G. Andrews, Service utilisation for anxiety in an Australian community sample, *Soc Psychiatry Psychiatr Epidemiol* **37** (2002), 153-163.

[21] G. Meadows, P. Burgess, E. Fossey, and C. Harvey, Perceived Need for mental health care, findings from the Australian National Survey of Mental Health and Wellbeing, *Psychol Med* **30** (2000), 645-656.

[22] D. Goldberg and P. Huxley, *Mental Health in the Community: The Pathways to Psychiatric Care*, Tavistock Publications, London, England 1980.

[23] D. Goldberg, Plato versus Aristotle: categorical and dimensional models for common mental disorders, *Compr. Psychiatry* **41** (2000), 8-13.

[24] S. Aoun, D. Pennebaker, and C. Wood, Assessing population need for mental health care: A review of approaches and predictors, *Ment Health Serv Res* **6** (2004), 33-46.

[25] J. Sareen, M. B. Stein, D. W. Campbell, T. Hassard, and V. Menec, The relationship between perceived need for mental health treatment, DSM diagnosis and quality of life: A Canadian population-based survey, *Can J Psychiatry* **50** (2005), 173-180.

[26] R. Mojtabai, M. Olfson, and D. Mechanic, Perceived Need and Help-Seeking in Adults with Mood, Anxiety or Substance Use Disorders, *Arch Gen Psychiatry* **59** (2002), 77-84.

[27] J. Rabinowitz, R. Gross, and D. Feldman, Correlates of a perceived need for mental health assistance and differences between those who do and do not seek help, *Soc Psychiatry Psychiatr Epidemiol* **34** (1999), 141-146.

[28] R. Mojtabai, M. Olfson, and D. Mechanic, Perceived need and help-seeking in adults with mood, anxiety or substance use disorders, *Arch Gen Psychiatry* **59** (2002), 77-84.

[29] G. Meadows, P. Burgess, E. Fossey, and C. Harvey, Perceived need for mental health care, findings from the Australian National Survey of Mental Health and Well-being, *Psychol Med* (2000), 645-656.

[30] J. Sareen, B. J. Cox, T. O. Afifi, I. Clara, and B. N. Yu, Perceived need for mental health treatment in a nationally representative Canadian sample, *Can J Psychiatry* **50** (2005), 447-455.

[31] T. O. Afifi, B. J. Cox, and J. Sareen, Perceived need and help-seeking for mental health problems among Canadian provinces and territories, *Can J Comm Mental Health* **24** (2005), 51-61.

[32] G. Meadows, P. Burgess, I. Bobevski, E. Fossey, C. Harvey, and S.-T. Liaw, Perceived Need for mental health care: influence of diagnosis, demography and disability, *Psychol Med* **32** (2002), 299-309.

[33] R. C. Bland, C. Newman, and H. Orn, Help-seeking for psychiatric disorders., *Can J Psychiatry* **42** (1997), 935-942-942.

[34] J. Sareen, W. Fleisher, B. J. Cox, S. Hassard, and M. B. Stein, Childhood adversity and perceived need for mental health care: findings from a Canadian community sample, *J Nerv Ment Dis* **193** (2005), 396-404.

[35] A. H. Crisp, M. G. Gelder, S. Rix, H. I. Meltzer, and O. J. Rowlands, Stigmatisation of people with mental illnesses, *Br J Psychiatry* **177** (2000), 4-7.

[36] A. Thompson, C. Hunt, and C. Issakidis, Why wait? Reasons for delay and prompts to seek help for mental health problems in an Australian clinical sample, *Soc Psychiatry Psychiatr Epidemiol* **39** (2004), 810-817.

[37] M. M. Weissman, A piece of my mind: Stigma, *JAMA* **285** (2001), 261-262.

[38] J. E. Wells, L. N. Robins, J. A. Bushnell, D. Jarosz, and M. A. Oakley Browne, Perceived barriers to care in St. Louis (USA) and Christchurch (NZ): Reasons for not seeking professional help for psychological distress, *Soc Psychiatry Psychiatr Epidemiol* **29** (1994), 155-164.

[39] S. Saldivia, B. Vicente, R. Kohn, P. Rioseco, and S. Torres, Use of mental health services in Chile, *Psychiatr Serv* **55** (2004), 71-76.

Section II

Diagnostic and Assessment Issues

Lowering Suicide Risk in Returning Troops
B.K. Wiederhold (Ed.)
IOS Press, 2008
© 2008 IOS Press. All rights reserved.
doi:10.3233/978-1-58603-889-2-45

A Review of the U.S. Army Soldier Suicides in Iraq

Carl A. CASTRO, PhD, Col[a,1], Dennis MCGURK, PhD, Maj. [b],
& Kathleen M. WRIGHT, PhD [b]

[a]*Medical Research and Materiel Command, Ft. Detrick, Maryland*
[b]*US Army Medical Research Unit – Europe, Walter Reed Army Institute of Research*

Note: The results and opinions presented in this report are those of the Mental Health Advisory Team IV members and do not necessarily represent the official policy or position of the Department of Defense, the United States Army, or the Office of The Surgeon General.

Abstract. The Mental Health Advisory Team (MHAT) IV was established by the Office of the U.S. Army Surgeon General at the request of the Commanding General, Multi-National Force-Iraq (MNF-I). The mission of MHAT IV was to (a) assess Soldier and Marine mental health and wellbeing, (b) examine the delivery of behavioral health care in Operation Iraqi Freedom (OIF), and (c) provide recommendations for sustainment and improvement to command. Part of the MHAT IV mission was to review the status of the theater's suicide prevention and surveillance programs, including an analysis of completed suicides. The MHAT IV assessed the mental health of the deployed force from August 28, 2006 to October 3, 2006. Recommendations are based on findings from anonymous Soldier (N = 1,320) and Marine (N = 447) surveys, and on behavioral health, primary care, and unit ministry team surveys; focus group interviews with Soldiers and Marines, as well as interviews and focus groups with Army and Navy behavioral health personnel; various secondary sources; and personal observations by team members.

Keywords. Suicide, suicide surveillance, suicide prevention, Mental Health Advisory Teams

1. Background

This document reviews U.S. Army Soldier suicides in Iraq and the status of the suicide prevention and surveillance programs established in-theater. Much of the information is contained in the full report representing the findings from the fourth Mental Health Advisory Team (MHAT IV). Such teams have deployed to Iraq and have conducted assessments since the beginning of Operation Iraqi Freedom (OIF) (see Operation Iraqi Freedom Mental Health Advisory Team Report, 2003; Mental Health Advisory Team II (MHAT-II) Report from Operation Iraqi Freedom II, 2004; Mental Health Advisory Team (MHAT-III) Operation Iraq Freedom 04-06, 2006; and Mental Health Advisory Team (MHAT) IV Operation Iraq Freedom 05-07). The mission and scope of activities of the MHAT IV were approved by the Commanding General (CG), Multinational

---

[1] Corresponding Author: COL Carl A. Castro. RAD III, Medical Research and Materiel Command, Ft. Detrick, Maryland, USA. Telephone: 001-301-619-7304; email: carl.castro@us.army.mil

Forces – Iraq (MNF-I). The MHAT IV members were assigned to the MNF-I and worked directly under the supervision and control of the Command Surgeon, MNF-I.

The MHAT IV mission statement was "MHAT IV assesses Soldier and Marine mental health and well-being; examines the delivery of behavioral health care in OIF; analyzes information obtained; provides recommendations for sustainment and improvement to command." The MHAT IV scope of activities included the following:

- Assess the mental health and wellbeing of the deployed force, building on the findings from previous MHATs. Focus on three populations: Soldiers, Marines, and Military Transition Teams. This is the first MHAT to assess the mental health and wellbeing of Marines and Military Transition Teams.
- Assess ethical issues faced by Soldiers and Marines to enhance future battlefield ethics training. This activity was included at the specific request of the CG, MNF-I. This is the first time that the topic of Battlefield Ethics has been systematically assessed in a combat environment since World War II (see Stouffer, et al. 1949).
- Compare findings from current OIF operations to previous OIF findings.
- Review behavioral health policies, programs, structure, and resources to ensure optimal integration/utilization, focusing on suicide prevention efforts.
- Review the status of the implementation of recommendations of previous MHATs, providing assistance where possible.

For the purpose of this document, the focus is on the status of the theater's suicide prevention and surveillance programs, including an analysis of completed U.S. Army Soldier suicides. Comparisons to previous MHAT observations over the course of Operation Iraqi Freedom are made where relevant. The first section of the document addresses the involvement of the Unit Ministry Teams in suicide prevention training. The next section discusses the theater's prevention and surveillance program, with particular attention to the Army Suicide Event Report (ASER), which was used as the reporting and tracking mechanism for Soldier completed suicides and non-lethal events that result in hospitalization and/or evacuation. The final section of the document reviews the suicide statistics for U.S. Army Soldiers in Iraq, which includes rates in theater over time, comparisons with overall Army rates, and analysis of suicides by month, to determine trends and clustering effects.

2. Suicide Prevention Training

Unit Ministry Team (UMT) staff members continue to be the primary personnel conducting suicide prevention training. Ninety-five percent (95%) of UMT members conducted suicide prevention training "at least once during this deployment". Eighty-nine percent (89%) of Soldiers reported receiving suicide prevention training, but only 63% of Soldiers reported being confident in identifying other Soldiers at risk for suicide. This highlights the need to ensure that suicide prevention training meets the goal of helping Soldiers recognize signs that a fellow Soldier may be suicidal.

3. Suicide Prevention Program Review

All of the previous MHATs have reviewed the status of the OIF theater's suicide prevention and surveillance program, including an analysis of completed suicides. The analyses of completed suicides was of particular interest during MHAT I due to an unanticipated increase in the rate of suicides occurring in OIF I compared to the U.S. Army 10-year average, with two significant "outbreaks" occurring in the months of July and October (see Table 1 and Figure 1). The MHAT IV conducted a similar review of MNF-I's prevention and surveillance program and a detailed analysis of completed suicides.

3.1. MNF-I Suicide Prevention Committee

The Command Surgeon of MNF-I serves as the chair of the MNF-I Suicide Prevention Committee. The charter of this committee is to (a) review suicide policies and procedures within MNF-I, (b) assess trends in suicides and suicidal behaviors within theater, and (c) advise Commanders and leaders in the prevention of suicides, to include training and education. This committee was formed in August 2006, and represents the first suicide prevention committee established in OIF.

3.2. Army Suicide Event Report (ASER)

The Army Suicide Event Report (ASER) is the reporting and tracking mechanism for completed Soldier suicides and non-lethal events that result in hospitalization and/or evacuation. The ASER was developed, and initial validation was conducted, by the U.S. Army Medical Research Unit- Europe as a means to track, in near real-time, suicides and suicidal behaviors of Army personnel within the U.S. Army, Europe (USAREUR) (Dolan, Schroeder, Wright, Thomas, & Ness, 2003). Following the recommendation of the Mental Health Advisory Team (MHAT) I, the U.S. Army Medical Command issued a policy directing that the ASER be used throughout the Iraqi theater of operations. The Suicide Risk Management & Surveillance Office (SRMSO), located at Fort Lewis, Washington, has operational oversight of the ASER, conducts routine data analyses and publishes reports of these findings. The SRMSO also has responsibility for updating changes to the ASER, with the latest update occurring in December 2005.

The SRMSO issued guidance for when an ASER is to be completed (Personal communication, September 8, 2006). ASERs are to be completed if they meet ALL of the criteria below:

- The person is in the Army, either the active or reserve component
- The Soldier completed suicide, was hospitalized, or evacuated
- The method used was lethal or believed by the person to be lethal
- The Soldier's intent was to die

To ensure that all required ASERs within the OIF theater of operations are completed every month, the MNF-I Behavioral Health (BH) Consultant reads the theater medical evacuations using the TRANSCOM Regulating and Command and Control Evacuation System (TRAC2ES) as well as all theater in-patient reports. The MNF-I BH Consultant then contacts the provider handling the case to ensure the ASER is submitted. According to SRMSO, from 1 JAN 2006 to 31 AUG 2006, there were 60

ASERs submitted for OIF 05-07. Forty-eight of the ASERs were for suicide attempts and 12 were for completed suicides. The SRMSO validates all ASERs submitted for a completed suicide with the Armed Forces Medical Examiner (AFME). Unfortunately, the SRMSO has no mechanism to ensure the accuracy of ASERs submitted for suicide attempts. The MNF-I BH Consultant noted that multiple ASERs are frequently submitted for the same Soldier and that ASERs are often submitted when they do not meet the criteria outlined previously. For example, in a review of the ASERs submitted for OIF 05-07 (from 1 JAN – 30 JUN 2006), the MNF-I BH Consultant was only able to validate 26 of 39 ASERS (67%), with 6 ASERs being duplicates and 7 ASERs failing to meet the criteria for completing an ASER (see previously cited criteria).

As noted earlier, the ASER was initially developed for use in garrison; and although the ASER has been subsequently modified for use in a deployed environment, additional revisions seem necessary. First and foremost, the ASER must include questions that will maximize the implementation of potential interventions in a deployed environment. While the ASER contains general questions about the deployment, questions regarding the relationship of the suicide or suicide attempt to key deployment events/experiences are missing. For example, the ASER contains no questions regarding whether the Soldier recently returned from mid-tour leave. Currently, all Soldiers leaving for mid-tour leave must receive a chaplain brief. If it could be demonstrated that suicides or suicide attempts are more likely to occur following mid-tour leave, then it might be sensible to require Soldiers to receive suicide prevention training upon returning from mid-tour leave.

The MNF-I is a multi-service headquarters. Therefore, the MNF-I Surgeon requires a suicide surveillance system capable of monitoring suicides and suicide behaviors across all services (Army, Navy, Marines, Air Force, and Coast Guard). The ASER is an Army system, and therefore ASERs are currently only being completed for Soldiers. A multi-service suicide surveillance system is urgently needed to facilitate joint interoperability of suicide tracking and reporting.

4. Suicide Statistics

Since the beginning of OIF, there have been 80 confirmed (as of 31 DEC 2006) Soldier suicides in Iraq. From 1 JAN to 31 DEC 2006, the Armed Forces Medical Examiner (AFME) confirmed 22 completed Soldier suicides in the OIF area of operations. The majority of these deaths involved single white male junior enlisted Soldiers, with the cause of death for all Soldiers being a self-inflicted gunshot wound (see Table 1). This profile of 2006 OIF Soldier suicides is consistent with previous OIF Soldier suicide profiles and with the 2005 Army suicide profile. When all OIF suicides (2003-2006) are considered, there appears to be more OIF suicide deaths resulting from gunshot wounds than the 2005 Army suicide profile (97% vs. 77%), as well as Soldiers being younger than 30 years of age (83% vs. 69%) and less likely to be married (47% vs. 26%).

Table 1. Summary of Demographics of Confirmed OIF 2003, OIF 2004, OIF 2005, OIF 2006 (thru 31 AUG 06) and Army 2005 Suicides

	2005 Army Suicides	2006 Army OIF Suicides	2005 Army OIF Suicides	2004 Army OIF Suicides	2003 Army OIF Suicides
Suicide by firearm/gunshot	77%	100%	95%	100%	96%
Male	96%	86%	89%	100%	92%
Age 30 or younger	69%	93%	68%	89%	79%
E-4 or below	61%	86%	63%	78%	71%
Married	47%	21%	32%	11%	38%
Minority (non- white)	21%	7%	26%	22%	42%

The Soldier suicide rates for OIF from 2003 (MAR) to 2006 (DEC) are shown in Table 2. The Soldier suicide rates in 2003, 2005, and 2006 were significantly higher than the U.S. Army ten-year average suicide rate (see Table 3). Analyses using the Poisson distribution for rare events confirmed this impression. For OIF 2003, OIF 2005, and OIF 2006, the suicide rates were 18.8, 19.9, and 17.3 per 100,000 Soldiers/year, respectively, compared to the U.S. Army's ten-year average of 11.6 suicides per 100,000/year. There was no significant difference between the suicide rate for OIF 2004 and the U.S. Army's ten-year average (9.6 vs. 11.6 suicides per 100,000 Soldiers/year). Thus, for three out of the four years, Soldier OIF suicide rates were higher than the U.S. Army's 10-year average suicide rate.

Table 2. OIF Soldier Suicides: 2003-2006

SUICIDE UPDATE	2003	2004	2005	2006
OIF Confirmed	25	11	22	22
OIF Pending	0	0	0	0
OIF Confirmed Adjusted Rate	18.8*	9.6	19.9*	17.3**

*Poisson, p< .01; **Poisson, p< .05

Table 3. U.S. Army Suicide Rates: Ten Year Average (1996-2005)

Calendar Year	Rate per 100,000
1996	12.4
1997	10.6
1998	12.0
1999	13.1
2000	12.1
2001	9.1
2002	11.1
2003	12.8
2004	11.0
2005	12.3
Average 1996-2005	11.6
U.S. Average	12.3*

*Crude, conservative U.S. population rate (Eaton et al., 2006)

Figure 1 shows the number of Soldier suicides by month from 2003 – 2006. As can readily be seen, there were three months in which the number of suicides "spiked," with 5 suicides in NOV 2003 and 6 suicides each month in July 2003 and October 2005. All three of these months represent a significant spike in suicides (Poisson, $p < .05$).

In fact, for each year (2003, 2005 and 2006) in which there was an increase in the OIF Soldier suicide rate compared to the U.S. Army suicide rate, there was at least one month in which 3 suicides occurred. In 2003, there were two months in which at least 3 suicides occurred and there were 5 suicides in both July and November 2003. In 2005, there were three months in which there were at least 3 suicides and there were 3 suicides in both May and July, and 6 suicides in October. The only year in which there was not at least once a month when three suicides occurred was 2004, which was the only year in OIF where the OIF suicide rate was not higher than the U.S. Army 10-year average suicide rate.

Furthermore, for those years when the OIF rates did differ from the U.S. Army rate, there appears to be a six-month "clustering" effect, beginning with the first month in which at least three suicides occurred. For instance, 16 of the 22 suicides that occurred in 2005 happened from May (the first month there were at least three suicides) until October, representing 73% of all suicides for the year. A similar pattern is also seen for 2003, where 18 of 26 suicides, representing 72% of all suicides, took place between July and December.

No previous MHATs have provided any indicators of Soldier suicide trends. One approach would be to monitor monthly suicides for any month in which three suicides occur, as this likely signifies a year in which suicide rates will exceed the 10-year Army average.

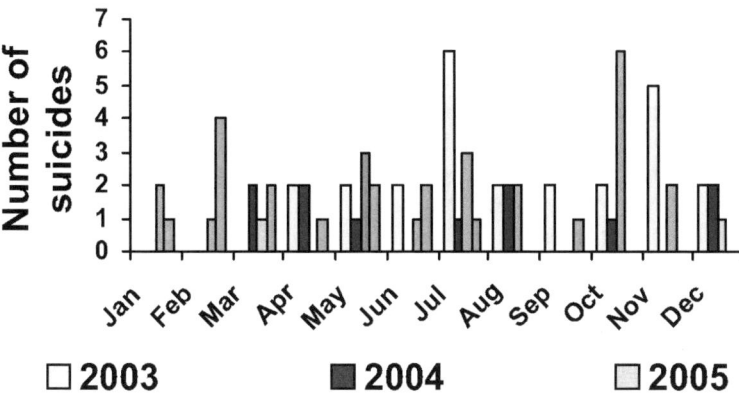

Figure 1. Monthly OIF Soldier Suicides for 2003- 2005.
*From 1 JAN – 1 OCT 2006

5. Summary of Findings

Since the beginning of OIF (March 2003), there have been 80 confirmed Soldier suicides in Iraq (as of 31 December 2006). The MNF-I has an active Suicide Prevention Committee that is chaired by the Command Surgeon. The current suicide training program being used was developed for a garrison Army and lacks relevance for a deployed (combat) environment. The Army Suicide Event Report (ASER) is being widely used in the theater by both Army and Marine behavioral health care providers, but only for suicides/suicidal gestures by Army personnel. However, there is confusion over when an ASER should be completed and there is concern over the relevance of the ASER in a combat environment. Although there are numerous service-specific mental health tracking systems, there is not a single joint tracking system capable of monitoring suicides, mental health evacuations, and the use of mental health/combat stress control services in a combat environment.

6. Recommendations: Suicide Prevention Program

- Sustain the MNF-I Suicide Prevention Committee, chaired by the senior theater medical officer.
- Expand the MNF-I Suicide Prevention Committee to include operational commanders and senior NCOs.

- Revise and field suicide awareness and prevention training so that it focuses on specific actions Soldiers (self-aid and buddy aid) and leaders can take in helping fellow unit members. Use real-world examples from a combat environment.
- Provide a detailed instruction manual for completing the ASER.
- Establish an in-theater review process of all ASERs before submitting to SRMSO to ensure that an ASER is required, and that the ASER is accurate.
- Update/modify the ASER so that it meets the needs of a deployed force. Ensure that the ASER committee members have practical and recent deployment experience. Ensure all modifications to the ASER facilitate the development of prevention activities in both a garrison and deployed environment.
- Establish a joint tracking system for the deployed environment to monitor suicides, mental health evacuations, and the use of mental health/CSC services.
- Establish a quality control process that ensures both internal (e.g., no duplicates) and external (e.g., completed suicides in the ASER database match those in the AFME database) validity.

References

[1] Dolan, C. A., Schroeder, E. D., Wright, K. M., Thomas, J. T., & Ness, J. W. (2003). *USAREUR suicide surveillance project: Data summary and program evaluation.* (USAMRU-E Technical Report). Heidelberg, Germany: U.S. Army Medical Research Unit-Europe.

[2] Eaton, K.M, Messer, S.C., Garvey-Wilson, A.L., & Hoge, C.W. (2006). Strengthening the Validity of Population-Based Suicide Rate Estimates: An Illustration Using U.S. Military and Civilian Data. *Suicide and Life Threatening Behavior*, 182-191.

[3] Mental Health Advisory Team II (MHAT-II) Report from Operation Iraqi Freedom II, chartered by The U.S. Army Surgeon General , December 30, 2004, available on www.armymedicine.army.mil.

[4] Mental Health Advisory Team (MHAT-III) Operation Iraq Freedom 04-06, chartered by the Office of the Surgeon General Multinational Forces-Iraq and Office of the Surgeon General United States Army Medical Command, May 29, 2006.

[5] Mental Health Advisory Team (MHAT) IV Operation Iraq Freedom 05-07, chartered by the Office of the Surgeon General Multinational Forces-Iraq and Office of the Surgeon General United States Army Medical Command, November, 17, 2006 available on www.armymedicine.army.mil.

[6] Operation Iraqi Freedom Mental Health Advisory Team (MHAT) report: chartered by U.S. Army Surgeon General and HQDA G-1. December 16, 2003, available on www.armymedicine.army.mil.

Lowering Suicide Risk in Returning Troops
B.K. Wiederhold (Ed.)
IOS Press, 2008
© 2008 IOS Press. All rights reserved.
doi:10.3233/978-1-58603-889-2-53

53

Integrative Diagnostic Model for PTSD and Suicidality

Dragica KOZARIĆ-KOVAČIĆ[a,1], Dragan GAMBERGER[b], Igor MARINIĆ[a], Mirjana GRUBIŠIĆ-ILIĆ[a], Željko ROMIĆ[c]

[a]*University Hospital Dubrava, Department of Psychiatry, Referral Centre for Stress-Related Disorders of the Ministry of Health and Social Welfare, Regional Centre for Psychotrauma, 10 000 Zagreb, Avenija Gojka Suska 6, Croatia*
[b]*Ruđer Bošković Institute, Department of Electronics, Laboratory for Information Systems, Bijenicka 54, 10 000 Zagreb, Croatia*
[c]*University Hospital Dubrava, Clinical Department of Laboratory Diagnostics, 10 000 Zagreb, Avenija Gojka Suska 6, Croatia*

Abstract. Suicide is one of top ten causes of death in most countries, and it has large impact both on families of victims and their environment. Suicide rate in Europe is 17.5 per 100,000 people and various activities from WHO and other organizations are underway with the goal of reducing suicide rates. Different underlying factors can contribute to suicide, and risk factors include both genetic and environmental factors, as well as probable existence of independent inheritance of a predisposition to suicidal behavior. In this paper we review actual epidemiological data on suicide behavior in Europe and Croatia, novel approaches and theories on suicidal behavior, and present our experiences in the diagnostic process. Some predictors of suicidality from our previous studies in PTSD patients are indicated. We reveal an integrative diagnostic model for PTSD and suicidality, based on integration of psychiatric, psychological, and biological markers. Preliminary algorithms for predicting suicidal behavior using data mining methods are shown, and some important variables are indicated. Further studies with larger numbers of patients and more parameters are needed for future development of this multidisciplinary approach to the assessment of suicidal behavior.

Keywords. Posttraumatic stress disorder, PTSD, suicidality, suicidal behavior

---

[1] The corresponding author: Prof. Dragica Kozarić-Kovačić, MD, PhD, University Hospital Dubrava, Department of Psychiatry, Referral Centre for Stress-related Disorders of the Ministry of Health and Social Welfare, Regional Centre for Psychotrauma, Avenija Gojka Suska 6, 10 000 Zagreb, Croatia, Phone no.: +385-1-290-26-18, Fax.: +385-1-290-3700, e-mail: dkozaric_kovacic@yahoo.com.

1. Introduction

Suicide is an act of deliberately initiated self-destruction. It ranks among the top ten causes of death for all ages in most countries [1, 2]. Suicide has a devastating emotional impact on the families of victims, friends, and the whole society. It frequently induces feelings of helplessness, isolation, and decline among people. Subsequently, close relatives of the victims have feelings of shame and guilt because of social stigma, and they need support because they pass through the process of mourning. In addition, a person who survived a suicide attempt needs support as well.

The causes of suicide are numerous and complex. The neurobiology of the brain, genetics, psychological traits, and social situations can contribute to suicide. Experts believe that external circumstances and events (divorce, loss of job, failure in school, etc.) are triggers rather than causes [3].

Natural disasters (earthquakes, floods, etc.) and wars have a similar impact on the suicide rate and burden individuals, families, and society as a whole [4, 5]. Suicide rates decrease during war or natural disasters [6-10]. According to Durkheim's theory, stronger social integration, such as during war and natural disasters, protects people from suicide because they are bound together and support each other against the external threat [11]. We found decreased numbers of male and female suicides during the war period in Croatia in the areas directly affected by war activities, compared to the areas indirectly affected by the war. The male to female suicide ratio was 2.8:1 in the war areas compared to 3.4:1 in the non-war areas [12].

2. Epidemiology of Suicide in Europe

According to the World Health Organization (WHO), Europe has the highest suicide rate and cases are rising among young people. Europe records 17.5 suicides per 100,000 people. In 2000 there were 873.000 suicides worldwide and 163.000 of those were in Europe [13]. Recent available data concerning global suicide prevention showed that almost 3,000 people every day commit suicide, and for every completed suicide in the world, there are 20 or more attempted suicides [14].

WHO's European Member States drafted a health policy document in 1984 in which the main goal is the reduction of suicide: "By the year 2000 there should be a sustained and continuing reduction in the prevalence of mental disorders, and improvement in quality of life of all people with such disorders and a reversal of the rising trends in suicide and attempted suicide" [15]. This goal was strongly reinforced as target 6 of HEALTH21 [16], ratified in 1988 by the European Ministries of Health and recently in the World Health Report 2001 [17].

The European multi-centre study began monitoring parasuicide/attempted suicide in 1989 in defined epidemiological catchment areas, stimulating initiation of suicide prevention programs, and the WHO European network on suicide prevention was established in December 2000 by the mental health program of the WHO Regional Office for Europe.

The main tasks of the network include research on and monitoring of suicide and attempted suicide in European countries, the initiation of suicide prevention programs, assistance in the development of new prevention strategies, and the development of new tools for evaluation of suicide prevention efforts and the establishment of educational programs [13].

The highest suicide rate in Europe is found in the Baltic countries and in the Russian Federation. These countries have more than 40 suicides per 100,000 people per year, followed by central European countries (Hungary, Slovenia), Ukraine and Belarus to the east and Finland to the north. The lowest suicide rate is in western and southern Europe, which is lower than 10 suicides per 100,000 per year (Figure 1) [18].

Figure 1. Standardized rate of suicide in Europe (HFA/WHO, June, 2005).

The international variation of suicide rates may be influenced through time and space by different factors: sociodemographic factors, ethnic differences, religious beliefs and affiliations, attitudes towards suicide, legislation regarding suicide, prevention strategies, and reliability and validity of death certification and reporting [19]. The cross-national variation arises in part because of different practices in the recording of the cause of death [20]. However, the majority of contemporary studies believe that these errors are randomized, at least to the extent that allows epidemiologists to compare rates between and within countries and over a period of time [1]. The so-called J-curve, which includes countries with a higher suicide rate, and starts in Finland and extends down to Slovenia, has opened the possibility that individuals of these ethnic groups, although possessing different traditional risk factors for suicide, could share the same ratio of European and Ural genes. These populations have a lower tolerance for alcohol and other characteristics possibly connected with suicidal behavior (aggressive and impulsive behavior, disinhibition) that may increase suicide risk [20].

Currently, traditional suicide risk factors, such as medical (mental disorders, specifically schizophrenia and depression), psychosocial, cultural, and socioeconomic factors, cannot explain the difference in suicide rates between countries because the most promising method for identifying risk factors for suicide is composed of genetic and environmental influences [21].

The suicide literature is slowly beginning to agree that there may be an independent inheritance of suicidal behavior [22, 23]. Recent molecular genetic studies indicate the serotonergic system in suicidality [24, 25]. An association has been found between suicidal ideation and tryptophan hydroxylase (TPH) [26], as well as between the severity of suicide attempts and alcoholism and polymorphism for the same enzyme [26, 27]. Speculation exists on the role of possible interactions between alcohol exposure and genetic vulnerability; it is possible that the groups of people living within the J-curve could share genes that may not tolerate excessive alcohol consumption, the combination of which is more likely to result in suicidal behavior [20, 21].

3. Epidemiology of Suicide in Croatia

Among the European countries, Croatia has a medium suicide-related mortality rate [3]. Studies from the Croatian National Institute of Public Health reported that the suicide mortality rate in Croatia did not change during the last 15 year period. It oscillated in the period from 1990 to 2003 for all ages, ranging from 23 (1995) to 17 (2003) per 100,000 people per year, and from 18 (1992) to 14 (2002) per 100,000 people per year for ages 0-64. According to the database of the "Health for All" program, the average suicide mortality rate in Croatia in 1995 was lower than the average suicide mortality rate in Europe, but higher than the average suicide rate in Central and Eastern Europe. Because of the decreasing trend of mortality due to suicide in Europe, the standard mortality rate in Croatia is higher than that in Europe (Figure 2) [28].

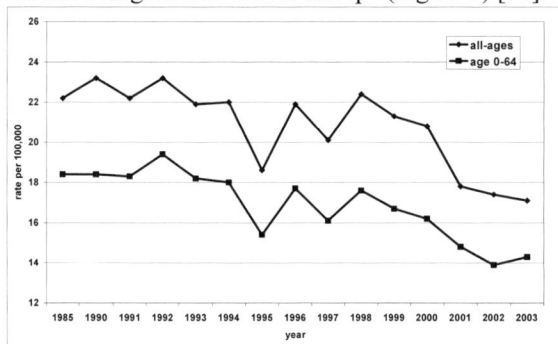

Figure 2. Age-standardized suicide rates for all ages and 0-64 years, Croatia, 1985 and 1990-2004 (Croatian National Institute of Public Health. Data obtained thanks to Maja Silobrcic Radic, MD).

4. Our Investigation

Our investigation was based on the Suicide Register of the Ministry of the Interior [10, 12, 29]. We found that the average suicide rate in Croatia in the pre-war, war, and post-war periods was 19.6 people per 100,000 per year. It is known that the accuracy of statistical data related to the suicide rate depends on the registers used, collection and procedures of evidence, definition of suicide, etc. There is a lot of criticism in the literature about official statistics of suicide and the comparison between countries and different registers [30].

According to our investigation, the data from the Croatian Suicide Register from the Croatian National Institute of Public Health, and the data from the Croatian Bureau of Statistics showed a higher frequency among young people between the ages of 15 and 19 and older persons over 65 years of age, which is similar to suicide data from the rest of Europe and the USA [31, 32]. In our study, men committed suicide more often than women in the 15-35 age group, and women more than men in the 15-25 age group. A higher suicide rate among men up to 35 years could be related to the increase in suicide among untreated war veterans who suffered from PTSD [29], because we examined suicide rates before the year 2000. After 2000, the network of psychotrauma centers developed across Croatia, and in the post-war period more war veterans received treatment than during the war and in the first years after the war [33]. The method of suicide changed during the war and post-war period. Although hanging was the most frequent method of suicide (50%), men used firearms and explosives more often than women. Medical problems were more often present among women than men, and alcoholism was more present among men (Table 1).

Table 1. Sociodemographic features, suicide methods and motives and some risk factors among people who committed suicide according to sex in the period between 1990 and 2000 (printed with copyright permission from *Društvena istraživanja*).

Features	Male %	Female %	χ^2-test	p
Current marital status			5.363	0.021
Married	70.1	76.7		
Other	29.9	23.3		
Having children			5.713	0.017
Yes	**20.0**	13.9		
No	80.0	86.1		
Employment			277.754	0.000
Employed	**50.1**	21.6		
Unemployed	4.4	**29.4**		
Retired	38.9	39.9		
Student	6.6	9.1		
Education			13.541	0.004
Did not finish school	0.6	0.6		

Elementary school	48.8	57.4		
High school	42.7	31.2		
Junior college/college	7.9	10.7		
Time of year			3.783	0.286
Autumn	24.4	24.9		
Winter	18.8	20.5		
Spring	28.8	26.8		
Summer	28.1	27.9		
Day of the week			4.767	0.574
Monday	16.1	15.4		
Tuesday	15.9	15.5		
Wednesday	14.2	14.3		
Thursday	14.6	13.0		
Friday	14.2	14.8		
Saturday	12.8	14.1		
Sunday	12.2	12.9		
Place of committing suicide			11.874	0.018
Place of living	72.5	75.7		
Other	27.5	24.3		
Suicide method			674.653	0.000
Hanging	53.8	53.4		
Jumping from heights	5.2	**14.2**		
Drowning	1.9	**11.3**		
Jumping in front of the train/car	2.7	**5.4**		
Firearms, explosive	**32.3**	7.7		
Combined	1.6	1.6		
Suicide motive			55.569	0.000
Medical condition	67.9	80.4		
Emotional difficulties	8.2	7.5		
Financial, economic hardship	**2.5**	0.8		
Family conflicts	8.5	6.5		
Problems at work	**0.8**	0.5		
To avoid jail	**1.3**	0.3		
Alcoholism	**9.8**	2.5		
School failure	0.6	**1.3**		
Drug addiction	**0.4**	0.2		
Suicide announcement			0.004	0.953

Yes	80.7	80.9		
No	19.3	19.1		
Suicidal message			1.238	0.235
Yes	7.4	8.1		
No	92.6	91.9		
Previous health condition			253.055	0.000
Healthy	**31.9**	22.7		
Mental disturbances	30.4	**59.8**		
Alcoholism	**20.0**	4.7		
Drug addiction	**0.8**	0.4		
Physical disorders	16.8	12.4		
Previous suicide attempts			0.953	0.004
Yes, once	8.3	**12.7**		
Yes, more times	7.7	**15.8**		
No	84.0	71.5		
Ongoing conflicts			5.206	0.023
Yes	**31.9**	20.6		
No	68.1	79.4		
Alcohol intoxication			68.016	0.000
Yes	**75.6**	25.4		
No	24.4	**74.6**		

The number of suicides decreased in the areas directly affected by war in the period from 1993-1998 (war and post-war period) in both genders; although more so in men than in women. Firearms and explosive devices were the methods used more frequently for suicides in the areas directly affected by war than in other areas, whereas hanging was more frequently used in the areas non-directly affected by war (Table 2 and 3) [12].

Table 2. Suicide rates according to the Registry of the Interior in the areas directly and indirectly affected by war.

Year	Areas						Total		
	Directly affected by war			Indirectly affected by war			n	%	Suicide rates
	n	%	Suicide rates	n	%	Suicide rates			

Average suicide number and rates during war period 1993 – 30 June 1996	348	13.5	14.74	465	16.3	19.17	813	14.9	16.96
Average suicide number and rates during non-war period 1 July 1996-1998	410	15.6	17.36	364	12.3	15.03	774	13.9	16.20

Chi-square=10.3245, d.f.=6, *p*=0.0017.

Table 3. Number of the suicides related to sex in the areas directly and indirectly affected by war activities.

Sex	Directly affected by war	Indirectly affected by war	Total
	N (%)	N (%)	N (%)
Male	1825 (45.5)	2191 (54.5)	4016 (100.0)
Female	646 (48.5)	687 (51.5)	1333 (100.0)
Total	2471 (46.2)	2878 (53.8)	5349 (100.0)

Chi-square=3.6697, d.f.=1, *p*=0.055.

Furthermore, firearms and explosive devices were used as the method of suicide among children [34]. According to the data recorded by the Ministry of the Interior of the Republic of Croatia, a total of 696 people were victims in 474 incidents caused by mines and destructive explosive devices during 1995, 1996, and 1997, i.e. each incident resulted in an average of 1.5 casualties. Out of the total number of casualties, 116 were children and adolescents who committed suicides; in 11% of those, death was caused by firearms (Table 4).

Table 4. Number of casualties with regard to circumstances (printed with copyright permission from *Croatian Medical Journal*).

Circumstances	Number of casualties				Number of children casualties			
	1995	1996	1997	Total	0-6	7-14	15-18	Total
Suicide	42	52	18	112 (17%)	-	4	8	12 (11%)
Children's play	7	22	1	30 (4%)	3	16	10	29 (27%)
Unauthorized handling of weapons	51	30	5	86 (13%)	-	6	13	19 (18%)
Dysfunctional arms and weapons	3	3	1	7 (1%)	-	1	-	1 (1%)
Daily activities	98	64	52	214 (32%)	2	5	12	19 (18%)
Shelling or rockets (projectiles)	71	0	0	71 (11%)	2	1	1	4 (4%)
Minesweeping and de-mining	13	9	22	44 (7%)	-	-	-	0 (0%)
Entering the minefield	9	3	1	13 (2%)	-	-	2	2 (2%)

Deliberate attack or murder	24	22	4	50 (8%)	2	-	7	9 (8%)
Self-injuries	2	4	0	6 (1%)	-	-	1	1 (1%)
Play with weapons	6	3	13	22 (3%)	-	9	2	11 (10%)
Child attacked parents	0	3	0	3 (0.5%)	-	-	-	0 (0%)
Use of explosives	1	2	0	3 (0.5%)	-	-	-	0 (0%)
No data	6	10	19	35	2	3	4	9
TOTAL	333	227	136	696 (100%)	11	45	60	116 (100%)

According to our investigation, almost 80% of suicide victims had previously announced the plan to commit suicide; thus such verbal announcement must be taken seriously. Prevention efforts should be focused on alcoholism, drug abuse, family crises, reduction of possession of firearms and explosives, improvement of socioeconomic status, mental disorders, previous suicide attempts, and treatment of persons with suicidal behavior.

The importance of social support and treatment in preventing suicide after a traumatic experience was clear from the data we collected during our expert evaluation of war veterans for compensation seeking, which was done from 2002 to 2004 at our institution. Our pilot study included 211 men and 13 women who experienced combat and war stress in 1991-1995. The mean age was 22.3 ± 7.4 years, the mean duration of their combat activity was 27.1 ± 18.7 months (range, 1-65 months), and 7-12 years had passed since they experienced combat traumas. We compared the psychiatric diagnoses made on the veteran's first visit to a local psychiatrist, the second diagnoses which were made during psychiatric treatment, and the third diagnoses which were established during the forensic evaluation by an expert team [35]. The PTSD diagnosis and comorbid diagnoses were made according to the International Classification of Disorders (ICD-10) criteria [36]. The Clinician Administrated PTSD Scale (CAPS) [37], the Clinical Global Impression scale (CGI) [38], Trauma Questionnaire [39], the Mississippi Scale for Combat-related PTSD [40], and the Minnesota Multiphasic Personality Inventory 201 [41] were also administered. The final diagnosis of lifetime and current PTSD and other mental disorders was reached when all sets of psychiatric and psychometric criteria were fulfilled. We then established the diagnoses, which are presented in Table 5.

Table 5. Comparison of the diagnoses made in 225 war veterans at three different assessments[*] (printed with copyright permission from *Croatian Medical Journal*).

	No. (%) of patients at assessment		
Diagnosis	first	second	third
PTSD[†]	93 (41)	100 (44)	43 (19)
Partial PTSD	12 (5)	5 (2)	6 (3)
PTSD with comorbid diagnoses	13 (6)	16 (7)	34 (15)
PTSD with personality change due to catastrophic experience	9 (4)	66 (29)	0 (0)

Personality change due to catastrophic experience	3 (1)	17 (8)	1 (0)
Other diagnoses	95 (42)	21 (9)	141 (63)
Total[‡]	225 (100)	225 (100)	225 (100)

[*]The first diagnosis was made at the first psychiatric appointment, the second diagnosis was made during psychiatric treatment, and the third diagnosis was made at the expert examination.
[†]PTSD – posttraumatic stress disorder.
[‡]Chi-square=250.359, d.f.=10, $p<0.001$; 1st vs 2nd diagnosis: chi-square=103.773, d.f.=5, $p<0.001$; 2nd vs 3rd diagnosis: chi-square=48.731, d.f.=5, $p<0.001$; 1st vs 3rd diagnosis: chi-square=198.402, d.f.=5, $p<0.001$.

In addition, in this period we evaluated a total number of 1,027 war veterans who applied for compensation seeking, 97.7% of which were men. During the forensic evaluation we diagnosed suicidal behavior in a small number of evaluated war veterans because they were under continuous psychiatric care and had social support. Over 90% of veterans were not suicidal, 8.2% had suicidal thoughts, and only 1.1% had suicidal intentions and previous suicide attempts, (unpublished data, Table 6).

Table 6. Suicidal behavior of war veterans during compensation seeking.

Suicidal behavior	%
Not suicidal	932 (90.7%)
Suicidal thoughts	84 (8.2%)
Suicidal intentions and previous suicidal attempts	11 (1.1%)
Total	1027 (100.0%)

Furthermore, we analyzed suicidal behavior in families of war veterans, which is presented in Table 7 (unpublished data). In the same group, 4.5% of the 1,027 evaluated veterans registered suicidal behavior in the family (suicide of mother, father, or member of close family).

Table 7. Suicidal behavior in families of war veterans.

Suicidal behavior in families	%
Suicide of mother	18 (1.7 %)
Suicide of father	16 (1.5%)
Suicide in close family	14 (1.3%)
Total	1027 (100.0%)

Attempted and committed suicide appears to be a familial behavior [42]. Risk factors for suicide are composed of genetic and environmental influences. Familial transmission of suicidal behavior may indicate shared environmental effects such as abuse or transmission of mental disorders [22, 23], although the heritability of suicide cannot be explained only by the transmission of heritable mental disorders, since suicide heritability persists after controlling for the presence of psychiatric disorders. Today there is more agreement that there may be an independent inheritance of suicidal behavior, while the tendency for a suicidal act, according to suicidal thoughts, may be a specific genetic component of suicidal behavior [26]. Recent molecular genetic studies that investigated candidate genes to explain heritability of suicidal behavior have implicated the serotonergic system [25, 26].

5. Some Predictors of Suicidality in PTSD Patients

There are no unique definitions of suicidal behavior. In addition, it is not easy to establish a diagnosis of suicidal behavior and recognize it, in clinical and research settings. In clinical practice this can have serious and complex consequences. We know that parasuicidal behavior can lead to suicidal behavior and that there are different steps in the escalation of suicidality from a single suicidal thought or ideation through suicidal ideas or gestures, and attempted suicide to completed suicide.

In one of our investigations we explored some predictors of suicidality among PTSD patients (213 men and 20 women) and 103 healthy control subjects with combat experience without psychiatric disorders including PTSD and suicidality (unpublished data) [43].

We administered the following psychometric instruments: General questionnaire, the Eysenck Personality Questionnaire (EPQ) – which consists of: extroversion, neuroticism, psychoticism, L, and C scale [44], the Coping Orientation to Problem Experienced (COPE) [45], Beck Depression Scale (BDI) [46], the Reasons for Living Scale (RFL-72) [47], the Scale of Stressful Events [48], and the Scale of Social Support [49].

We found some predictors of suicidality after regression analysis. We named these predictors "reasons for living" (Table 8).

Table 8. Predictors of suicidality.

Positive predictors	Positive assessment of stress adjustment
	Actual social support
	Using of mental unengagement as a coping mechanism
	Religion
Negative predictors	Psychoticism as a dimension of personality
	High level of depression
	Behavioral unengagement

In this study positive and negative predictors of suicidality were found. Positive factors were protective, and they included positive subjective assessment of the adjustment to a stressful situation and the presence of actual social support, meaning that people who found more reasons for living had a wider social network and a need to extend that network. Furthermore, religious and coping mechanisms such as mental unengagement were also found to be positive predictors and significantly associated with finding more reasons for living. The more a patient is involved in a social network with family, friends or religious associations the more adequate his or her coping would be. Negative predictors of suicidal behavior included the personality dimension of psychoticism, with rigidity and weak adaptation, and a high level of depression. Behavioral unengagement as a coping mechanism, which is not an adequate mechanism for coping with a stressful situation, was also found to be a negative predictor. Patients using these negative factors should be more closely monitored in the process of suicide prevention.

6. Integrative Diagnostic Model for PTSD and Suicidality

Predicting suicidal behavior is a complex task and many different risk factors are involved, such as various sociodemographic parameters (social and marital status, employment, education), developmental factors, physical and mental health, biological and genetic factors, and correct assessment of a suicidal patient is very important in everyday clinical work. The main question is how to make a more precise diagnosis of suicidal behavior.

As stated above, a lot of effort has been invested in the work to predict and prevent suicide attempts on various levels. In our project "Integrative diagnostic model for stress related mental disorders" (TP-03/01, principal investigator Prof. D. Kozarić-Kovačić, MD, PhD, supported by the Croatian Ministry of Science, Education, and Sports) that aimed at developing diagnostic algorithms for diagnosing stress-related disorders using recent diagnostic criteria and instruments and integration of biological, psychological, clinical, and functional markers, several models regarding suicidal behavior were built using the novel approach of intelligent data analysis.

Data mining is a process of extraction of implicit, previously unknown, and potentially useful information from data [50], and data mining algorithms can be used for analyzing large sets of data, such as various data collected from the patient [51, 52]. It is important to point out that, while data mining algorithms are based on statistical principles, there is a difference in the approach from traditional statistics such that these algorithms can be used in finding associations between different parameters, classification of data, discovering knowledge [42, 53, 54] and non-obvious patterns in available data [55], and for generating rules and conditions applicable in everyday clinical practice [54]. Some authors point out that machine learning methods are blind and unbiased [42]. Especially relevant are approaches that reveal information in a form understandable to humans [53], and using a Data Mining Server we were able to describe specific groups of patients by means of specific attributes.

This approach allowed the integration of biological, psychological, and clinical markers in a process of differentiating suicidal and non-suicidal psychiatric patients as well as sorting out some of the relevant attributes regarding suicidal behavior. It is important to point out that this is one of the first applications of data mining methods in psychiatry, as they have mostly been used in basic biomedical research [56-58]. In our previous study [53] we used different data mining algorithms to detect relevant attributes for PTSD diagnosis.

Our intent was to find associations between attributes of suicidal behavior and posttraumatic disorder, define rules that describe risk groups using available descriptors, and generalize the defined rules for prediction of future, unseen patient data. The result of the induction process is the set of rules that describe the target class. Sensitivity and specificity are given for each rule. It is important to notice that, when data mining methods are applied, the interpretation of results by experts in the detection and interpretation of relevant and novel models is necessary [59].

Models shown are preliminary results of our study and they are unpublished so far. They were built using data mining methods implemented in the Data Mining Server software, which allowed us an induction of rules that described relevant subgroups of patients with suicidal behavior [59]. The study included 102 patients, 51 with confirmed combat PTSD and 51 with psychiatric diagnoses other than PTSD. Various information from each patient was collected such as main and comorbid diagnosis, medical history data (age, sex, demographic and social data, work history, family, combat experience, previous medical and psychiatric conditions, previous and current psychiatric problems and treatment). Data was included from the administered psychiatric and psychological scales and questionnaires (Clinician Administered PTSD Scale – CAPS [37], Positive and Negative Syndrome Scale – PANSS [60], Hamilton Anxiety Scale – HAMA [61], Hamilton rating scale for depression – HAMD-17 [62], Harvard trauma questionnaire – HTQ [39], Mississippi Scale for Combat Related PTSD – M-PTSD [40], Minnesota Multiphasic Personality Inventory-2 – MMPI-2 [41] Los Angeles Symptom Checklist – LASC [63]), and several biological parameters were measured (lipid status questionnaire regarding risk factors for cardiovascular diseases [64], lipid status – triglycerides, cholesterol, LDL, HDL, levels of apolipoprotein A, apolipoprotein B, oLAB, and levels of blood homocystein, serotonin and monoamine oxydase activity). We included only patients without risk factors for lipid status (cardiovascular risks in family and in patients, hypertension, increased glucose, dietary habits, daily activities and exercise, body mass index, fasting 12 hours before blood sampling, etc.) and they were drug free for the serotonergic agents for between 2-6 weeks before inclusion in the research.

6.1. Model Based on Structured Psychiatric Interview, Psychiatric and Psychological Scales

Based on data from the structured psychiatric interview and psychiatric and psychological questionnaires and scales (CAPS, PANSS, HAMA, HAMD-17, MMPI-2, HTQ, LASC and M-PTSD) three rules for identifying suicidal PTSD patients were generated (Table 9). They described suicidal PTSD patients as having higher depressive characteristics (with total HAMD-17 score over 19.5) and higher scores on PANSS negative scale (more than 9.00) (first rule). Second, suicidal PTSD patients endorsed feelings of guilt (HAMD-17 item 2 more than 0.50), a shorter duration of current employment (fewer than 10.50 years), an absence of alcohol-related problems, and one or more children (second rule). Finally, the third rule stressed symptoms of agitation (HAMD-17 item 9 more than 1.50), participation in a fight with civil

Table 9. Rules for identifying suicidal PTSD patients based on structured psychiatric interview and psychiatric and psychological scales.

	Combination of characteristics				Sens. (%)	Specif. (%)
Rule	Characteristic 1	Characteristic 2	Characteristic 3	Characteristic 4		
1.	Total HAMD -17 score more than 19.50	PANSS negative scale more than 9.00			68.8	97.1
2.	HAMD-17 item 2 (feelings of guilt) more than 0.50	Duration of current employment status fewer than 10.50 years	Absence of problems regarding alcohol consumption	One or more children	62.5	97.1
3.	HAMD-17 item 9 (agitation) more than 1.50	HTQ item 9 (fight with civil casualties) more than 0.50	HTQ item 30 (forced hiding) less than 1.50		62.5	94.3
	Total				100.0	91.4

casualties (HTQ item 9 more than 0.50), and rare or never forced hiding (HTQ item 30 less than 1.50). All three rules combined together acquired high sensitivity (correctly recognizing 100.0% of suicidal PTSD patients) and specificity (correctly recognizing 91.4% of non-suicidal patients).

6.2. Model Based on Biological Parameters

A model built on psychiatric and biological parameters (lipid status questionnaire, lipid status – triglycerides, cholesterol, LDL, HDL, levels of apolipoprotein A, apolipoprotein B, oLAB, levels of blood homocystein and serotonin, monoamine oxydase activity) also generated three rules for predicting suicidal PTSD patients (Table 10). They indicated a cluster of psychotic comorbid diagnosis (Schizophrenia F20, Persistent delusional disorders F22, Acute and transient psychotic disorders F23, Unspecified nonorganic psychosis F29) (first rule), more than 24 months of combat experience, a blood level of apolipoprotein B, and a moderate frequency of exercising (once monthly or more) (second rule), and a decrease in physical activity as from a previously frequent tendency to exercise (once daily), to a present decline (occasionally or not exercising). All the rules together achieved sensitivity of 100.0% and specificity of 85.7%.

Table 10. Rules for identifying suicidal PTSD patients based on biological parameters.

	Combination of characteristics			Sens. (%)	Specif. (%)
Rule	Characteristic 1	Characteristic 2	Characteristic 3		
1.	Comorbid group of diagnosis - Schizophrenia F20, Persistent delusional disorders F22, Acute and transient psychotic disorders F23, Unspecified nonorganic psychosis F29			43.8	97.1
2.	Frequency of exercising once monthly or more	Duration of combat experience more than 24 months	Blood level of apolipoprotein B	37.5	94.3
3.	Previous frequency of exercising once daily	Frequency of exercising occasionally or not exercising		43.8	91.4
	Total			100.0	85.7

6.3. Important Parameters in Suicidal Non-PTSD Patients

The data mining software also allowed us to detect some important biological parameters in discriminating suicidal from non-suicidal non-PTSD patients. They included (as presented in Table 11): a history of smoking (more than 15 cigarettes per day), current smoking (more than 12 cigarettes per day), age over 40.5 years, blood levels of serotonin, monoamine oxidase activity, absence of an anxiety disorder, and presence of mood disorders (Bipolar affective disorder F31, Depressive episode F32, Recurrent depressive disorder F33, Persistent mood disorders F34, Other mood disorders F38). These parameters should also be carefully evaluated in suicidal PTSD patients in future studies.

Table 11. Relevant attributes in discriminating suicidal from non-suicidal non-PTSD patients.

Characteristic	Sens. (%)	Specif. (%)
Smoking more than 12.50 cigarettes per day	88.9	57.1
Blood level of serotonin	77.8	73.8
History of smoking more than 15.00 cigarettes per day	88.9	42.9
Monoamine oxidase activity	44.4	88.1
History of previous smoking	88.9	38.1
Absence of anxiety and depressive disorder	55.6	59.5
Age over 40.5 years	66.7	61.9
Presence of mood disorders (Bipolar affective disorder F31, Depressive episode F32, Recurrent depressive disorder F33, Persistent mood disorders F34, Other mood disorders F38)	33.3	83.3

In general, these and other models pointed out several biological parameters that could be measured from the blood samples of patients. They include blood levels of serotonin, monoamine oxidase activity, oLAB, apolipoprotein A and apolipoprotein B levels.

Various studies have shown that the level of serotonin is an important marker in mood disorders and suicidal behavior [65, 66], and it contributes to a vulnerability to commit suicidal acts [67]. Furthermore, lower levels of the serotonin metabolite 5-hydrohyindoleacetic acid (5-HIAA) in cerebrospinal fluid also correlates with lethality of suicide attempts in patients with major depression [68-70]. Different studies investigating serotonin synthesis, transmission and genetics were performed and various abnormalities have been found in the serotonergic system in suicide attempters and completers [66, 67].

In close association with serotonin function is monoamine oxidase, an important enzyme in the degradation of serotonin, which was found to be associated with suicidal behavior in some studies [71]. Genetic polymorphisms of the MAO gene are associated with sensitivity to environmental insults in children [71-73].

The roles of apolipoprotein A and apolipoprotein B are somewhat less studied, but there is evidence that some polymorphisms of apolipoprotein A are connected with depression [74] while increased oxidation and oxidizability of lipoproteins containing apolipoprotein B was found in major depressive disorder [75].

It is important to point out that various other biological parameters are undoubtedly important as well, such as lipid status (including levels of cholesterol and other lipids [76,77]), but in this study group and using this particular method of intelligent data analysis, the above mentioned parameters were shown as more appropriate in forming the models with high specificity and sensitivity. If only the biological parameters obtained from blood samples were used (lipid status – triglycerides, cholesterol, LDL, HDL, levels of apolipoprotein A, apolipoprotein B, oLAB, levels of blood homocystein and serotonin, monoamine oxydase activity), they would be more highlighted in specific rules, but sensitivity and specificity of those rules would be lower than those presented.

Besides the potential relevance that each of these rules and patient models represent separately, it is interesting to note that the detection of three relevant rules means that the population of PTSD patients is not homogenous. Although they may share common properties, significant differences among the subpopulations can be expected. Detailed analysis of each of these subpopulations by automatic data analysis approaches is not appropriate because of very small numbers of patients in each group, but this fact may be relevant for medical practice.

The preliminary findings of this study mostly confirm previously known attributes of suicidal behavior, but a novel and important contribution is the use of novel data mining methodology and the integration of biological, psychological, clinical and functional markers in the process of assessing suicidal patients. Further studies are needed on larger numbers of patients and using even more parameters. The development of such integrative and multidisciplinary diagnostic models for PTSD and suicidality is important for future understanding and development in this complex field.

Acknowledgments

Data presented is part of a technological project "Integrative diagnostic model for stress related mental disorders," (TP-03/01), principal investigator Prof. D. Kozarić-Kovačić, MD, PhD, supported by the Croatian Ministry of Science, Education, and Sports. Authors would like to thank Tanja Jovanović, PhD, for the language proofing.

References

[1]   R.F. Diekstra, The epidemiology of suicide and parasuicide, *Acta Psychiatr Scand (Suppl.)* **371** (1993), 9-20.
[2]   U. Bile-Brahe, Suicide in relation to other causes of death in Denmark, 1992-1991, *Nord J Psychiatry.* **48** (1994), 257-61.
[3]   L.A. Berman, *Suicide*, [CD-ROM], Microsoft, Encarta Encyclopedia, 2000.
[4]   E.G. Krug, M. Kresnow, J.P. Peddicord, L.L. Dahlberg, K.E. Powell, A.E. Crosby, J.L. Annest, Suicide after natural disasters, *N Engl J Med.* **338** (1998), 373-378.
[5]   D. Lester, B. Yang, The influence of war on suicide rates, *J Soc Psychol.* **132** (1992), 135-137.
[6]   D. Lester, Suicide rates before, during and after the world wars, *Eur Psychiatr.* **9** (1994), 262-264.
[7]   T. Shioiri, A. Nishimura, H. Nushida, Y. Tatsuno, S.W. Tang, The Kobe earthquake and reduced suicide rates in Japanese males, *Arch Gen Psychiatry.* **56** (1999), 282-3.
[8]   M. Definis Gojanovic, V. Capkun, A. Smoljanovic, Influence of war on frequency and patterns of homicides and suicides in South Croatia (1991-1993), *Croatian Med J* **38** (1997), 54-58.
[9]   V. Skorupan, V. Petrovecki, J. Skavic, Suicide epidemiology before and during the war in Croatia, *Croatian Med J* **38** (1997), 59-63.
[10] D. Kozaric-Kovacic, M. Grubisic-Ilic, F. Grubisic, Z. Kovacic, Suicide rates and methods before, during and after the war in Croatia (1985-2000), *Natl Med J India.* **15** (2002), 356-7.
[11] E. Durkheim, *Suicide, a study in sociology*, In: Spaulding JA, Simpson, editors, Routledge & Kegan Paul Ltd, London, 1952.
[12] M. Grubisic-Ilic, D. Kozaric-Kovacic, F. Grubisic, Z. Kovacic, Epidemiological study of suicide in the Republic of Croatia-comparison of war and post-war periods and areas directly and indirectly affected by war, *Eur Psychiatry.* **17** (2002), 259-264.
[13] World Health Organization, *Suicide Prevention in Europe. The WHO monitoring survey on national suicide prevention programmes and strategies,* WHO Regional Office for Europe, 2002.
[14] World Health Organization, *World sucide prevention day,* Statement WHO, WHO, 2007.
[15] World Health Organization, *Targets for health for all. Targets in support of the European regional strategy for health for all (European Health for All, Series N 1),* WHO Regional Office for Europe, Copenhagen, 1985.
[16] World Health Organization, *HEALTH21. The Health for all policy framework for the WHO European Region (European Health for All, Series N 6),* WHO Regional Office for Europe, Copenhagen, 1999.
[17] World Health Organization, *The world health report 2001: mental health: new understanding, new hope,* WHO, Geneva, 2001.
[18] World Health Organization, *Atlas of Health in Europe,* WHO Library Cataloging in Publication Data, 2003.
[19] A. Schmidtke, Perspective: Suicide in Europe, *Sucide Life Threat Behav.* **27** (1997), 127-136.
[20] A. Marusic, History and Geography of Suicide: Could Genetic Risk Factors Account for the Variation in Suicide Rates?, *Am J Med Genet C Semin Med Genet.* **133C** (2005), 43-47.
[21] A. Marusic, A. Farmer, Genetic risk factors as possible causes of the variation in European suicide rates, *Br J Psychiatry.* **179** (2001), 194-196.
[22] D.A. Brent, J.J. Mann, Family genetic studies, suicide, and suicidal behavior, *Am J Med Genet C Semin Med Genet.* **133C** (2005), 13-24.
[23] M. Leboyer, F. Slama, L. Siever, F. Bellivier, Suicidal disorders: a nosological entity per se? *Am J Med Genet C Semin Med Genet.* **133C** (2005), 3-7.

[24] E. Baca-Garcia, C. Vaquero, C. Diaz-Sastre, A. Ceverino, J. Saiz-Ruiz, J. Fernandez-Piquera, et al., A pilot study on a gene-hormone interaction in female suicide attempts, Eur Arch Psychiatry Clin Neurosci. 253 (2003), 281-285.

[25] J. Stefulj, A. Buttner, M. Kubat, P. Zill, M. Balija, W. Eisenmenger, et al., 5HT-2C receptor polymorphism in suicide victims. Association studies in German and Slavic populations, Eur Arch Psychiatry Clin Neurosci. 254 (2004), 224-227.

[26] J.J. Mann, K.M. Malone, D.A. Nielsen, D. Goldman, J. Erdos, J. Gelernter, Possible association of a polymorphism of the tryptophan hydroxylase gene with suicidal behavior in depressed patients, Am J Psychiatry. 154 (1997), 1451-1453.

[27] D.A. Nielsen, M. Virkkunen, J. Lappalainen, M. Eggert, G.L. Brown, J.C. Long, et al., A tryptophan hydroxylase gene marker for suicidality and alcoholism, Arch Gen Psychiatry. 55 (1998), 593-602.

[28] V. Hrabak-Zerjavic, Z. Folnegovic, M. Silobrcic-Radic, I. Brkic, Epidemioloski prikaz izvršenih samoubojstava u Hrvatskoj u razdoblju od 1985. do 1998. godine (Epidemiological overview of suicides in Croatia in period 1985-1998), In: V. Folnegovic-Smalc, B. Gogic, D. Kocijan-Hercigonja editors, Zbornik sažetaka 1. hrvatskog kongresa o suicidalnom ponašanju (Book of Abstracts, 1st Croatian congress on suicidal behavior), Marko M., Zagreb, 2000, 56.

[29] D. Kozaric-Kovacic, M. Grubisic-Ilic, F. Grubisic, Z. Kovacic, Epidemiological indicators of suicide in the Republic of Croatia, Društvena istraživanja 57 (2002), 155-170.

[30] B. Barraclough, Differences between national suicide rates, Brit J Psychiatr. 122 (1973), 95-96.

[31] C. Pritchard, New patterns of suicide by age and gender in the United Kingdom and the Western World 1974-1992; an indicator of social change?, Soc Psychiatry Psychiatr Epidemiol. 31 (1996), 227-234.

[32] D. Brent, M. Baugher, J. Bridge, T. Chen, L. Chiappetta, Age and sex-related factors for adolescent suicide, J Am Acad Child Adolesc Psychiatry. 38 (1999), 1497-1505.

[33] D. Kozaric-Kovacic, D. Kocijan-Hercigonja, A. Jambrosic, Psychiatric help to psychotraumatized persons during and after war in Croatia, Croat Med J. 43 (2002), 221-228.

[34] D. Kozaric-Kovacic, M. Grubisic-Ilic, Lj. Bakic-Tomic, L. Rutic, Children's awareness dangers from firearms, land mines and other explosive devices in Croatia, 1996, Croat Med J. 3 (1997), 335-364.

[35] D. Kozaric-Kovacic, M. Bajs, S. Vidosic, A. Matic, A. Alegic Karin, T. Peraica, Change of diagnosis of post-traumatic stress disorder related to compensation-seeking, Croat Med J. 45 (2004), 427-433.

[36] World Health Organization, The ICD-10 Classification of Mental and Behavioral Disorders; Clinical Descriptions and the Diagnostic Guedelines, WHO, Geneva, 1992.

[37] F.W. Weathers, T.M. Keane, J.R. Davidson, Clinician-administered PTSD scale: a review of the first ten years of research, Depress Anxiety. 13 (2001), 132-56.

[38] W. Guy, Clinical global impressions, In: Early clinical drug evaluation unit assessment manual for psychopharmacology, Rev. ed., U.S. Department of Health, Education, and Welfare, Public Health Service, Alcohol, Drug Abuse, and Mental Health Administration, National Institute of Mental Health Psychopharmacology Research Branch, Division of Extramural Research Programs, Rockville, MD, 1976, 79-86.

[39] R.F. Mollica, Y. Caspi-Yavin, P. Bollini, T. Truong, S. Tor, J. Lavelle, The Harvard Trauma Questionnaire. Validating a cross-cultural instrument for measuring torture, trauma, and posttraumatic stress disorder in Indochinese refugees, J Nerv Ment Dis. 180 (1992), 111-116.

[40] T.M. Keane, J.M. Caddell, K.L. Taylor, Mississippi Scale for Combat-related Posttraumatic Stress Disorder: three studies in reliability and validity, J Consult Clin Psychol. 56 (1988), 85-90.

[41] S.R. Hathway, J.C. McKinley, Minnesota multiphasic personality inventory, 1st ed., University of Minnesota, Mineapolis, MN, 1989.

[42] E. Baca-Garcia, M.M. Perez-Rodriguez, D. Saiz-Gonzalez, I. Basurte-Villamor, J. Saiz-Ruiz, J.M. Leiva-Murillo, et al., Variables associated with familial suicide attempts in a sample of suicide attempters, Prog Neuropsychopharmacol Biol Psychiatry. 31 (2007), 1312-1316.

[43] A. Alegic, V. Matulic-Karadole, Neki prediktori suicidalnosti kod osoba oboljelih od PTSP-a (Some predictors of suicidality in PTSD patients), In: V. Folnegovic-Smalc, B. Gogic, D. Kocijan-Hercigonja editors, Zbornik sažetaka 1. hrvatskog kongresa o suicidalnom ponašanju (Book of Abstracts, 1st Croatian congress on suicidal behavior), Marko M., Zagreb, 2000, 56.

[44] H.J. Eysenck, S.B.G. Eysenck, P. Barrett, A revised version of the psychoticism scale, Personality and Individual Differences 6 (1985), 21-29.

[45] C.S. Carver, M.F. Scheier, J.K. Weintraub, Assessing coping strategies: a theoretically based approach, J Pers Soc Psychol. 56 (1989), 267-83.

[46] A.T. Beck, C.H. Ward, M. Mendelson, J. Mock, J. Erbaugh, An inventory for measuring depression, Arch Gen Psychiatry. 4 (1961), 561-71.

[47] M.M. Linehan, J.L. Goodstein, S.L. Nielsen, J.A. Chiles, Reasons for staying alive when you are thinking of killing yourself: the reasons for living inventory, *J Consult Clin Psychol.* **51** (1983), 276-86.

[48] V. Matulić, *Socijalna podrška, stres i zdravlje kod starijih osoba* (Social support, stress and health in elderly people) [M. Sc. degree], University of Zagreb, Faculty of Philosophy, Depratment of psychology, Zagreb, 1995.

[49] T. H. Holmes, R. Rahe, The social readjustment rating scale, *J Psychosom Res.* **11** (1967), 213.

[50] W.J. Frawley, G. Piatetsky-Shapiro, C.J. Matheus, Knowledge discovery in databases: an overview, *AI Magazine.* **13** (1992), 57-70.

[51] D. Gamberger, N. Lavrac, G. Krstacic, Active subgroup mining: a case study in coronary heart disease risk group detection, *Artif Intell Med.* **28** (2003), 27-57.

[52] D.M. Coulter, A. Bate, R.H. Meyboom, M. Lindquist, I.R. Edwards, Antipsychotic drugs and heart muscle disorder in international pharmacovigilance: data mining study, *BMJ.* **322** (2001), 1207-9.

[53] I. Marinic, F. Supek, Z. Kovacic, L. Rukavina, T. Jendricko, D. Kozaric-Kovacic, Posttraumatic stress disorder: diagnostic data analysis by data mining methodology, *Croat Med J.* **48** (2007), 185-97.

[54] P. Perner, Intelligent data analysis in medicine-recent advances, *Artif Intell Med.* **37** (2006), 1-5.

[55] J.R. Baker, D. Gamberger, J.R. Mihelcic, A. Sabljic, Evaluation of artificial intelligence based models for chemical biodegradability prediction, *Molecules.* **9** (2004), 989-1004.

[56] H. Liu, Z.Z. Hu, M. Torii, C. Wu, C. Friedman, Quantitative assessment of dictionary-based protein named entity tagging, *J Am Med Inform Assoc.* **13** (2006), 497-507.

[57] Y. Qi, Z. Bar-Joseph, J. Klein-Seetharaman, Evaluation of different biological data and computational classification methods for use in protein interaction prediction, *Proteins.* **63** (2006), 490-500.

[58] C.S. Goh, N. Lan, S.M. Douglas, B. Wu, N. Echols, A. Smith, et al., Mining the structural genomics pipeline: identification of protein properties that affect high-throughput experimental analysis, *J Mol Biol.* **336** (2004), 115-30.

[59] D. Gamberger, T. Šmuc, N. Lavrač, Subgroup discovery: on-line data mining server and its application, *Proc. of Simulations in Biomedicine V* (2003), 433-442.

[60] S.R. Kay, A. Fiszbein, L.A. Opler, The positive and negative syndrome scale (PANSS) for schizophrenia, *Schizophr Bull.* **13** (1987), 261-76.

[61] M. Hamilton, The assessment of anxiety states by rating, *Br J Med Psychol.* **32** (1959), 50-5.

[62] M. Hamilton, A rating scale for depression, *J Neurol Neurosurg Psychiatry.* **23** (1960), 56-62.

[63] L.A. King, D.W. King, G.A. Leskin, D.W. Foy, The Los Angeles Symptom Checklist: a self-report measure of posttraumatic stress disorder, *Assessment* **2** (1995), 1-17.

[64] T. Sairenchi, H. Iso, F. Irie, K. Yamagishi, H. Takahashi, H. Noda, et al., Development of a tool for assessment of local government health policy, *Nippon Koshu Eisei Zasshi.* **52** (2005), 1032-44.

[65] J.J. Mann, D.A. Brent, V. Arango, The neurobiology and genetics of suicide and attempted suicide: a focus on the serotonergic system, *Neuropsychopharmacology.* **24** (2001), 467-77.

[66] H.I. Kaplan, B.J. Sadock, *Kaplan & Sadock's Synopsis of Psychiatry: Behavioral Sciences/Clinical Psychiatry*, 9th ed., Lippincott Williams & Wilkins, Philadelphia, PA, 2003.

[67] J.J. Mann, The neurobiology of suicide, *Nature Med.* **4** (1998), 25–30.

[68] A. Roy, J. De Jong, M. Linnoila, Cerebrospinal fluid monoamine metabolites and suicidal behavior in depressed patients. A 5-year follow-up study, *Arch Gen Psychiatry.* **46** (1989), 609–612.

[69] L. Träskman-Bendz, C. Alling, L. Oreland, G. Regnéll, E. Vinge, R. Öhman, Prediction of suicidal behavior from biologic tests, *J Clin Psychopharmacol.* **12**, 2 Suppl (1992), 21S–26S.

[70] P. Nordström, M. Samuelsson, M. Åsberg, L. Träskman-Bendz, A. Aberg-Wistedt, C. Nordin, et al., CSF 5-HIAA predicts suicide risk after attempted suicide, *Suicide Life Threat Behav.* **24** (1994), 1–9.

[71] J.B. Savitz, C.L. Cupido, R.S. Ramesar, Trends in suicidology: personality as an endophenotype for molecular genetic investigations, *PLoS Med.* **3** (2006), e107.

[72] X. Ni, T. Sicard, N. Bulgin, R. Bismil, K. Chan, S. McMain, et al., Monoamine oxidase a gene is associated with borderline personality disorder, *Psychiatr Genet.* **17** (2007), 153-7.

[73] A. Caspi, J. McClay, T.E. Moffitt, J. Mill, J. Martin, I.W. Craig, et al., Role of genotype in the cycle of violence in maltreated children, *Science.* **297** (2002), 851–854.

[74] T.F. Ejchel, L.M. Araújo, L.R. Ramos, M.S. Cendoroglo, M. de Arruda Cardoso Smith, Association of the apolipoprotein A-IV: 360 Gln/His polymorphism with cerebrovascular disease, obesity, and depression in a Brazilian elderly population, *Am J Med Genet B Neuropsychiatr Genet.* **135** (2005), 65-8.

[75] A. Sarandol, E. Sarandol, S.S. Eker, E.U. Karaagac, B.Z. Hizli, M. Dirican, et al., Oxidation of apolipoprotein B-containing lipoproteins and serum paraoxonase/arylesterase activities in major depressive disorder, *Prog Neuropsychopharmacol Biol Psychiatry.* **30** (2006), 1103-8.

[76] D. Lester, Serum cholesterol levels and suicide: a meta-analysis, *Suicide Life Threat Behav.* **32** (2002), 333-46.
[77] J. Brunner, K.G. Parhofer, P. Schwandt, T. Bronisch, Cholesterol, essential fatty acids, and suicide, *Pharmacopsychiatry.* **35** (2002), 1-5.

Section III

Prevention

Lowering Suicide Risk in Returning Troops
B.K. Wiederhold (Ed.)
IOS Press, 2008
© *2008 IOS Press. All rights reserved.*
doi:10.3233/978-1-58603-889-2-75

Interdisciplinary Joint Approach to Suicide Prevention of Warfighters

Krešimir ĆOSIĆ [a,1], Ph.D., LTG (Ret.), Miroslav SLAMIĆ [a], Ph.D.,
Siniša POPOVIĆ [a], M.S., Svjetlana DORIČIĆ [b], M.A., COL

[a] *University of Zagreb, Faculty of Electrical Engineering and Computing, Croatia*
[b] *Ministry of Defense, Croatia*

Abstract. Intense multi-factorial stresses faced by participants in combat operations may cause high levels of psychological suffering that may progress to serious mental disorders or even suicide. Therefore, the impact of stress and mental disorders on modern military is analyzed, including the role and importance of military training and leadership in protecting warfighters from devastating combat-related psychological disorders. Mental health indicators and stress-related impact factors, extended with known risk and protective factors for suicide, lead to a comprehensive mental health profile. In order to address the issues of psychological suffering and potential suicide of warfighters, the need for an interdisciplinary approach and joint institutional efforts has been stressed. Finally, an integrated strategy of suicide risk detection and prevention is proposed, based on longitudinal acquisition of an extended vector of comprehensive mental health indicators and appropriate probabilistic analyses. Regressive analysis of the individuals' databases is the starting point for identification of various psychological disorders, degraded operational performance, and potential suicide risk.

Keywords. combat operations, stress inoculation training, stress exposure training, virtual reality exposure therapy, psychophysiological measurements, comprehensive mental health indicators, interdisciplinary approach, posttraumatic stress disorder, suicide risk assessment, suicide prevention

Introduction

Stressful and chaotic combat environments impose an entire range of extraordinary demands on every individual, particularly soldiers. Destruction, injuries, and deaths mixed with deep emotions like fear, hate, frustration, anger, guilt etc. may cause serious mental problems. These acute or chronic invisible mental injuries may trigger posttraumatic stress disorder or even suicide. Combat stressors may also cause severe operational casualties, reducing individual as well as unit, operational performance and effectiveness during a combat military mission. Even in such highly stressful environments, the main tasks and objectives of military forces are to reach and maintain maximum effectiveness. This means that, despite technological advances, humans continue to be the central element in combat military operations. Maintaining soldier emotional, cognitive, and behavioral control in combat operations is crucially

---

[1] Corresponding Author: Prof. Dr. Krešimir Ćosić; University of Zagreb, Faculty of Electrical Engineering and Computing; Head of the Delegation of Croatian Parliament to the NATO Parliamentary Assembly; E-mail: kcosic@sabor.sabor.hr.

important to ensure their own safety and the safety of subordinates. Severe forms of operational stresses related to extreme trauma, like injuries, deep wounds, massacres, death etc., may significantly reduce soldiers' ability to perform tasks effectively in the uncertainties of combat operations. Leadership abilities in such stressful environments are critical for survival, performance, and the morale of subordinates and units. Therefore, optimization of unit operational effectiveness and operational tempo in combat operations requires maximization of the mental health potential of every individual soldier and their leaders. Important indicators of military readiness like cognitive, emotional, behavioral, and physical performance must be continuously assessed before deployments. Estimation of soldier motivation, self-esteem, personality hardiness, stress resistance, and self-control are also very important parameters of their readiness. Stress reactions and stress symptoms as well as coping strategies are crucial characteristics of every individual in the highly unpredictable and ambiguous environment of combat operations. It is logical to expect that high intensity combat periods and high fatalities or deaths during combat operations will be directly proportional to mental health problems among soldiers like depression, posttraumatic stress disorder (PTSD), or even suicide. Combat stressors may cause soldiers to become mentally and physically weary and listless, pre-occupied and unable to remember details, indifferent, easily startled and confused, and tense and irritable to all stimuli. Current peacekeeping and peace enforcement deployments can also be associated with increased rates of long-lasting mental distress and mental illness in the form of PTSD, depression, alcohol abuse, anxiety disorders, and panic disorder. They can also be associated with higher levels of medically unexplained physical symptoms including musculoskeletal pain, cognitive dysfunction, sleep disturbance, and digestive complaints. Therefore, better post-deployment screening is important since it can decrease the burden of deployment-related health problems. Appropriate post-deployment screening can more easily and quickly identify and treat individuals suffering from deployment-related illnesses, particularly mental health problems. Quick treatment may truncate the period of suffering and may mitigate the personal, family, social, and occupational consequences of an untreated illness. To minimize combat stress effects, it is critical to recognize the mental health needs of each individual as soon as possible and to initiate assistance even during combat deployments. Stressful emotions and thoughts can strongly affect soldier behavior and may be critical elements for mission success. A deeper understanding of psychological operational stress disorders is very important, as are coping strategies, which are the right tools to use to prevent the negative impact of stressors on troops. Alarming individual behavioral health problems in combination with various mental health indicators, like ideations of self-harm, can point to the need for suicide prevention efforts. Depression, anxiety disorders, aggressive behaviors, alcohol, drugs etc. among soldiers may also strongly affect soldiers' families, as well as entire societies in general.

1. Role and Importance of Stress Management in Military Training

Performance of well-trained soldiers and units significantly exceeds performance of those not adequately prepared for stressful combat uncertainties and challenges. Traditional military training focuses on skill acquisition, and the development of technical proficiency, discipline, strength, endurance, and teamwork. Training skills, leadership, and teambuilding through tough training and hazardous conditions also speeds up the learning of military tactical skills and leadership techniques.

In addition to physical and technical skills, important prerequisites of good military performance are the mental ability to function effectively under stressful combat conditions and resilience against psychological problems associated with combat stress. This section presents an overview of these topics. A more detailed treatise can be found in Thompson and McCreary (2006) [1]. Military leaders play a critical role in enhancing the effectiveness of their units in military operations by providing the best training and rigorous disciplines, which sustain high personal motivation and morale. Modern military leaders also need to know how to manage operational stress and how to provide psychological support in order to mitigate negative impacts of combat involvements and maintain the psychological readiness of their units. Unit stress management and team building skills strengthen unit cohesion and reduce the overall effects of the shocking combat environment and experience. Many military leaders, however, associate stigma with stress-related issues and particularly help-seeking behavior. Stereotypes that psychological problems reveal inherent character weakness may cause the leaders' general resistance toward the relevance of psychological support in professional military units. Indeed, this mindset is prevalent in traditional military cultures that explicitly value only physical fitness and technical skills. Despite these significant obstacles, military leaders must address the issue of developing the baseline psychological resilience of their soldiers due to consistent evidence that such resilience ensures more health and well-being of their units and is a vital operational prerequisite for success. Considerable effort, time, and money have also been spent on military psychological screening programs at the recruiting level in order to maximize performance and minimize psychological casualties. However, stress injuries continue to be responsible for a high percentage of operational casualties and tactical failures.

Learning how to control thoughts and emotions represents a critical element of operational effectiveness in highly stressful combat environments and provides the military with individuals who are more capable of coping with the demands of professional military life. Lack of psychological skills and readiness may significantly increase operational risks due to certain stress-related reactions of individuals. Links between thoughts, emotions and behavioral responses, and abilities to control them determine the stress-coping potential of each individual soldier. Development of coping capabilities is particularly important for novice soldiers who may lack coping resources, which may lead them to a greater degree of arousal. Their limited coping potential, including their high physiological arousal, gives them less capacity to cope with combat risks and dangers. On the other hand, experienced soldiers have developed the coping and adaptive strategies that enable them to have greater control of their arousal levels and more cognitive resources for better combat effectiveness in life-threatening situations.

For the outlined reasons, improving the stress resilience of troops through military training programs is necessary. To increase the baseline psychological resilience, it is important to promote stress awareness and stress training in ways that are meaningful and immediately relevant to military personnel. Providing concrete and specific information related to recognition and management of psychological stress reactions needs to go beyond academic management briefings, lectures, and discussions of a generic stress model. The development of training programs that successfully prepare personnel for the psychologically rigorous operations, in addition to the physical and technical demand, is important for operational effectiveness in high-stress environments and for maintaining the wellbeing of individual soldiers and their units. Training programs must be designed to build soldier self-confidence, mental toughness, and inner strength to face adversity, fear, and hardship during combat with confidence, resolution and courage. Soldiers subjected to stressful conditions in training should experience, later on, less stress in real combat circumstances. A multi-stressor training environment that realistically simulates combat conditions is, therefore, an important element of psychological preparation.

Mental Readiness Training, Stress Inoculation Training, and Stress Exposure Training are powerful cognitive behavioral tools to reach high mental readiness in professional military forces. The most popular among them is Stress Inoculation Training (SIT), which is an intensive, multi stage process designed to change maladaptive or harmful thoughts and behaviors in stressful situations. Stress Exposure Training (SET) was developed to expand the scope of SIT beyond its traditional clinical applications in order to enhance the performance of healthy people in stressful working environments (Figure 1).

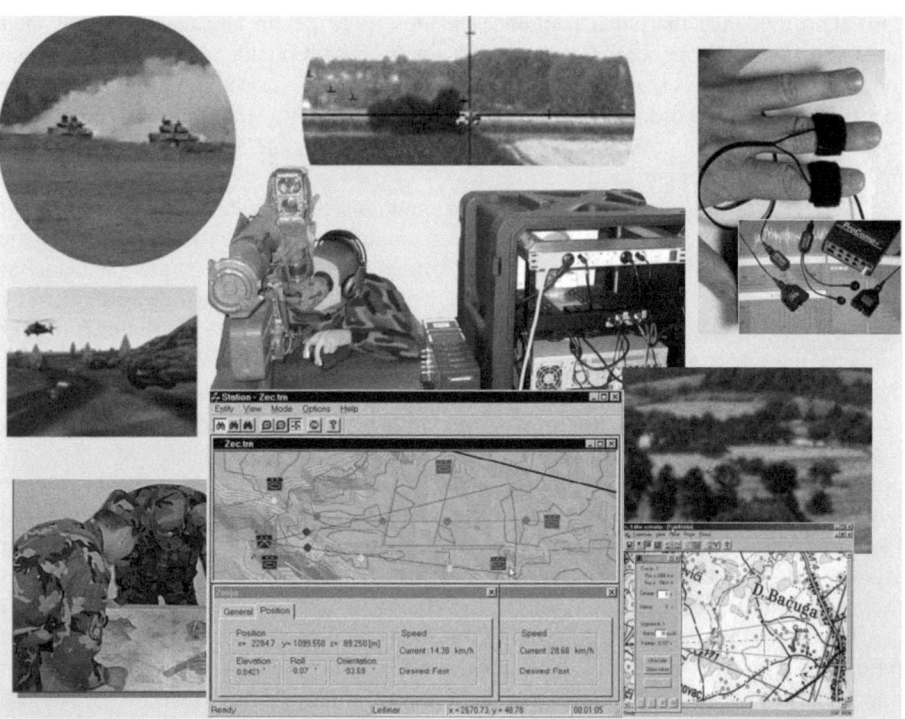

Figure 1. Stress exposure training that incorporates psychophysiological monitoring of AT guided missile trainees and corresponding tactical commanders

Consistent with SIT, the goal of SET is to develop the ability to maintain awareness of stress reactions via feedback sensors and to develop cognitive, emotional and behavioral control strategies for specific stressful environments. The important element that SET adds onto traditional military training of core skills is simulation of highly stressful situations, in order to enhance psychological and physiological fidelity of training. In addition to the relevance of SET for direct combat involvement, SET adjusted for tactical decision making is also important, since inability to maintain decision-making performance under stress may ultimately lead to unpredictable casualties. Technologies like virtual reality (VR) and psychophysiological monitoring are being tested and applied for SET [2-3], as well as for assisting individuals who already suffer from psychological consequences of combat, like PTSD [4-9].

In essence, the mental readiness training is a process of acquiring toughness, courage, and strength using cognitive and behavioral skills to learn how to cope and how to successfully manage and prevail in stressful combat situations. The notion that mental readiness is a trainable skill that can be acquired and developed, much like physical fitness, is a real innovation in comparison with the traditional view that psychological performance is a time invariant characteristic of the individual's temperament. Training of maintaining cognitive, emotional, and behavioral control is regarded as important in training of core technical proficiencies. Soldiers who over-learn and instinctively embed principles of mental readiness training are more successful and effective in professional military operational duties. Mental readiness training may provide significant preventative mental health benefits by providing a higher baseline resilience level for military personnel that would reduce the impact of acute operational stress. Altogether, intense, rigorous, and frequent comprehensive training may protect warfighters from the adverse psychological and physiological effects of acute stress and its long-term chronic consequences in the form of PTSD or even suicide.

2. Comprehensive Mental Health Indicators and Necessity of an Interdisciplinary Joint Approach

Adverse effects of combat on mental health emphasize the responsibility of military organizations to provide extraordinary mental care for their personnel. Military training that merges learning of technical competencies and stress-coping techniques is one aspect of such mental care. Another aspect is systematic and comprehensive monitoring of a number of variables related to military personnel mental wellbeing, in order to make and implement prompt and appropriate decisions. Rationale for such monitoring comprises several potential benefits. First of all, comprehensive information facilitates assessing the readiness state of each individual, as well as operational performance of military units. In addition, gathered information may help with assessing the individual's risk of potential future psychological problems. If the risk assessment is sufficiently reliable and accurate, then very scarce psychological expert resources may be rightfully allocated to individuals in need. Thus, the problems may be resolved before serious psychological morbidity sets in, or the serious psychological morbidity may be treated early enough to have a good prognosis. Suicide in warfighters represents the terminal phase of inability to cope with real life circumstances, and it is associated with certain psychological and psychiatric disorders. Moreover, there is still only a vague understanding of the interplay between all risk and protective factors that ultimately leads to the tragic act of committing suicide. Various risk and protective factors have been identified, but it is difficult to predict which person in high-risk populations will actually commit suicide, unless the individual has reported a suicidal plan [10]. The best predictive value for imminent suicide is the reported intention to die, existence of a suicidal plan, and availability of means to carry out suicide, as well as despair and hopelessness; comorbid depression and alcoholism indicate a short-term risk of suicide even if suicidal behavior is not exhibited [10]. Therefore, prediction of suicide before an individual exhibits suicidal or other critical behaviors is a daunting task, which most likely requires monitoring of a considerable number of different factors, including psychological and psychiatric disorders, like depression and PTSD. In this regard, systematic comprehensive monitoring also holds potential for better suicide risk assessment and prevention. Furthermore, prompt and appropriate action based on comprehensive information may help minimize negative social impact of combat-related psychological consequences in a broader sense, such as divorces, early retirements from service, legal problems etc. The decreases in homicides, accidental deaths, and severe and moderate family violence following implementation of the U.S. Air Force suicide prevention program [11] support these expectations.

The proposed comprehensive mental health profile of an individual consists of snapshots taken at various times during the individual's military career. A snapshot contains values of indicators relevant for mental wellbeing, which are classified into eight functional groups (Figure 2): **Service Indicators (*Srv*)**, related to military service, **Physical Indicators (*Phs*)**, related to physical issues, **Psychological/Psychiatric Indicators (*Psy*)**, related to psychological or psychiatric issues, **Psychophysiological Indicators (*Ppho*)**, **Biological Indicators (*Bio*)**, **Cognitive Indicators (*Cog*)**, **Personality Indicators (*Prs*)**, and **Sociodemographic Indicators (*Sdem*)**. From the perspective of design of the database that holds the comprehensive mental health profiles, the functional groups are non-overlapping because of the need to minimize data redundancies, even if some groups may be regarded as logically overlapping (*Psy* and *Prs* groups, for instance). In this sense, the functional groups are one large set of indicators (where no duplicates exist by definition), which has been partitioned into eight groups for easier comprehension and structured discussion of its elements. Since the eight functional groups contain risk and protective factors for various outcomes of interest, indicators can be further clustered according to the outcomes (Figure 2).

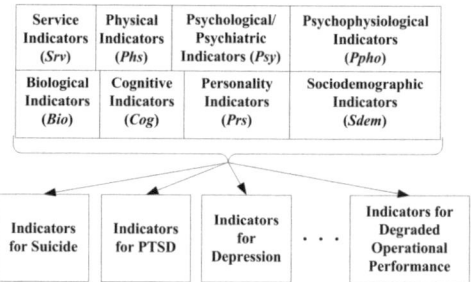

Figure 2. Organization of the comprehensive mental health indicators into eight functional disjunctive groups and outcomes of interest

Figure 3 illustrates the contents of the functional groups of indicators. *Srv* group reflects the known impact of the various events during the military career on the mental health of the individual. Some examples include exposures to various traumatic combat-related events, intensity of combat operations that the individual has been involved with, existence of pending disciplinary action etc. Physical issues that may seriously affect mental health are gathered under the *Phs* group; prime examples are amputations, burns, and other physical damages and illnesses with debilitating and irreversible consequences. Relevance of *Psy* group for monitoring the mental wellbeing of military personnel is self-evident. Group *Ppho* of psychophysiological indicators facilitates insight into the physiological state of the individual, by measurements without stimuli, with startle auditory and visual stimuli, and with stimuli depicting various combat-related events, some of which may be directly relevant to previous combat experiences of the individual. The ability to control psychophysiological reactivity in stressful situations seems intuitively desirable, as it may indicate less susceptibility to stress and resistance to performance degradation in stressful situations. Thus, psychophysiology may be important in the wider context of monitoring the stress-related state of the individual. Preliminary testing has shown better control of physiological arousal and better performance during VR testing of combat medics who were previously trained in stressful VR conditions versus those training in no-stress VR conditions [12]. Psychophysiological monitoring is also important for PTSD [13] and stress exposure training [2]. Although no psychophysiological characteristic seems to be included in prominent risk and protective factors for suicide, electrodermal reactivity to auditory stimuli in a habituation experiment has discriminated suicidal action from suicidal thinking with no suicidal thoughts in depressed patients [14]. Biological group, *Bio*, is included since various psychological or psychiatric problems have biological correlates in body or brain. Elevated levels of cortisol are indicators of prolonged stress [15], PTSD patients exhibit certain biological differences with regard to healthy controls [16-17], hereditary predisposition may be important for some psychiatric disorders and so on. Cognitive indicators (*Cog* group) are relevant since cognitive impairments may be indicators of degraded operational performance for soldiers and commanders alike. Despite the majority of psychological casualties occurring at the levels directly involved in combat, higher-level decision-making stress is also substantial, as mistakes caused by bad judgment in high-stress situations cost lives. Moreover, the severity of casualties from erroneous decision making generally grows with the level at which decisions are made. For these reasons, the military needs careful and regular monitoring for cognitive impairments on different levels of rank hierarchy. Personality traits in *Prs* group may make some people more susceptible to certain psychological problems. Association of impulsivity and aggression with suicide [18] supports this view. Sociodemographic indicators, gathered into *Sdem* group, are considered to play a role in various psychological problems, including suicide [10], PTSD [19], and depression [20]. Many of the items within functional groups are groups themselves, which have not been further decomposed due to space limitations. The "suicidality & self-harm" item within *Psy* group is one example, as it contains items about suicidal and self-harm behavior, history, and history in the family (cf. Figure 4).

In Figure 4, indicators for suicide observed in the literature have been drawn together, noting their memberships with regard to the functional groups. Rather than enumerating all indicators relevant for suicide, the intention is to illustrate their functional breadth. In this regard, five of the eight functional groups are represented among suicide indicators with more than one item, **Bio** and **Cog** groups have contributed one item, and **Ppho** is the only unrepresented group. **Ppho** group, however, is relevant in the context of risk assessment for PTSD and assessment of the individual's mental readiness.

Srv Group Indicators	*Phs* Group Indicators	*Psy* Group Indicators	*Ppho* Group Indicators
Unit of an individual	Physical illness	Despair	Baseline measurements
a) Unit1	a) Illness1	Guilt	Heart rate/ECG
b) Unit2	b) Illness2	Hopelessness	Skin resistance
...	...	Anxiety	...
Rank	Physical injuries	Alcoholism	Reactions to startle stimuli
a) Rank1	a) Amputations	Drug abuse	Reactions to traumatic stimuli
b) Rank2	a) Hand	PTSD	Individual's combat-
...	b) Foot	Depression	related events
Operation involvements	...	Cluster B personality disorder	Other events
Op1, Op2 ...	b) Burns	Suicidality & self-harm	...
Combat-related events	Type	Psychiatric hospitalization	
a) Friend killed in action	Surface area	...	*Sdem* Group Indicators
b) Treated casulties	Body parts		Sex
...	...		Age
Pending transitions		*Prs* Group Indicators	Race
a) Retirement	...	Big five personality traits	Marital status
b) Discharge		Agreeableness	Children
c) Promotion	*Cog* Group Indicators	Conscietiousness	Parents
...	Memory	Extraversion	Childhood
Bio Group Indicators	Attention	Neuroticism	Education
Blood testing	Perception	Openness to experience	Religion
Genetics	Action	Aggression & anger	Financial status
Imaging	Problem solving	Self-esteem	Interests and activities
...	...	...	...

Figure 3. Sketch of the contents of the functional groups of indicators

Indicators for Suicide	
Suicidality & self-harm (*Psy*)	Within 1 month of discharge from psychiatric
Intention to die	hospital (*Psy*)
Suicidal plan	PTSD (*Psy*)
Availability of means	Male sex (*Sdem*)
History of suicide attempts	Age 20-24 (*Sdem*)
History of suicide or suicide attempts in	Parental loss before age 11 (*Sdem*)
family	Decline of interests and activities (*Sdem*)
History of deliberate self-harm	Childhood physical/sexual abuse (*Sdem*)
Suicide triggers	Marital isolation (*Sdem*)
Onset or acute worsening of a	Not living with child under 18 (*Sdem*)
psychiatric disorder (*Psy*)	Pending transitions (*Srv*)
Financial troubles (*Sdem*)	Rank (*Srv*)
Job problems (*Sdem*)	Unit (*Srv*)
Legal difficulties (*Sdem* or *Srv*)	Combat-related events (*Srv*)
Despair (*Psy*)	Blood cholesterol (*Bio*)
Guilt (*Psy*)	Serious physical illness (*Phs*)
Hopelessness (*Psy*)	Serious physical injuries (*Phs*)
Depression (*Psy*)	Rational thinking loss (*Cog* or *Psy*)
Cluster B personality disorder (*Psy*)	Unrealistic expectations (*Prs*)
Alcoholism (*Psy*)	Aggression & anger (*Prs*)
Drug abuse (*Psy*)	Low self-esteem (*Prs*)
	...

Figure 4. Indicators relevant for suicide, obtained by selection of indicators from basic functional groups

Extensiveness of the profile calls for an interdisciplinary approach across several disciplines. Acquisition of data from the eight functional groups, via psychological, psychiatric, sociodemographic, service-related, and personality questionnaires, psycho-physiological data acquisition, cognitive testing and biological and physical assessments, spans different disciplines. In order to monitor the mental health of military professionals longitudinally during their careers, computerized databases are necessary. The data needs to be organized for efficient retrieval of information for analytic purposes. Data may then be analyzed to determine predictive values of various combinations of indicators in the comprehensive mental health profile for degraded operational performance, psychological disorders and suicide. Prevention of suicide can further be facilitated by early identification and treatment of psychological and psychiatric disorders associated with increased suicide risk.

It is important to acquire data in structured and unambiguous, categorized, or quantitative form, avoiding free natural language in the data. This would assist the research and development of decision-support systems with partially or fully automated risk analyses in two ways. First, research of comprehensive risk assessment models for outcomes of interest would be facilitated. More importantly, after the appropriate models are found, implementation of these models into decision-support systems may be feasible only if the database is sufficiently well structured. Otherwise, the amount of data preprocessing that decision-support systems need to implement may become impractical. Thus, in the context of the taxonomy for data sharing described in Walker et al. [21], the storage of the comprehensive mental health profiles needs to comply with Level 3 (machine-organizable data) and ideally Level 4 (machine-interpretable data).

The data acquisition should also be as automated as possible. Questionnaires are expected to be widely utilized for data acquisition in *Psy*, *Prs*, *Srv*, *Sdem* groups, as their administration is resource and time efficient, and they can be mostly automatically converted into a suitable electronic form for later retrieval and analyses. Acquisition of data in other groups and their conversion into appropriate digital format is generally more difficult to automate and it is more resource and time intensive in comparison to questionnaire-based data acquisition.

For analysis of data acquired during comprehensive monitoring, application of data mining techniques holds promise [22]. Data mining is the extraction of implicit, previously unknown, and potentially useful information from data [23]. One aspect of data mining, particularly interesting in the context of this paper, is related to making quality predictions regarding future events based on the available data. Specifically, the raison d'être of comprehensive mental health profile monitoring and analysis is early identification of individuals with a higher probability of degraded and risky performance in combat and of contracting serious psychological morbidity or committing suicide, in order to provide them prompt and efficient allocation of scarce expert help. Longitudinal comprehensive monitoring intends to facilitate development and testing of predictive models over various indicators in order to find the best predictive models and indicators for degraded operational performance, serious psychological disorders or suicide. There is a multitude of methods available for these purposes, with many publications and books dedicated to individual methods and their applications. Artificial neural networks, support vector machines, logistic regression, and Bayesian networks are a subset of the potentially applicable methods.

Taken together, monitoring and analyzing the comprehensive mental health indicators of individuals in the military requires joint efforts of various institutions. These efforts include interdisciplinary collaboration of military personnel, military training instructors, psychologists, psychiatrists, cognitive scientists, neuroscientists, computer scientists, engineers, statisticians etc. Equally important, the efforts include decisions that need to be made at appropriate policy level in order to ensure the necessary longevity of this undertaking. Furthermore, all monitored data must be handled with the highest level of confidentiality to avoid negative impact on individual military careers, or even the potential leak of such data to the adversary side.

3. Integrated Strategy of Suicide Risk Detection and Prevention

An integrated strategy of suicide risk detection and prevention in warfighters relies on comprehensive mental health profiles and an interdisciplinary joint approach. Major activities of the strategy are presented in Figure 5.

The central element in the figure is the Comprehensive Mental Health Profile Database, containing the profiles of individual warfighters. Processes or procedures making use of the profile roughly include data acquisition, analyses and aggregation, and decision-related processes.

First, the profile elements need to be measured for an individual warfighter at service entry time, comprising the initial snapshot of the profile. This is represented by Initialization process in Figure 5. The exact protocol of longitudinal acquisition of the profile snapshots depends on a variety of factors, like availability of time, human and financial resources. However, it is possible to envision that the snapshot acquisitions (henceforth also referred to as "profile updates") may be motivated by relevant events in the individual's military career or personal life, as well as performed periodically if no specific events take place for a longer time. These distinctions are represented by the processes Regular Data Acquisition and Event-Driven Data Acquisition.

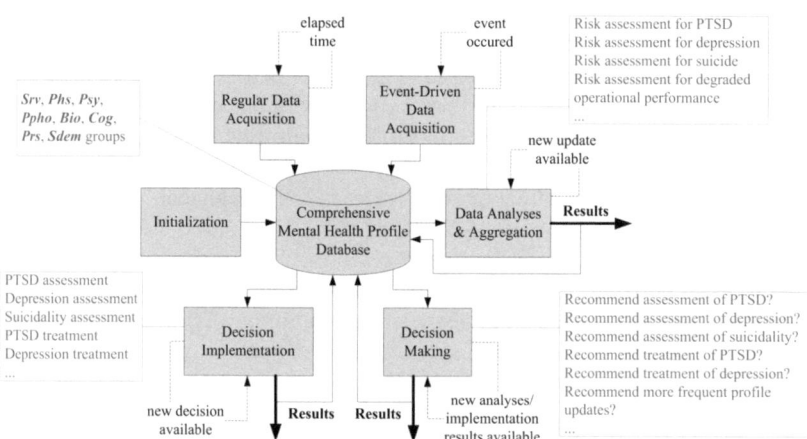

Figure 5. Comprehensive Mental Health Profile Database and the activities of the integrated strategy of suicide risk detection and prevention

Approaching deployment might be one event that justifies the profile updates in order to assess the readiness of troops for an operation at the individual and unit levels. Likewise, monitoring of the profile during deployment and after return from deployment (e.g. 3 or 4 months post-deployment [24]) is indicated due to early identification of changes in indicators of psychological morbidity. Traumatic personal events, such as a loss of a beloved person, can have serious impact on mental wellbeing of any person; therefore, profile updates are indicated at such critical events in personal life.

Figure 6 illustrates the abstract protocol of longitudinally performed profile updates. Initial screening corresponds to the Initialization process in Figure 5. For simplicity, Figure 6 shows all unit members having initial screening performed at the same time. Regular unit monitoring refers to the regular acquisition of profile snapshots, which happens every ΔT units of time (for example, ΔT may equal 1 year). All members of the unit have their profile updated at these times. Some individuals may have different ΔT than the rest of the unit, which is not illustrated in the figure. For example, an individual considered at high risk of some psychological morbidity, with the expert assessment showing that diagnosis is not yet present, may need more frequent monitoring of the profile. When a relevant event for the entire unit takes place, such as deployment to an operation, or a return from deployment, it may also be appropriate to update the profiles of all unit members. For personal events, relevant to particular individuals, updates are performed only on the profiles of the affected individuals.

Data Analyses & Aggregation process may start when at least one snapshot of the individual's profile has been acquired. This process is particularly focused on the risk assessments for degraded performance in an approaching operation, various psychological problems, or suicide. Furthermore, through aggregation of data on the unit level, it may be possible to observe the readiness state of the units, their strengths and weaknesses, their combat experience, vulnerability to adverse psychological consequences etc. Individuals can be clustered by various criteria and differences between groups investigated via longitudinal study designs. In particular, abundant data from diverse set of indicators, collected by systematic longitudinal monitoring, helps investigate feasibility of predicting various psychological disorders, operational performance degradation, or suicide.

Individual risk assessment of psychological morbidity, degraded operational performance or suicide, as the major aspect of Data Analyses & Aggregation process, is illustrated in Figure 7. Based on the comprehensive mental health profile of a particular individual, risk assessment can be envisioned to produce several types of results. One result report may indicate the severity of risk (state), and the direction of change with respect to the previous risk assessment (state trend). This type of reporting is particularly suitable for further automated decision making, such as deciding who needs to visit a human expert for a thorough diagnostic and/or treatment procedure. Classifying numerical values of risk into red-yellow-green states will need expert opinion and preferably scientific data supporting the chosen classification. Experts and scientific evidence are also needed if using a result report that contains the values of the prominent indicators for an outcome of interest. Here, knowledge is required regarding which indicators are prominent enough to be reported.

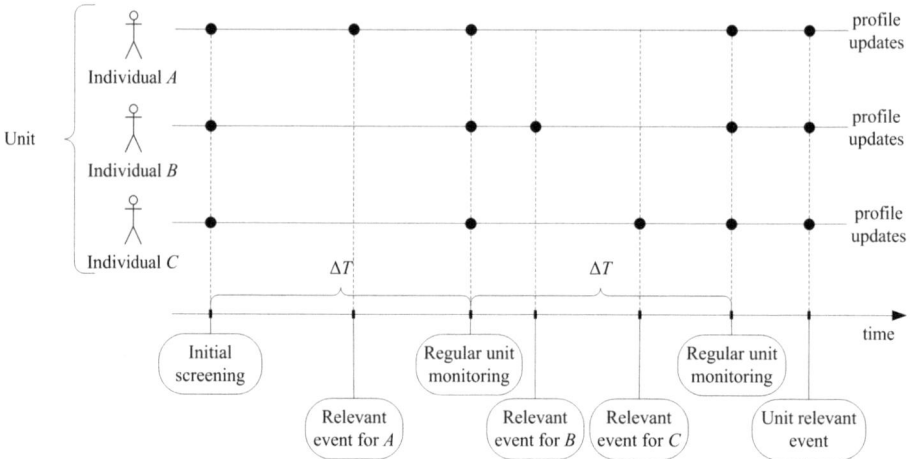

Figure 6. Abstract protocol of updates to the individuals' comprehensive mental health profiles

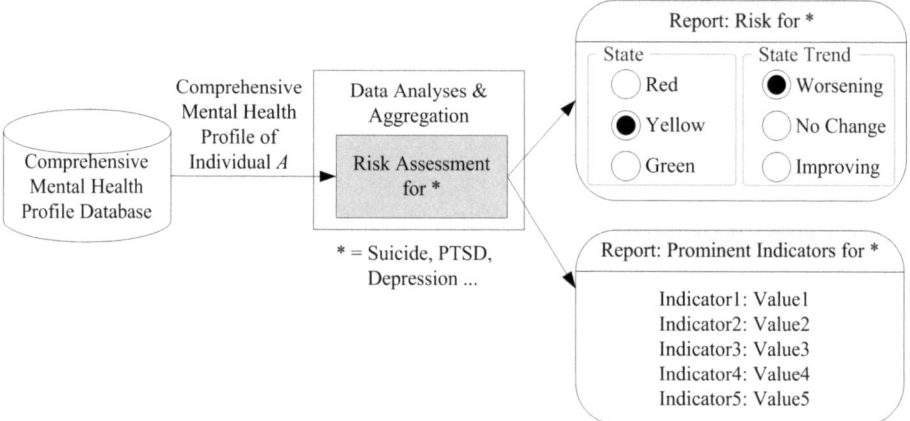

Figure 7. Possible outputs of risk assessment

The Decision Making process involves interpretation of the risk assessments in order to make decisions about committing scarce human expert resources to the individual whose risk is assessed as high. For example, individuals with high risk of already having PTSD, as indicated by the results of PTSD screening, can be directed to go through a "gold-standard" PTSD assessment. If PTSD diagnosis is confirmed, initiating the treatment may be the next reasonable decision. Decision Making may also involve decisions other than scheduling expert assessments or treatments of certain disorders. Individuals with a significantly increased risk of contracting some disorder in the future, but not of imminent disorder, may instead be scheduled more frequent updates of the profile. The complexity of decision-making depends on the result report from the risk assessment; the report with red-yellow-green states and state trends is simpler for decision-making than the report with the prominent indicators.

The Decision Implementation process represents following through with the decisions. This process requires considerable involvement from human experts, since it involves conducting the diagnosis or treatment of psychological disorders and suicide. As decisions are being implemented, new data are usually created, which are important to be stored in the profile of the affected individual. Examples are the results of the diagnosis of PTSD or other disorders, and, if a diagnosis is confirmed, the progress of the treatment.

4. Conclusion

This paper has presented the concept of comprehensive monitoring and analysis of relevant information regarding the mental wellbeing of military personnel in military organizations. This proposal may improve military readiness at individual and unit levels, as well as assessment of potential risks of various psychological problems and even in-theater suicide. Such an initiative may increase the effectiveness of military operations and decrease post-operational psychological casualties, simultaneously minimizing the associated negative social consequences.

The comprehensive mental health profile discussed in this paper is similar to an electronic health record [25], which has a broader scope. The proposed approach can also be considered as continuation of the work of authors who have performed longitudinal studies on military populations for mental health reasons. Longitudinal comprehensive monitoring, analysis and decision-making, integrated into the policy of military organization, will be very important and valuable, but also resource intensive.

At present, prediction abilities for psychological breakdown during the battle, on an individual or even unit level, and future psychological morbidity are rather weak [26]. Therefore, we strongly believe that the proposed approach is the appropriate answer on many different mental health challenges and uncertainties related to the current peacekeeping and peacemaking operations.

Acknowledgments and Disclaimer

This research has been partially supported by the Ministry of Science, Education and Sports of the Republic of Croatia. The authors are also grateful to Pavao Golubović for his assistance regarding figures. The opinions, views, and ideas expressed in this paper are those of the authors and do not necessarily reflect the position or policy of the sponsor or the institutions with which the authors are affiliated.

References

[1] Thompson MM; McCreary DR. Enhancing Mental Readiness in Military Personnel. Human Dimensions in Military Operations – Military Leaders' Strategies for Addressing Stress and Psychological Support. Meeting Proceedings RTO-MP-HFM-134, Paper 4. Neuilly-sur-Seine, France: RTO; 2006. p. 4-1 – 4-12. Available from: http://www.rto.nato.int/abstracts.asp.

[2] Wiederhold BK, Bullinger AH, Wiederhold MD. Advanced technologies in military medicine. In: Roy M, editor. Proceedings of NATO Advanced Research Workshop on Novel Approaches to the Diagnosis

and Treatment of Posttraumatic Stress Disorder; 2005 Jun 13-15; Cavtat-Dubrovnik, Croatia. Amsterdam: IOS Press; 2006. p. 148-60.

[3] Stetz MC, Long CP, Schober Jr WV, Cardillo CG, Wildzunas RM. Stress assessment and management while medics take care of the VR wounded. Annual Review of CyberTherapy and Telemedicine. Forthcoming 2007.

[4] Wood DP, Murphy J, Center K, McLay R, Reeves D, Pyne J et al. Combat-related post-traumatic stress disorder: a case report using virtual reality exposure therapy with physiological monitoring. Cyberpsychology & Behavior 2007 Apr;10(2):309-15.

[5] Rothbaum BO, Hodges LF, Ready D, Graap K, Alarcon RD. Virtual reality exposure therapy for Vietnam veterans with posttraumatic stress disorder. J Clin Psychiatry 2001 Aug;62(8):617-22.

[6] Difede J, Hoffman HG. Virtual reality exposure therapy for World Trade Center posttraumatic stress disorder: a case report. Cyberpsychol Behav 2002;5:529-35.

[7] Rizzo A, Pair J, Graap K, Manson B, McNerney PJ, Wiederhold B et al. A virtual reality exposure therapy application for Iraq War military personnel with post traumatic stress disorder: from training to toy to treatment. In: Roy M, editor. Proceedings of NATO Advanced Research Workshop on Novel Approaches to the Diagnosis and Treatment of Posttraumatic Stress Disorder; 2005 Jun 13-15; Cavtat-Dubrovnik, Croatia. Amsterdam: IOS Press; 2006. p. 235-47.

[8] Josman N, Garcia-Palacios A, Reisberg A, Somer E, Weiss PLT, Hoffman H. Virtual reality in the treatment of survivors of terrorism in Israel. In: Roy M, editor. Proceedings of NATO Advanced Research Workshop on Novel Approaches to the Diagnosis and Treatment of Posttraumatic Stress Disorder; 2005 Jun 13-15; Cavtat-Dubrovnik, Croatia. Amsterdam: IOS Press; 2006. p. 196-204.

[9] Botella C, Quero S, de la Vega NL, Banos R, Guillen V, Garcia-Palacios A et al. Clinical issues in the application of virtual reality to treatment of PTSD. In: Roy M, editor. Proceedings of NATO Advanced Research Workshop on Novel Approaches to the Diagnosis and Treatment of Posttraumatic Stress Disorder; 2005 Jun 13-15; Cavtat-Dubrovnik, Croatia. Amsterdam: IOS Press; 2006. p. 183-95.

[10] Sher L. Preventing suicide. QJM 2004;97:677-80.

[11] Knox KL, Litts DA, Talcott GW, Feig JC, Caine ED. Risk of suicide and related adverse outcomes after exposure to a suicide prevention programme in the U.S. Air Force: cohort study. British Medical Journal 2003;327:1376-81.

[12] Wiederhold BK, Wiederhold MD. Virtual reality as a tool in early interventions. Human Dimensions in Military Operations – Military Leaders' Strategies for Addressing Stress and Psychological Support. Meeting Proceedings RTO-MP-HFM-134, Paper 45. Neuilly-sur-Seine, France: RTO; 2006. p. 45-1 – 45-8. Available from: http://www.rto.nato.int/abstracts.asp.

[13] Orr SP, Metzger LJ, Miller MW, Kaloupek DG.. Psychophysiological assessment of PTSD. In: Wilson JP, Keane TM, editors. Assessing Psychological Trauma and PTSD. 2nd ed. New York: Guilford Publications; 2004. p. 289-343.

[14] Wolfersdorf M, Straub R, Barg T, Keller F, Kaschka WP. Depressed inpatients, electrodermal reactivity, and suicide – a study about psychophysiology of suicidal behavior. Archives of Suicide Research 1999;5:1-10.

[15] Lieberman HR, Caruso CM, Niro PJ, Bathalon GP. Acute effects of battlefield-like stress on cognitive and endocrine function of officers from an elite Army unit. In Human Dimensions in Military Operations – Military Leaders' Strategies for Addressing Stress and Psychological Support. Meeting Proceedings RTO-MP-HFM-134, Paper 33. Neuilly-sur-Seine, France: RTO; 2006. p. 33-1 – 33-14. Available from: http://www.rto.nato.int/abstracts.asp.

[16] Pivac N, Kozarić-Kovačić D, Mück-Šeler D. Biological markers in Croatian war veterans with combat related posttraumatic stress disorder. In: Roy M, editor. Proceedings of NATO Advanced Research Workshop on Novel Approaches to the Diagnosis and Treatment of Posttraumatic Stress Disorder; 2005 Jun 13-15; Cavtat-Dubrovnik, Croatia. Amsterdam: IOS Press; 2006. p. 3-12.

[17] Nutt D, Ballenger J, editors. Anxiety disorders: generalized anxiety disorder, obsessive-compulsive disorder, and post-traumatic stress disorder. Oxford: Blackwell Publishing; 2005. p. 176-85.

[18] Dumais A, Lesage AD, Alda M, Rouleau G, Dumont M, Chawky N. Risk factors for suicide completion in major depression: a case-control study of impulsive and aggressive behaviors in men. Am J Psychiatry 2005;162:2116-24.

[19] Fairbank JA, Ebert L, Costello EJ. Epidemiology of traumatic events and post-traumatic stress disorder. In: Nutt, D, Davidson JRT, Zohar J, editors. Post-traumatic Stress Disorder: Diagnosis, Management and Treatment. London: Martin Dunitz; 2000. p.17-27.

[20] Roy A. Five risk factors for depression. The British Journal of Psychiatry 1987;150:536-41.

[21] Walker J, Pan E, Johnston D, Adler-Milstein J, Bates D, Middleton B. The value of health care information exchange and interoperability. Health Affairs, Web Exclusive [Internet]. 2005 Jan 19 [cited 2007 Nov 12]. Available from: http://content.healthaffairs.org/cgi/content/full/hlthaff.w5.10/DC1.

[22] Marinić I, Supek F, Kovačić Z, Rukavina L, Jendričko T, Kozarić-Kovačić D. Posttraumatic stress disorder: diagnostic data analysis by data mining methodology. Croatian Medical Journal 2007;48:185-97.

[23] Witten IH, Frank E. Data mining: practical machine learning tools and techniques. 2nd ed. San Francisco, CA: Morgan Kaufmann Publishers; 2005.

[24] Bliese PD, Wright KM, Adler AB, Thomas JL. Psychological screening validation with soldiers returning from combat. In: Roy M, editor. Proceedings of NATO Advanced Research Workshop on Novel Approaches to the Diagnosis and Treatment of Posttraumatic Stress Disorder; 2005 Jun 13-15; Cavtat-Dubrovnik, Croatia. Amsterdam: IOS Press; 2006. p. 78-86.

[25] Electronic health record definition, scope, and context [Internet]. ISO/TC 215 Technical Report, Second Draft; 2003 Aug [cited 2007 Nov 12]. Available from: http://www.cihi.ca/cihiweb/en/downloads/infostand_ihisd_isowg1_mtg_denoct_contextdraft.pdf.

[26] Wessely S. Risk, psychiatry and the modern military. Keynote 2. Human Dimensions in Military Operations – Military Leaders' Strategies for Addressing Stress and Psychological Support. Meeting Proceedings RTO-MP-HFM-134; Neuilly-sur-Seine, France: RTO; 2006. p. KN2-1–KN2-16. Available from: http://www.rto.nato.int/abstracts.asp.

Lowering Suicide Risk in Returning Troops
B.K. Wiederhold (Ed.)
IOS Press, 2008
doi:10.3233/978-1-58603-889-2-90

Lowering Suicide Risk: Situation and Prevention Measures in the Lithuanian Armed Forces

Capt. Danute LAPENAITE[1], Capt. Ramute VAICAITIENE, PhD[2]
Military Medical Service of the Lithuanian Armed Forces, Vytauto av. 49, LT-44331
Kaunas, Lithuania
[1] *E-mail: danute.lapenaite@mil.lt*
[2] *E-mail: ramute.vaicaitien@mil.lt*

Abstract. In spite of the fact that the suicide rate in Lithuania decreased during the past years, it is still one of the highest in Europe. 1 to 1.5 thousand people commit suicide in Lithuania every year. In 2006, the suicide rate was 30.9 per 100,000 people. Men commit 84% of all suicides. The number of male suicides is six times higher than that of female suicides. Men of average age living in rural areas have the highest risk of suicide. The ratio of attempted suicides to committed suicides is 10:1. Official data on suicide in the Lithuanian Armed Forces has existed since 1993. There have been few suicide cases in the Lithuanian Armed Forces since then. The amount of suicides are spread nearly equally among conscripts, officers, and non-commissioned officers. The suicide rate ranged from 0.15 to 0.34 per 1,000 servicemen for several years. Since 2004, the rate remains more or less level and does not exceed 0.2 per 1,000 servicemen. There is a need for suicide prevention measures, both in the country and in the Armed Forces, in spite of the fact that suicide rates in the military are not as high as in the civilian population. Suicide prevention measures should be applied not only to conscripts but to military professionals as well as officers and non-commissioned officers who are deployed. Scientific research findings [1] have shown an above average prevalence of suicidal behavior among servicemen, a low level of knowledge about suicide, inappropriate attitudes toward suicide, and a positive view on suicide prevention in the military, which became the background for the Program of Psychological support in the Lithuanian Armed Forces. The Program, with a wide spectrum of prevention measures, include: training, education, psychological support for servicemen and their families, additional care of personnel with psychological problems, and/or the risk of suicide, and monitoring of servicemen's psychological wellbeing, is in progress. The efficiency of this program is now being assessed. Since 2006, incident handling for service personnel by psychological support professionals has been organized not only in Lithuania but in the mission area as well. The concept of psychological support for service personnel and their families across the deployment cycle was validated and is now being successfully implemented.

1. Suicide Rates in Lithuania

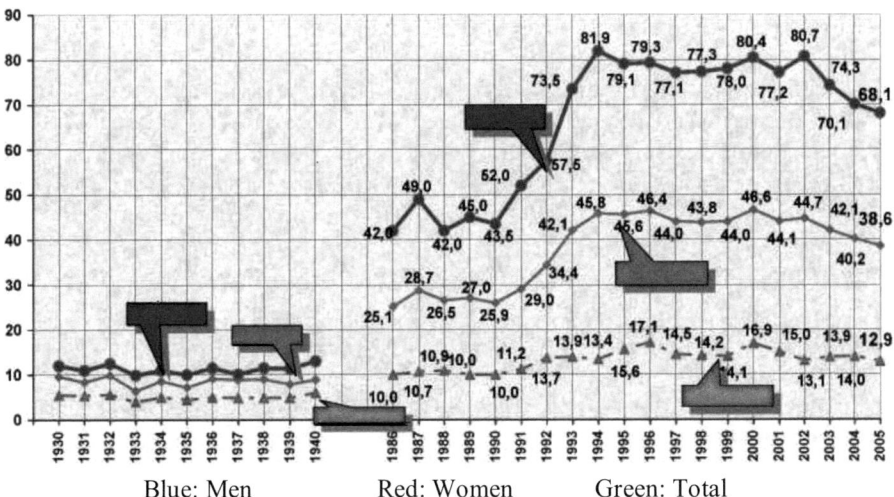

Blue: Men   Red: Women   Green: Total

Figure 1. Total suicide rates per 100,000 in Lithuania between 1930-1940 and between 1986-2005.

Source: The Statistics Department at the State Government of the Republic of Lithuania

In spite of the fact that the suicide rate in Lithuania has decreased during the past years, it is still one of the highest in Europe. 1 to 1.5 thousand people commit suicide in Lithuania every year. In 2006, the suicide rate was 30.9 per 100,000 people. Men commit 84 % of all suicides. The number of male suicides is six times higher than that of female suicides (Figure 1). Men of average age living in rural areas have the highest risk of suicide. The ratio of attempted suicides to committed suicides is 10:1.

2. Suicides in the Lithuanian Armed Forces

Official data on suicide in the Lithuanian Armed Forces has existed since 1993. There have been few suicide cases in the Lithuanian Armed Forces since then. The amount of suicides are spread nearly equally among conscripts, officers, and non-commissioned officers. The suicide rate ranged from 0.15 to 0.34 per 1,000 servicemen. Since 2004, the rates have remained more or less level and do not exceed 0.2 per 1,000 servicemen.

3. Preconditions of Suicidal Behavior in the Lithuanian Armed Forces [1]

3.1. Goal

The goal of the research was to assess service personnel's:
1. Prevalence in relation to cases of suicide.
2. Level of knowledge on how to recognize the risk of suicide.
3. Attitude toward suicide.
4. Status of psychological health.

3.2. Respondents

550 conscripts, officers, and non-commissioned officers were questioned.

3.3. Findings

The findings of the research show the preconditions of suicidal behavior in the Lithuanian Armed Forces.

1. The relation to suicide can strengthen the positive attitude towards it and even increase the risk of suicide.

The problem of suicide was important for most of the respondents. Thirty percent of respondents reported that they had met people with a high risk of suicide in their close environment. Six percent of respondents reported that they acknowledged people who had been thinking about suicide at the moment of investigation. Thirty-five percent of respondents had acquaintances who had committed suicide.

At least 25 respondents (6.1%, only conscripts) attempted to commit suicide once in their life. Ten of them had tried to commit suicide during the year before the investigation. The number of conscripts' attempts to commit suicide in the Lithuanian Armed Forces was almost the same as in the male rural population (5.3%).

Eight percent of conscripts, 2% of non-commissioned officers, and no officers had serious thoughts about suicide during the last year (when they were questioned).

In addition, 42.9% of conscripts, 18% of non-commissioned officers, and 32.3% of officers had a risk of suicide (i.e. respondents reported that they have had thoughts about committing suicide at least once in their life, but in reality would not complete the act).

2. It was found that service personnel had a low level of basic knowledge about the assessment of risk of suicide and sources of support.

Respondents received 10 statements about suicide. They had to choose between "true" or "false" statements. No respondent marked all 10 statements correctly. The number of correct answers to incorrect statements ranged from 33.8% to 74.9%. Officers and non-commissioned officers had even less knowledge about suicides than conscripts (65%, 61%, and 55% of false answers respectively). The statement that suicide could be an accepted solution and the statement that people who talked about suicide would never commit suicide were marked true by officers more often than other servicemen (Figure 2).

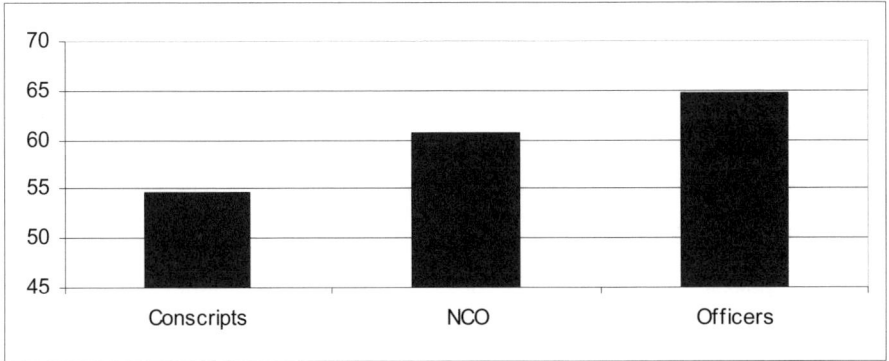

Figure 2. False answers to the statement "People who talk about suicide will never commit suicide." (percentage)

3. The attitude of most respondents was negative towards suicide prevention. The respondents (especially conscripts) did not believe that it was possible to foresee the danger of suicide or to help an individual. Furthermore, respondents thought that suicide was acceptable in some cases. The most important finding was that the majority of servicemen were ready to help a person in a suicidal crisis.

4. Service personnel's state of psychological health was much better than men in the civilian population. This finding is reasonable because of the strict selection of people recruited to the Armed Forces. Comparing the results of service personnel with different positions, it was found that conscripts' status of psychological health was worse than that of officers and non-commissioned officers (Figure 3).

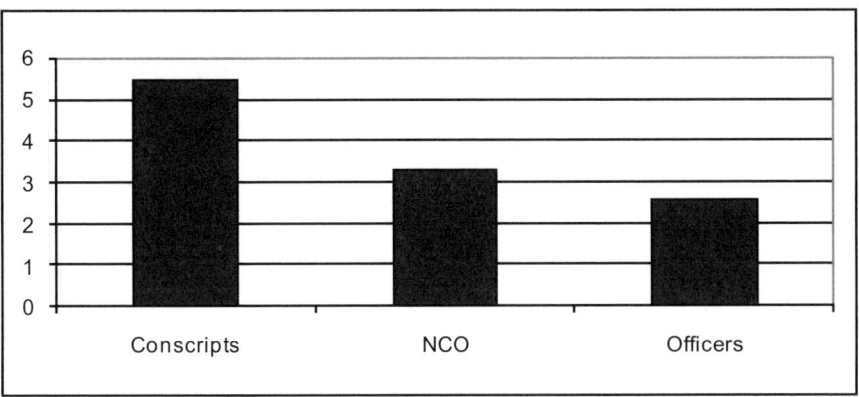

Figure 3. Service personnel's level of despair (pessimism). (Beck Scale of Despair)

4. Prevention Measures in the Lithuanian Armed Forces

4.1. Program of Psychological support in the Lithuanian Armed Forces (2005-2008)

4.1.1. Aim

The aim of the Program is to prevent the development of psychological problems and mental disorders in service personnel and to lower the risk of suicide in the Lithuanian Armed Forces.

4.1.2. Tasks

The tasks of the Program are:
1. To improve psychological selection during recruitment to the Armed Forces.
2. To educate service personnel (conscripts, officers, non-commissioned officers, and military medical doctors) about stress and suicide prevention, suicidal behavior identification, and psychological support during crisis, etc.
3. To create longitudinal care and monitoring of service personnel's psychological wellbeing.
4. To create a management system of service personnel's psychological support.

4.1.3. Target results of the Program in the Lithuanian Armed Forces

1. The improvement of psychological selection during recruitment to the Armed Forces.
2. The implementation of a permanent psychological educational system for service personnel.
3. The development of access to psychological support professionals to servicemen with suicide risk or any psychological problems.
4. The improvement of psychological support for service personnel before, during, and after deployments.
5. The implementation of personnel's families' psychological support before, during, and after deployments.
6. Decreasing the number of servicemen leaving the Armed Forces because of psychological problems or discharged from service due to mental disorders.
7. The implementation of longitudinal care and monitoring of service personnel's psychological wellbeing.
8. Improved psychological wellbeing, not only of servicemen, but in the civilian population as well.

4.1.4. What is done already?

• Field of service personnel's psychological training and education:
Military medics are trained to educate service personnel about suicide behavior identification, stress, depression, suicide prevention and intervention, and psychological support during a crisis. They are also trained how to change personnel's attitude toward suicide and suicide prevention. The courses for military medics are organized every 4 years. The courses for service personnel, which are given by military medics, take place every year. The duration of the courses is:

• 7.5 hours for military leaders;

- 6.5 hours for officers and non-commissioned officers;
- 5.5 hours for conscripts.

Before deployment, service personnel receive 16 hours of psychological training and education) where he or she receives additional knowledge about crisis, suicide and depression, and drug and alcohol abuse prevention, etc. Brochures and printed material prepared by specialists of the Military Medical Service are given to every person pre-deployment.

- Implementation of prevention measures for personnel with psychological problems and/or the risk of suicide:

The monitoring of service personnel's psychological wellbeing is in progress now. Psychological support professionals (or medics if there is no psychological support professional in the unit) take care of the service personnel military medics, who are trained to recognize the signs of possible suicide, can act as individual suicide risk assessors, can advise military leaders, and can conduct basic interventions. Also, medical personnel have learned when to bring in more specialized support from psychological support professionals.

- Changes in the amount of service personnel leaving the Armed Forces because of psychological problems or service personnel discharged due to mental disorders:

The amount of personnel leaving the Armed Forces because of psychological problems or those who are discharged due to mental disorders has been slowly decreasing every year since 2005.

- Experience in management of incident handling:

1. During Deployment in the Operation Theater

Two psychologists are appointed to every unit that is preparing for deployment. They begin collaboration with service personnel before deployment and psychologically prepare them, educate, and take part in their military training. After a traumatic incident, these psychologists, as a psychological emergency team, are sent to the mission area within a short amount of time (5 to 10 days, depending on the deployment area). Medical personnel and the chaplain, in some cases, are available during deployment. They are the first to make a basic intervention in the Operation Theatre until the arrival of psychological support professionals. Psychologists provide psychological support in the individual and unit levels in the mission area during a period of one to two weeks.

2. In the Home Country

After a traumatic incident in Lithuania (as well as after suicides), a psychological emergency team of at least 2 people is sent to the unit (if there is no psychologist present) within one to three days after the incident. Psychological support professionals provide psychological support on an individual and unit level. Critical incident stress debriefing is organized for survivors, witnesses, colleagues, and friends of the deceased.

4.1.5. Human resources for the implementation of the Program

Currently, six psychologists and six psychiatrists are taking part in the recruitment process of service personnel at four Enrollment Centers. Special post-deployment support is given by one psychologist in a Rehabilitation Center. There are four psychologists in the military units and two psychologists in the Department of Health Care Programs. Chaplains and trained military medics are also involved in providing psychological support for service personnel.

4.2. Concept of Psychological Support for Service Personnel and their Families across the Deployment Cycle

The Lithuanian Armed Forces support and participate in modern military operations, which take place in Iraq, Afghanistan, and Kosovo. Although military personnel have received some psychological support during the deployment process since 2002, the management system of psychological support before, during, and after deployments was not established until this year. That is why it was essential to have a national concept of stress and psychological support. This concept was validated in January of 2007.

The main psychological support trends throughout the deployment process are:
Before deployment:

- Assessment of individuals' mission fitness;
- Assessment of unit mission fitness;
- Defining rules and making agreements that will ensure cooperation between military leaders and psychological support professionals;
- Psychological education and training;

1. During deployment:
   - Monitoring of psychological wellbeing at the personnel level;
   - Immediate post-incident support (critical incident stress management);
   - Psychological support upon demand;
   - Providing a mechanism for reporting problems and concerns that offers a certain degree of confidentiality and does not stigmatize the individual;
2. After deployment:
   - Assessment of individual wellbeing post-deployment;
   - Middle and long term monitoring of psychological wellbeing for all service personnel who have been deployed;
   - A structured homecoming and reintegration program for service personnel with further support and information tailored to the nature of the operational demands;
3. Across the deployment cycle:
   - Home front support well in advance of deployment, throughout deployment and, after deployment;
   - Maintaining a professional network of psychological support professionals in the Lithuanian Armed Forces.

It is predicted that all aforementioned measures directed toward strengthening psychological health of servicemen and the development of a psychological support management system across the deployment cycle will be successfully continued and will decrease suicide risk in the Lithuanian Armed Forces.

5. Conclusions

1. The suicide rate in Lithuania is still one of the highest in Europe, which is why there is a need for suicide prevention measures both in the country and in the Armed Forces, in spite of the fact that since 2004 the suicide rates do not exceed 0.2 per 1,000 servicemen.
2. Since 1993, there has been almost the same amount of suicides among conscripts, officers, and non-commissioned officers in the Armed Forces. Therefore, suicide prevention measures should be applied not only to conscripts (as it was done previously) but also to military professionals as well as officers and non-commissioned officers who are deployed.
3. The findings of scientific research [1] have shown a higher than average prevalence of suicidal behavior in servicemen, a low level of knowledge about suicide, inappropriate attitudes toward suicides, and a positive view of suicide prevention in the military, which became the background for the Program of Psychological support in the Lithuanian Armed Forces.
4. The Program of Psychological support in the Lithuanian Armed Forces, with a wide spectrum of prevention measures, include: training, education, psychological support for servicemen and their families, additional care of personnel with psychological problems and/or the risk of suicide, and monitoring of servicemen's psychological wellbeing, is in progress and the efficiency of this program is now being assessed.
5. Since 2006, the incident handling for service personnel by psychological support professionals has been organized not only in Lithuania but in the mission area as well.
6. The concept of psychological support for service personnel and their families during the deployment process was validated and is currently being successfully implemented.

References

[1] Gailiene, D., Skruibis, P. (2004). The Prevalence of Servicemen Suicidal Behavior in the Lithuanian Armed Forces. II. Vilnius University, Vilnius.
[2] Gailiene, D. (1998). They didn't have to die. Lawrence Erlbaum: Mahwah, NJ.
[3] NATO RTO HFM Task Group HFM 081/RTG "SPSIMMO" (in press). A Leader's Guide to Psychological Support Across the Deployment Cycle.
[4] Total suicide rates per 100 000 in Lithuania in 1930-1940 and 1986-2005 (2007). http://www.savizudybes.lt/vidinis.asp?DL=L&TopicID=12
[5] Wasserman, D., Rutz, E. M., Rutz, W., Schmidtke, A. Suicide prevention in Europe. The WHO European monitoring survey on national suicide prevention programmes and strategies. NASP Swedish National and Stockholm Country Council's Centre for Suicide Research and Prevention of Mental III-Health.

Lowering Suicide Risk in Returning Troops
B.K. Wiederhold (Ed.)
IOS Press, 2008
© *2008 IOS Press. All rights reserved.*
doi:10.3233/978-1-58603-889-2-98

Prevention Of Suicides In The United States Army

MAJ Todd M Yosick
Chief, Battlemind Training Office
Chief, Combat Stress Actions Office
United States Army Medical Department Center and School

Abstract: The annual report of the United States (U.S.) Army Suicide Event Report (ASER) allows for detailed Army-wide statistical reports on suicide events, including attempts and completions. The report submitted as of March 1st 2007 provided statistics for Calendar Year (CY) 2006 indicating a suicide rate of 16.91 (per 100,000) for the overall Army-Active Component only – the highest they have been since 1991. Historically, the U.S. Army annual average is 12 suicides per 100,000 Soldiers.

Data from ASER note the most frequently reported stressors included failed or failing relationships (especially marriage) followed by legal problems, work-related problems, and excessive debt. In addition, almost two-thirds of suicide completions had a history of at least one deployment to Iraq or Afghanistan; however, multiple deployments were relatively rare among those with suicide behaviors. The data also noted almost a third of completed suicides occurred in a deployed environment.

For this reason, the Department of the Army (DA), the Office of the Surgeon General (OTSG), Behavioral Health Proponency Office, Walter Reed Army Institute for Research (WRAIR), U.S. Army Center for Health Promotion and Preventive Medicine (CHPPM), U.S. Army Medical Department Center & School (AMEDDC&S), Battlemind Training Office (BTO), U.S. Army Medical Command (MEDCOM), the Suicide Prevention Office (SPO), the Chaplain Corps, and the U.S. Army Training and Doctrine Command (TRADOC) have collaborated to conduct ongoing research and training and policy development and implementation regarding suicide prevention in the U.S. Army.

The development of the Battlemind Training System serves as a collaborative effort at building Soldier resiliency through all phases of the deployment cycle, life cycle, and support cycle of military service. Battlemind may be defined as a Soldier's inner strength to face adversity and fear in combat with confidence and resolution; the will to persevere and win. Battlemind skill developed through military training serves as the cornerstone for resiliency of the American Soldier on and off the battlefield, and addresses a strength-based approach for the greater military communities in which they serve.

Suicide prevention in the U.S. Army remains a Commander's program and utilizes the guidance laid out in Army Regulation (AR) 600-63: *Army Health Promotion, Suicide Prevention and Psychological Autopsy*, DA Pamphlet (PAM) 600-24: *Suicide Prevention & Psychological Autopsy* and DA PAM 600-70: *Guide to the Prevention of Suicide and Self-Destructive Behavior*. The U.S. Army remains committed to assisting Soldiers at every level.

Despite the U.S. Army's commitment to assisting Soldiers, stigma and institutional barriers remain the major factors in Soldiers' reluctance to seek care. When stigma exists, Soldiers fail to seek help out of concern that they will lose standing in their unit or because seeking help will negatively impact their career. To address the issue of stigma in the Army, and build Soldier resiliency, WRAIR developed the Battlemind Training System. The Battlemind Training Office, which has now transitioned to the AMEDD Center & School, produces outcome-based training which reduces stigma by normalizing the effects of Combat and Operational Stress Reactions (COSR). The training gains its relevance by using information obtained through current and developing research conducted by WRAIR.

Battlemind is the process of developing a Soldier's inner strength to face fear and adversity with courage, and has two key components. The first is *Self Confidence*, which is a Soldier's ability to calculate and handle risk while working through challenges. The other key component is *Mental Toughness*, or a Soldier's ability to learn from and overcome past setbacks during times of difficulty or challenge.

In combat, Soldiers push themselves to their physical and psychological limits for their missions and their fellow Soldiers. As with physical pain, Soldiers will often try to "tough things out," or handle their personal struggles on their own. These actions serve as the cohesive glue that pushes units toward victory in battle, but can have a negative impact on Soldier safety and mission capability. Soldiers typically do not want to let their buddies and leaders down, and as a result, may hide signs or symptoms of greater problems.

Battlemind training emphasizes that leaders and Soldiers must look out for each other. It is based on the idea that Soldiers know each other the best and are in the best position to recognize changes in behavior in a fellow Soldier and to get them the help they need. Battlemind training also emphasizes self-awareness and duty to report problems if Soldiers are experiencing problems in themselves as well. The importance of establishing a climate where seeking help is a sign of strength rather than weakness is essential to unit level care.

Battlemind training builds on existing Soldier strengths and skills using real-life examples which Soldiers can easily relate to. Action focused training uses skill development in addition to education while placing an emphasis on normalizing misunderstood physical, psychological and emotional reactions to abnormal events. A major theme of Battlemind is that a team works best when it works together.

Battlemind training is also outcomes based, integrating real-time lessons learned in the Global War on Terror. The ultimate goal of the Battlemind mission is to provide the most innovative strengths-based and resiliency enhancing behavioral health training programs to Soldiers, Sailors, Airmen, Marines, their Families and other special populations who are directly affected by or involved in supporting Service Members in military operations at all levels.

The Battlemind Training System is organized into three separate categories: deployment cycle, life cycle, and support cycle.

Deployment cycle training products provide tools and concepts that are important for all Soldiers during all phases of deployment, from pre-deployment to during deployment and post-deployment.

Life cycle training provides tools and concepts for Soldiers and Leaders throughout all traditional phases of a Soldier's career training. Training products are targeted for all initial entry level training courses, all leadership development courses, pre-command courses, and senior leadership courses.

Support cycle training training provides tools and concepts which incorporate considerations for the full spectrum of support for all military operations. Training is geared toward Families, U.S. Army Reserve and Army National Guard Soldiers, Joint Services, Veterans Affairs, Department of Defense personnel, Wounded Warriors, and for both military and civilian healthcare professionals involved in supporting U.S. Armed Forces.

There are currently three Battlemind training products related to suicide prevention which have been fielded, and there are an additional four products currently in development. Each training product is aimed at the specific requirements of different Soldier populations. The information listed below describes the differences between the products.

Deployment Cycle Suicide and Related Training Products

Battlemind Tactical Suicide Prevention training is a priority and is currently under phased development. Based on research conducted in Iraq and Afghanistan, a suicide prevention training specific to a combat environment has become a necessary initiative. Soldiers are exposed to different risk factors such as repeated deployments, compounded relational stressors based on separation and personal loss, as well as long-term access to lethal means of acting on impulsive suicidal thoughts. All of the stresses of combat become additional pressures which compound pre-existing factors on the home front. Leader and buddy actions are the initial focus for prevention and intervention.

Life Cycle Suicide Prevention and Related Training Products

Battlemind for Junior Leaders: Warrior Leader Course (WLC) and Basic Officer Leader Course (BOLC): The "Be, Know, Do" model of leadership trains our Army leaders to be tactically and technically proficient. Leaders have a vital role for caring for their Soldiers, and effective leader actions may very well prevent an avoidable suicide. This training product builds on the tactical and technical proficiencies by emphasizing the interpersonal aspects of leadership. These skills are often subtle and difficult to teach. In order to build these skills among junior leaders, items such as effective leadership behaviors versus characteristics of poor leadership, education on different leadership approaches, and on how leaders impact their Soldiers' total well-being are addressed.

Suicide Prevention for Junior Leaders is a product which has been tailored to junior leaders during WLC and BOLC. The suicide prevention training focuses on the importance of getting to know ones Soldiers and staying involved, addressing their problems and making sure they are taken seriously, importance of self and buddy checks, and how to access and utilize additional resources.

As stated earlier, Battlemind products are developed and tailored through a massive collaborative effort. CHPPM has currently fielded a number of suicide prevention training modules, posters and tip cards. The Battlemind Training Office has also filmed educational training video on the Army Suicide Prevention Program (ASPP) for Garrison and Combat environment. The objective is to provide numerous media outlets for training that is relevant to the targeted audience and maximizes Soldier contact.

The ACE acronym is an easy to remember but important suicide intervention tool created for the US Army by CHPPM.

The "A" stands for "ASK." Battlemind training requires every leader to educate subordinates that the best way to ask someone if they are suicidal is to do just that "Are you suicidal?" It emphasizes that it takes loyalty, duty and personal courage to confront a Soldier who may be in crisis and impulsively considering suicide.

The "C" in ACE stands for "CARE." Battlemind training teaches Soldiers that upon recognition that a fellow Soldier is feeling suicidal, the buddy needs to convey that they care about the Soldier while maintaining control of the situation and their personal reaction as their anxiety may impact their ability to successfully intervene. Training also focuses on remaining calm and respectful of the distressed Soldier. Once the situation is under control, leaders and buddies are trained to care for the Soldier and to stay involved with their Soldier before and during the crisis. This will demonstrate to the distressed individual that people do care about them and that they are not an expendable asset.

The "E" in ACE stands for "ESCORT." Battlemind teaches Soldiers that they should never leave a suicidal Soldier alone. It draws on comparison to the U.S. Army's Warrior Ethos of never leaving a fallen comrade behind. This is done by staying with the Soldier and escorting them to help or assistance. Soldiers are also taught that failure to stay involved at this point can have a devastating impact on the Soldier's present and future health and stability. Staying involved and demonstrating care may reduce the risk of the Soldier acting impulsively on suicidal intent.

The ACE of Hearts Card is a playing card-sized tip card distributed to Soldiers. The face of the ACE of Hearts outlines the ACE acronym and provides guidance and examples of things Soldiers can say when they encounter a fellow Soldier in crisis. The back side of the card outlines common risk factors and behaviors which are warning signs of impulsivity, depression and suicide. These cards have been fielded and are given to all Soldiers deploying to combat zones. Additional cards can be found anywhere there are Chaplains or behavioral health assets.

The Army Suicide Prevention Program (ASPP) video was produced and filmed at AMEDD Television, a local media resource for the AMEDD Center & School. This 20 minute video is available for download on the Army Knowledge Online (AKO) behavioral health web page. It highlights the importance of getting to know Soldiers and how understanding what issues may be causing them stress can help them take steps to regain control before it gets to a crisis level. The video also outlines what to do, using the ACE acronym, if that Soldier feels as if they have lost that control and actually begin to consider suicide as their primary solution.

In conclusion, the Army supports suicide prevention interventions, and views suicide as a preventable incident. More importantly, one preventable suicide is one too many.

*The above overview of Battlemind was provided by Major Yosick based on the Mental Health Advisory Team (MHAT) IV data. Supported references provided upon request.

Lowering Suicide Risk in Returning Troops
B.K. Wiederhold (Ed.)
IOS Press, 2008
© 2008 IOS Press. All rights reserved.
doi:10.3233/978-1-58603-889-2-102

Suicide Prevention Among Polish Veterans of Multinational Missions

Stanislaw ILNICKI [a, 1]

*a Department of Psychiatry and Combat Stress of the Military Institute
of the Medical Services, Warsaw, Poland*

Abstract. This paper presents some outcomes of the participation of Polish Military Contingents (PMC) in multinational missions and military operations within the UN, OSCE, EU and NATO mandate. The suicide risk among soldiers serving both in country and abroad is discussed. Selected legal issues and organization of the combat stress disorders prevention system in the Polish armed forces were presented. In particular, prevention activity before deployment, during deployment and after returning home was highlighted. Achievements and challenges in PTSD prevention and treatment in the PMC were discussed.

Keywords: multinational military operations, veterans, suicides, Poland.

1. Polish Participation in the Multinational Military Missions and Operations

54 years have passed since the moment when the first group of the Polish military officers joined the United Nations Supervisory Commission in Korea. From that time more than 64,000 soldiers and civilian MoD employees participated in 66 missions within mandate of the UN, OSCE, EU and NATO, taking place in 39 countries. On these missions 72 soldiers died and more than 600 were disabled [1, 2].

In the period of 1997-2002, each year an average of 2,500 soldiers and civilian employees participated in the missions. This constitutes about 1.4% of the total strength of the Polish armed forces. Since 2003, this participation increased by a factor of more than two. At present approximately 3.8% of the total strength of the Polish armed forces serves abroad. (See Figure 1) [3].

Currently, the personnel of Polish Military Contingents (PMC) consists of nearly 90% professional career soldiers, while the percentage of professional soldiers in the Polish armed forces amounts to approximately 55%. (See Figure 2) [3].

Nowadays 3,521 soldiers and civilian MoD employees serve outside Poland (See Table 1) [3].

---

[1] Corresponding Author: Stanisław Ilnicki, Department of Psychiatry and Combat Stress of the Military Institute of the Medical Services, ul. Szaserow 128, 00-909 Warszawa, Poland; E-mail: ilnickis@wim.mil.pl

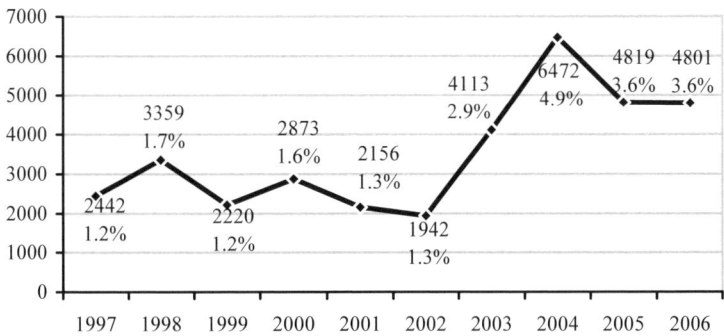

Figure 1. Polish Military Contingents in absolute numbers and as a percentage of the total manpower [3]

Table 1. Personnel of the Polish Military Contingents in 2007 [3]

Name of Mission	Number of Soldiers
EUFOR, Bosnia and Herzegovina	220
KFOR, Kosovo	310
ISAF, Afghanistan	1,200
Multinational Force, Iraq	900
UNIFIL, Lebanon	500
UNDOF, Golan Heights	367
Other	24
Total	**3,521**

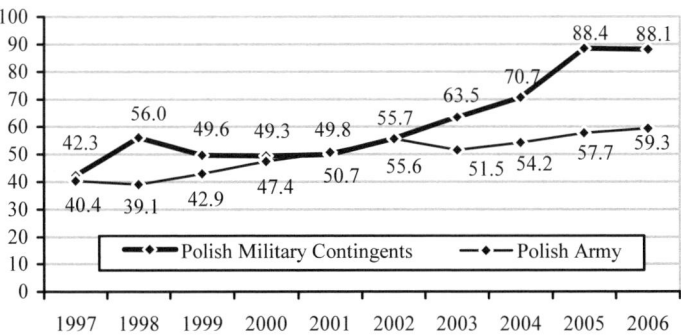

Figure 2. Percentage of professional soldiers in Polish Military Contingents and in the Polish armed forces [3]

2. Suicides in the Polish Armed Forces

In the decade of 1997 – 2006, the average rate of suicides committed in the Polish armed forces ranged from 11.2 to 29.2 and on average amounted to 22.6 per 100,000. As the duration of conscript service was gradually reduced from 12 to 9 months, the actual number of soldiers serving in this period was used as a base for calculation of the suicide rate in the years 2004 – 2006. This number exceeded the authorized standard personnel number by approximately 20 - 30%. (See Table 2)   [3]

Table 2. Suicides committed in Polish Armed Forces

Year	Strength of Polish Armed Forces	Number of Suicides Committed by Soldiers	Rate of Suicides per 100.000 Soldiers
1997	205,587	41	19.9
1998	200,604	25	12.4
1999	188,097	36	19.1
2000	177,681	52	29.2
2001	164,984	40	24.2
2002	144,867	40	27.6
2003	141,962	24	16.9
2004	130,706	32	24.5
2005	135,024[a]/146,448[b]	21	13.8
2006	133,319[a]/151,238[b]	17	11.2
Total	1,446,792	328	22.6

Source: Data of the Ministry of National Defense [4] - [a] authorized strength, [b] actual strength

In the period considered, the suicide rate among professional soldiers ranged from 8.9 to 22.6 and the average rate was 14.6. In case of conscript soldiers the rate ranged from 13.8 to 40.4 and the average rate was 25.1. In the same period the suicide rate for a general male population, aged 20 – 49, was changing within the range of 25.8 – 32.6 and its average value was 29.5. Thus the average values of the suicide rate for both professional and conscript soldiers in the period of 1997 - 2006 were lower than in a comparable group of males in the general population [3].

What is striking in comparison to the relatively stable and gradually declining general male suicide rate is a large fluctuation of the suicide rate among soldiers, both career and conscript. A particularly big difference occurred in the period of 2000 - 2002, in which the average suicide ratio for conscript soldiers (35.5) significantly exceeded values of this rate for males in general (28.7). This can be explained by the restructurization changes taking place in the Polish armed forces in this period.

At the end of the decade considered, suicide rates of both professional and conscript soldiers decreased significantly below the long-term average (correspondingly 8.9 and 13.8) and came close to each other. (See Figure 3) [3].

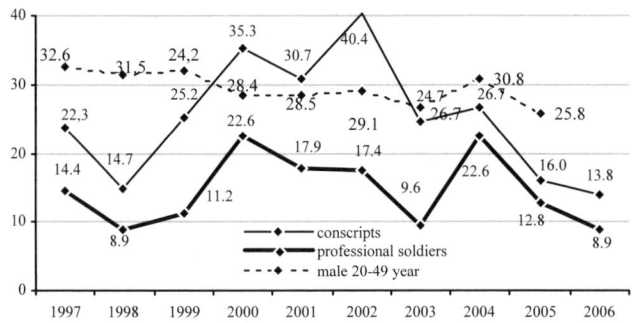

Figure 3. Suicide rates for professional soldiers, conscripts and males in general, in the age group of 20 – 49, for the period of 1997 - 2006. Source: Data of the Ministry of National Defense and [3].

Table 3. Suicides committed by Polish soldiers during and after deployment within multinational missions, 1997 to 2006

Year	Total Number of Soldiers	Number of Suicides		Rate of Suicides per 100,000 Soldiers
		During Deployment	Post-deployment	
1997	2,442	1	0	40.9
1998	3,359	0	0	0
1999	2,220	0	0	0
2000	2,873	1	0	35.2
2001	2,156	0	0	0
2002	1,942	0	0	0
2003	4,113	0	0	0
2004	6,472	0	1	15.5
2005	4,819	1	0	20.7
2006	4,810	1	1	41.5
Total	**35,206**	**4**	**2**	**17.0**

Source: Data of the Ministry of National Defense and [3]

During more than fifty years of service within multinational missions, 8 PMC soldiers committed suicide. In relation to 64,000 Polish mission participants this makes the rate 12.5. Four soldiers out of a total 35,206 Polish mission participants took their lives in the decade of 1997 – 2006; that makes the ratio 11.4.

Based on an analysis conducted by the Supreme Military Prosecutor's Office it was discovered (for the needs of this paper) that in the period of 2002 – 2007 two cases of suicide among veterans after their return to Poland occurred, and both victims were professional soldiers. The first suicide was directly connected with a divorce adjudicated by a court to be the fault of the veteran, while the other was an outcome of depression following an alcohol-related traffic accident on the eve of a re-deployment to Iraq.

Unfortunately, at present there are no statistical data on suicides of retired veterans. A database allowing for tracking their further life histories after leaving the service is being built.

3. Legal Bases of Mental Health Protection Organization in the Polish Armed Forces

The legal basis for preventive activity in the area of health care for servicemen serving both in country and outside Poland as well as veterans who, as a result of injuries suffered on deployment, became unfit for further service is provided by the five following Acts: 1) Act on the Common Obligation to Defend the Republic of Poland [5], 2) Act on the Military Service of Professional Soldiers [6], 3) Act on Protection of Mental Health [7], 4) Act on the Pension System for Professional Soldiers and Their Families [8] and 5) Act on Allowances for Disabled Servicemen, War Victims and Their Families [9].

Based on the first two Acts, the Minister of National Defense issued ordinances that specify the organization and procedures of military medical commissions as well as defines criteria for evaluation of fitness for military service in country and outside Poland. According to these ordinances only professional servicemen who hold a health certificate issued by the military medical commissions are assigned for service in the Polish Military Contingents (PMC) [10,11]. In accordance with the relevant regulations even slight mental disorders and deficiencies rule out service outside Poland. Mental health of professional soldiers is evaluated based on mandatory prophylactic examination by medical specialists, conducted at least once every three years (if necessary, a psychologist and psychiatrist participate in the examination) as well as examinations conducted directly before deployment and after returning home [10].

The Act on Protection of Mental Health obliges organization and performance activities in the area of mental health promotion and prevention of mental disorders in the armed forces. Based on the MoD decision dated February 17, 1997, a corps of psychologist prevention consultants to military unit commanders was established [12, 13]. This corps has no counterpart in other European armed forces. At present it consists of 213 specialists including 15 officers and 198 civilian employees. Ninety-five percent of them are women. The general ratio is 1 psychologist per 1000 soldiers, while in missions abroad one psychologist is assigned to several hundred soldiers (see Table 5). Besides the preventive psychologists, mental health protection is also provided by a team of 90 psychologists who provide screening and selection of candidates for specified military positions and specialties.

The last two out of the above-mentioned Acts provide material security to disabled veterans and their families. Polish regulations distinguish a few categories of mental disorders, closely connected with combat stress. They provide the basis for receiving a one-time compensation for suffering damage to one's health and, at the same time, the basis for being included in one of the three disability groups (with a disability pension ranging from 40% up to 90% of the previous salary) [8, 9].

These legal acts provide conditions for the health prophylactics that cover, among other things, suicide prevention during all phases of missions and military operations as well as after the veterans leave the service.

4. Psycho-education in Suicide Prevention

One of the primary tasks of military unit psychologists is psycho-education, including suicide prevention. Auxiliary data were developed for lectures on this subject in the form of a plan-synopsis of two 45-minute lectures with charts for soldiers, available on the Internet [14]. The following issues are covered: 1) Basic terms in suicide problems, 2) Symptoms of presuicidal syndrome, 3) Risk factors of suicidal behaviors, 4) Identification of auto-aggressive dispositions among soldiers, 5) Counteracting autodestructive behaviors in soldiers, 6) Procedures for commanders taking action in relation to suicide-exposed soldiers, and 7) Information on where to find help.

Figure 4. Title page of the plan-synopsis for lectures on suicide prevention.

5. Prevention of Combat-stress Related Mental Disorders

5.1. Prevention before Deployment

During exercises preceding a deployment to areas of armed conflict, soldiers attend an educational course and undergo training in psychological aid. Soldiers in special forces are covered by a 16-hour training conducted by a team of experts who work for the Armed Forces. This training includes issues related to operations under extreme conditions (see Table 4) [15, 16].

In addition, psychologists deployed for missions are trained on a regular basis. This educational program includes the Critical Incident Stress Debriefing, group forms of crisis intervention, work with a person exposed to suicide risk, handling an aggressive person, work with a violent perpetrator and victim, aid to persons who suffered a "loss" (e.g. death, divorce, etc.), and rendering aid by telephone. Both the training and education is provided by psychologists who have been deployed many times to missions outside Poland and by invited civilian experts, both from Poland and abroad [15].

In the preparatory period before deployment both the military unit commander and psychologist meet the soldiers' families to inform them about the deployment and the means of contacting them if they need help. This is the task of the informal Family Support Teams established on-location where the unit is stationed [15].

Table 4. Program of Psychological Preparation of Soldiers for Deployment in Armed Conflict Areas [15]

Subject	Period	
	Lectures	Exercises
Factors affecting mental life during service on the military missions	1	
Separation problems	1	
Adaptation – getting to know with subordinates and colleagues	1	
Causes of conflicts, conflict prevention and resolution	2	
Responses to stress – courage, anger, panic prevention, fear overcoming	1	
Defusing and reduction of battlefield stress	2	
Effective command and control		2
Practical ways of defusing and stress reduction		2
Psychological crisis – violence, aggression and depressive states		2
Losses, suicidal behavior, aid to a person exposed to suicide risk	1	
Alcohol and drugs – their detrimental effect on soldier's discipline and behavior	1	
Total	**10**	**6**

5.2.   Prevention during Deployment

Psychologists deployed to missions abroad are formal members of the Polish Military Contingent. In 2000 the first psychologist was assigned to the Polish Military Contingent within the SFOR. So far 31 psychologists have participated in tours of duty with Polish troops in Iraq. There were 5 or 6 psychologists assigned to the initial rotations while at present, due to a change of the nature of the mission into training, there is one psychologist attached to the troops. Following an intensification of the fighting during Rotation 8, the number of psychologists assigned to the Contingent was increased to 2 (see Table 5).

Basic subjects of psychological intervention during the deployment are: debriefing, defusing after operations, resolving of family-related problems, mourning experience, separation from family, threat to life and health as well as social and climatic conditions.

The psychologists, together with a psychiatrist and a chaplain, form the informal Psychological Support Team. Examples of the psychologist's interventions during Rotation 2 of Polish Military Contingent to Iraq: 938 individual conversations, 449 team meetings including 43 debriefings, and 190 defusing sessions and pre-operation briefings.

Table 5. Psychologists assigned to the Polish Military Contingents in Iraq

Rotation	Period	Number of Psychologists	Number of Soldiers per 1 Psychologist
1	July 2003 – Jan. 2004	6	387
2	Febr. 2004 - Aug. 2004	6	407
3	Aug. 2004 - Febr. 2005	5	472
4	Febr. 2005 - Aug. 2005	6	265
5	July 2005 - Jan. 2006	4	347
6	Jan. 2006 – July 2006	1	900
7	July 2006 - Jan. 2007	1	887
8	Jan. 2007 – July 2007	2	450
	Total	**31**	**413**

Source: data of the Ministry of National Defense and [3]

In the preventive and therapeutic treatment of soldiers with Combat and Operational Stress Reaction (COSR) the psychologists and psychiatrists observe the BICEPS and triage rules based on assumptions of the Combat and Operational Stress Control [17, 18]. Due to this, the number of soldiers with the COSR who require evacuation to Poland ahead of their end date does not exceed 3 per 1000 (see Table 6).

Table 6. Injured soldiers of the Polish Military Contingent in Iraq evacuated to Poland early, July 2003 to July 2007

Casualty category	n =12.800	per 1.000 Soldiers
Combat casualties	42	3.3
Non-combat casualties and diseases	67	5.2
Combat and Operational Stress Reaction (COSR)	38	2.9
Total	**147**	**11.5**

Source: Military Health Service Inspectorate

5.3. Post-Deployment Prevention

Within 7 days after coming back to Poland, the soldiers undergo a mandatory medical examination by the same military medical commission that examined them before the deployment [10]. The short time available for the examination, and the reluctance of soldiers to confide in medical personnel (as they are anxious to see their loved ones) does not allow for a precise evaluation of their mental condition. Because of this the next psychological examination (a survey) is conducted within 30 days in their home military units; if needed these examinations are supplemented with an individual psychological or psychiatric examination [15].

Since 2004, veterans with precursor symptoms of stress disorders, on request of the psychologist or psychiatrist, can go for a free 14-day preventive and treatment stay in one of the four Military Rehabilitation and Treatment Hospitals – in Krynica, Busko-Zdrój, Ciechocinek or Lądek-Zdrój. They can be accompanied by a spouse or partner (who needs to pay for the stay) [10, 15].

Approximately 12% of the veterans were qualified for these stays in the period of 2004 - 2006 and approximately 11% made use of them (see Table 7).

Table 7. Polish Military Contingent (PMC) veterans participating in the preventive and therapeutic tours, 2003-2005

Year	Number	Qualified		Participated	
	n	n	%	n	%
2004	4113	496	12.1	437	10.6
2005	6472	659	10.2	589	9.1
2006	4819	742	15.4	685	14.2
Total	**15,404**	**1,897**	**12.3**	**1,711**	**11.1**

Source: Military Health Service Inspectorate

Veterans with developed post-traumatic stress disorder who need to be treated or observed for purposes of the health condition certificate are hospitalized in one of the psychiatric departments of military hospitals in Bydgoszcz, Cracow, Wrocław and in the Psychiatric and Combat Stress Department of the Military Institute of the Medical Services in Warsaw that is the main therapeutic and formal mental health evaluation center for veterans of the Polish Military Contingents. Within 1.5 years of operation, the Department has provided treatment and issued mental health certificates for approximately 100 veterans. In 2007, due to a partnership established with the Virtual Reality Medical Center of San Diego, virtual reality enhanced PTSD treatment was launched.

Soldiers who, due to health-related reasons, are unfit for service for 3 months are sent by the military unit commander for a medical examination by the military medical commission. The commission may grant a six-month health-recovery leave in order to continue treatment. After this time, depending on the opinion of the psychiatric consultant of the commission, the soldiers are deemed fit for further military service or retire [6].

An overwhelming majority of the Polish Military Contingent's veterans are interested in continuation of their military service and follow a trend of hiding their PTSD-related disorders out of a fear that disclosure of these disorders may have a detrimental effect on their military career. If they cannot cope with their problems they use alcohol as a "remedy" or contact physicians outside of the armed forces. A change of this negative attitude is one of the goals of preventive activity in this area in the Polish armed forces.

A veteran certified by the commission as unfit for service due to health-related reasons is retired and at the same time classified to one of the three disability groups, becoming eligible for a disability pension. Type and amount of the pension depends on a connection between the disability and military service and with unique features of the service.

6. Psychological and Social Support to Soldiers and Veterans after Retirement

The preventive and therapeutic activity is supplemented by supportive actions being provided by the Team for Supporting Families of Fallen Soldiers and the Injured during Missions, operating within the Land Forces Command. This team consists of a physician, chaplain, and social welfare and financial experts. The team monitors the current situation of the veterans, coordinates and analyzes support actions, as well as maintains permanent contact with the injured, families of the fallen soldiers, and with commanders of their home military units. In order to provide direct contact between the injured, their families and the Land Forces Command, an emergency confidence telephone desk was created. A similar team has been functioning in the Military Peace-Keeping Mission Centre [15].

Another source of a mental support to the veterans is veteran associations. One of them is the Association of the UN Peace-Keeping Missions in Poland (SKMP ONZ). Goals of this association include an integration of the combatant community, representation and defense of peace-keeping mission combatants in relation to governmental administration as well as military and local government authorities, ensuring material help to those in need and promotion of issues related to veterans of peace-keeping operations. Currently the Association has more than 1500 members organized in 40 branches all over Poland [1, 19].

Since its establishment in 1999, the Association has been undertaking efforts aimed at recognition of disability incurred as a result of injuries and diseases suffered during war-zone service upon the UN, NATO, OSCE and EU mandate as a war-related disability. Lack of such an official regulation results in the fact that support rendered to the veterans is perceived by friendly observers as a kind of a noble charity rather than a fulfillment of due obligations towards soldiers who have lost their health on deployments on behalf of the Polish State.

In the existing legal situation, aid to veterans of peace-keeping missions who are in a particularly bad material situation is provided by the *Servi Paci* foundation.

7. Conclusions

There are many models explaining suicidal behaviors of soldiers, from the classical socio-cultural Emil Durkheim's model to medical ones, interpreting a suicide as an outcome of mental disorders, in particular depression and personality disorders. There is no doubt that this phenomenon depends on both biological and psycho-social factors, the contribution of which is individually differentiated in each case [4, 20, 21].

A reduction of the suicide risks in the armed forces can be achieved effectively only by comprehensive activities focusing on a minimization of both individual and environmental suicidogenic factors. An example of such an activity selecting for professional military service only those candidates that feature mental characteristics adequate for their future missions. Other preventive activities include elimination of factors interfering with adaptation to conditions of military service such as bullying, physical violence, alcohol abuse or drugs. Also an early recognition of mental crises in soldiers (including so called pre-suicide syndrome) is very effective as it allows for timely intervention including provision of a personal safety to the soldier and rendering quick psychological or psychiatric help. All this must be supplemented by building a system of psycho-social and material support for the veterans after they leave the armed forces.

All these elements of the suicide prevention policy are included in the above-mentioned program of mental health protection in the Polish armed forces, both in country and on deployments outside Poland.

8.   References

[1]   A. Florkowski et al., Evaluation of Psychopathological Factors and Origins of Suicides Commited by Soldiers, 1989 to 1998, *Milit. Me*d. **166** (2001), 44-47.
[2]   Z. Bednarski, *Poles in the Service of Peace*. Department Wychowania i Promocji Obronności MON, Warszawa 2005.
[3]   *Decyzja Nr 24/MON Ministra Obrony Narodowej z 17.02.1997 r. w sprawie utworzenia w jednostkach organizacyjnych Sił Zbrojnych Rzeczpospolitej Polskiej stanowiska koordynatora do spraw psychoprofilaktyki oraz konsultanta dowódcy jednostki wojskowej do spraw psychoprofilaktyki* (Dz. Rozk. MON z 1997 r., poz. 16).
[4]   FM 6-22.5. *Combat Stress*. Headquarters, Department of the Army. 23 June 2000

[5]   FM 4-02.51. *Combat and Operational Stress Control*. Headquarters, Department of the Army. July 2006.

[6]   B. Hołyst, *Suicydologia*, Wydawnictwo Prawnicze Lexis Nexis, Warszawa 2002.

[7]   S. Ilnicki, *Poles in the service of peace 1953-2003*, 3rd Northern European Conference on Veterans Support, Vordinborg, Denmark, 16-19.10.2003, www://skmponz.w.interia.pl/index1.htm

[8]   *Rozporządzenie Ministra Obrony Narodowej z dnia 16 czerwca 2004 r. w sprawie badań lekarskich żołnierzy zawodowych skierowanych do służby poza granicami państwa oraz powracających do kraju po zakończeniu tej służby.* (Dz.U. Nr 148, poz. 1557).

[9]   *Rozporządzenie Ministra Obrony Narodowej z dnia 29.11.2005 r. w sprawie orzekania o zdolności do zawodowej służby wojskowej oraz właściwości i trybu postępowania wojskowych komisji lekarskich w tych sprawach* (Dz.U. nr 253, poz. 2130).

[10]   *Służba żołnierzy i funkcjonariuszy służb państwowych wykonujących zadania w warunkach ekstremalnych.* Departament Wychowania i Promocji Obronności MON-Polskie Towarzystwo Naukowe Kultury Fizycznej, Warszawa 2004.

[11]   R. Staniszewski, *Injury and illness analysis among soldiers of The Polish Military Contingent in Iraq*, Ph.D. thesis, Military Institute of the Medical Services, Warsaw 2007.

[12]   *Statistical Yearbooks of the Republic of Poland, 1998-2007*, Central Statistical Office, Warsaw.

[13]   *Stres i pomoc psychologiczna w misjach wojskowych*, Ministerstwo Obrony Narodowej, Departament Wychowania i Promocji Obronności, Warszawa 2002.

[14]   *Ustawa o powszechnym obowiązku Rzeczpospolitej Polskiej z 21.06.1967 r.* (Dz.U. z 2004 r., Nr 241, poz. 2416)

[15]   *Ustawa z 29.05.1974 r. o zaopatrzeniu inwalidów wojennych i wojskowych oraz ich rodzin* (Dz.U. Nr 9, poz. 87 z późn. zm.)

[16]   *Ustawa z 10.12.1993 r. o zaopatrzeniu emerytalnym żołnierzy zawodowych oraz ich rodzin* (Dz.U. Nr 8, poz. 66 z późn. zm.)

[17]   *Ustawa z dnia 19.08.1994 r. o ochronie zdrowia psychicznego* (Dz. U. Nr 111, poz. 535 z późn. zm.).

[18]   *Ustawa z dnia 11 września 2003 r. o służbie wojskowej żołnierzy zawodowych* (Dz. U. Nr 179 poz. 1750)

[19]   *Wytyczne Sekretarza Stanu – I Zastępcy Ministra Obrony Narodowej z 11.04.1997 r. w sprawie prowadzenia działalności psychoprofilaktycznej w rodzajach sił zbrojnych, okręgach wojskowych i jednostkach wojskowych* (Dz. Roz. MON z 1997 r., poz. 35).

[20]   *Zdrowie psychiczne żołnierzy*, A. Florkowski, W. Gruszczyński (red.), Wojskowa Akademia Medyczna, Łódź 2000.

Lowering Suicide Risk in Returning Troops
B.K. Wiederhold (Ed.)
IOS Press, 2008
© *2008 IOS Press. All rights reserved.*
doi:10.3233/978-1-58603-889-2-113

Mobile Narratives for Combating Battlefield Stress: Rationale, Preliminary Research and Protocol

Giuseppe RIVA[1-2], Alessandra GORINI[1], Alessandra GRASSI[2], Daniela VILLANI[1-2]

[1] *Applied Technology for Neuro-Psychology Lab.,*
Istituto Auxologico Italiano, Milan, Italy
[2] *ICE-NET, Università Cattolica, Milan, Italy*

Abstract: Battlefield stress is the consequence of man being exposed to the hostile environment of combat. Combat stress is specifically caused by man's fear of the dangers of combat, and is fueled and tempered by other variables such as morale, cohesion, fatigue, confidence, training and intensity of the combat. Treatment is often as simple as giving soldiers time to rest for a few hours or days, to get a shower and some sleep, and to talk about the feelings they have in the presence of a counselor. Only in rare cases do soldiers undergo more serious psychological treatment. One of the best strategies for dealing with stress is learning how to relax. However, relaxing is difficult to achieve in the battlefield. In this paper we suggest the use of mobile multimedia technology--PDA/cellular phones--for providing advanced coping techniques suitable to the battlefield context. Specifically, we developed a protocol based on mobile narratives, to be experienced on mobile multimedia technology: 3G cellular phones, IPODs or PDAs. Mobile narratives are audio-visual experiences, implemented on mobile devices, in which the narrative component is a critical aspect to induce a feeling of presence and engagement. Through the link between the feeling of presence and emotional state, mobile narratives may be used to improve mood state in their users. The rationale of the approach, a preliminary test of the proposed method, and a protocol for its use on the battlefield are presented and discussed.

Keywords: Battlefield stress, cellular phones, PDAs, Mobile Narratives

Introduction

Battlefield stress is the consequence of man being exposed to the hostile environment of combat [1]. Combat stress is specifically caused by man's fear of the dangers of combat, and is fueled and tempered by other variables such as morale, cohesion, fatigue, confidence, training and intensity of the combat.

History shows that a stressed soldier may be a significant problem. In the battles of Faid-Kasserine, the first major engagements of US forces in World War II, 20%-34% of casualties were caused not by direct wounds and disease, but by battlefield stress [2]. And the situation has not significantly changed. As demonstrated recently by Morgan

---

[1] Corresponding Author: Prof. Giuseppe Riva, Ph.D., Dipartimento di Psicologia, Università Cattolica del Sacro Cuore, Largo Gemelli 1, 20123 Milan, Italy, e-mail: giuseppe.riva@unicatt.it, web-site: http://www.neurotiv.org

and colleagues [3], acute stress may impair working memory and visuo-spatial ability even in elite soldiers. In their study, including 184 Special Operations warfighters, stress exposure impaired visuo-spatial capacity and working memory of the sample, potentially reducing performance of duty.

For these reasons, stress management is a critical issue for the US Army. As underlined in the Army Regulation 600-63, stress, its effects, and its management are concerns for leaders at every level [4]. Specifically, Field Manual 26-2 provides different techniques and consideration for the management of stress in Army operations [5].

The Field Manual depicts three different and increasing levels of support (Stress Management Module) based on installation resources:

- *Level one* is designed as a minimum program that includes placement of pamphlets/brochures/posters around the military community, making sure that welcome packets are provided to all new members and ensuring sponsorship of new arrivals.
- *Level two* includes level one plus community education classes (learning new skills and activities) and the use of radio/TV spots.
- *Level three* includes level one and level two plus specific intervention programs conducted by qualified health care professionals. These programs include relaxation techniques, problem solving, cognitive restructuring and clarification of life goals.

Given the limited number of qualified professionals on the battlefield, treatment is often as simple as giving soldiers time to rest for a few hours or days, to get a shower and some sleep, and to talk about the feelings they have in the presence of a counselor.

In general, management efforts that emphasize replenishment of physiological needs, structured occupation, and support of the affected soldier's occupational roles have yielded better results [6]. Nevertheless, in rare cases soldiers undergo more serious psychological treatment.

Another critical issue is providing stress coping techniques. In the civilian sector there is a broad spectrum of techniques available for individual to use. However, the possible techniques are significantly fewer when applied in the battlefield. Duration of stress and intensity of battle usually reduce imagination and relaxation abilities. This makes stress coping even more challenging.

In this paper we suggest the use of mobile multimedia technology – PDA/cellular phones – for providing advanced coping techniques suitable for the battlefield context.

1. Stress Management and Technology

Stress management techniques can be used to moderate the build-up of stress. As stress levels rise throughout the day, we can employ relaxation methods to reduce the build-up and return to lower, more manageable levels. However, *"stress management"* is an umbrella term including many different methods and tools. Analyzing more than 100 research articles, Ong and colleagues [7] categorized the most commonly used techniques in three approaches.

The first approach involves imagery, relaxation, and meditation. Frequent applications are diaphragmatic breathing, directive and receptive imagery, yoga, progressive muscle relaxation, autogenic training, and massage therapy.

The second involves cognitive–behavioral approaches, where strategies include emotion-focused or problem-focused coping, self-monitoring of stress intensity, thought recordkeeping and rewriting, cognitive reappraisal, time management, assertiveness training, systematic desensitization, and various didactic and educational topics.

The last category is represented by systemic approaches. They are focused on altering the external factors which contribute to create stress in the individual, such as social, environmental, or political factors.

Box-score analysis in the review indicates that the most commonly employed components in a stress management program involve multi-component cognitive-behavioral therapy (CBT) or relaxation-oriented techniques.

Given the wide availability of different methods, the most effective stress management approach may not be to impose a single approach on all subjects, but to carefully tailor a set of approaches to each individual. Here, technology can play an important role.

CDs of calming music have shown positive effects on stress reduction by achieving psychological benefits including distraction, sense of control over symptoms, and relaxation. Music interventions also have reported good results to reduce state and trait anxiety, to ease stress, and to increase relaxation [8]. These CDs combined the positive effect of calm, sedative music with relaxation techniques to achieve enhanced effects. To increase effectiveness, commercial relaxation DVDs have also integrated visual stimuli. In such a delivery, the visual representation of the scenario supports the process of relaxation, creating an isolated context in which the subject can feel safe [9].

2. A New Stress Coping Technique: Mobile Narratives

Cellular telephones and hand-held personal digital assistants (PDAs) are multi-purpose computing devices for which 3D content will simply be one more feature, but not necessarily the most important feature (a cell phone, for example, will be used primarily as a phone by most people). Because the combined market size of cell phones and PDAs is massive, however, the financial opportunity for successfully deployment of 3D hardware and software to this segment of the market is also potentially massive.

A necessary precondition for 3D graphics to make any impact is the availability of open-standard, well-performing Application Programming Interfaces (APIs) that are supported by handset manufacturers, operators and developers alike. Actually, there are two main industry efforts that aim to standardize APIs for animated 3D graphics in mobile phones (see Figure 1): *OpenGL ES* and Mobile 3D Graphics API for J2ME.

Although the most significant advances in 3D mobile hardware are yet to come, some cell phones and PDAs are already shipping with enough raw horse power to deliver a good 3D experience today: *Power VR MBX* (Nokia N93/N95, Ericsson P990, Apple IPhone) and *NVidia GoForce 5500/6100* (Samsung P910/920, HTC Foreseer, Motorola Maxx).

These devices allow the provision of *mobile narratives*: 3D audio-visual experiences, implemented on mobile devices, in which the narrative component is a critical aspect to induce a feeling of presence and engagement. The developed narratives include different relaxation techniques adapted to the battlefield context: breathing control, progressive relaxation, mindfulness, etc.

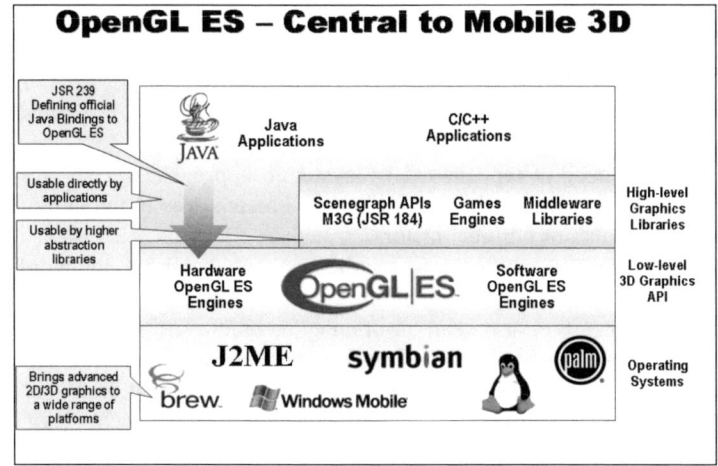

Figure 1: 3D Graphics for mobile devices (courtesy of Khronos, http://www.khronos.org/opengles/)

Through the link between the feeling of presence and the emotional state, mobile narratives may be used to improve the mood state in their users [9]. Future devices will also allow immersion, through the use of headsets (already possible on Nokia N93/N95 phones) and tracking.

3. Testing the concept: commuting stress

Following the above guidelines, we developed a specific protocol based on mobile narratives - multimedia narratives experienced on multimedia UMTS/3G phones - to reduce stress in non-comfortable situations.

To test the concept, we planned a controlled trial involving an experimental sample of 17 male and 16 female commuters (N=33) of the Italian regional train line "Milano-Saronno", aged between 20-25 years (M=23.82+/-0.72). The sample was randomly divided among the following three conditions:
- MN - Mobile narratives: the sample experienced four mobile narratives based on a trip in a desert tropical beach (see Figure 2);
- NA - New age videos: the sample experienced four commercial videos with new age music (see Figure 2). The videos were selected for their similar visual content (a tropical beach) to the mobile narratives;
- CT - Control group: no treatment.

The sample was tracked for two days. During each trip the experimental samples experienced the multimedia content on a Multimedia UMTS cellular phone (screen size: 208x320 pixels). The total length of each experience was 6 minutes. Before and after each trip the subjects completed the following questionnaires: STAI: State-Trait Anxiety Inventory [10]; VAS: Visual Analog Scale [11]; PANAS: Positive and Negative Affect Schedule [12]; ITC-Sopi: Sense of Presence Inventory [13].

The first significant result was the difference in anxiety between the three groups. Only the MN group experienced a significant reduction in the anxiety level (STAI: z=2,943, p<0.01) and an increase in the relaxation scale (VAS: z=-2,842; p<0.01) at the end of the trial. Also, the anxiety reduction in the MN group was significantly higher than the ones achieved by the other two groups (STAI: Chi-square: 20.749, p<0.01).

Figure 2. The visual content of the Mobile Narratives (left) and the New Age video (right)

The second relevant result is related to the level of presence experienced by the two experimental groups. The level of "engagement" and "spatial presence" was significantly higher in the MN group. These data suggest that the efficacy of the MN may be related to the higher level of presence induced by mobile narratives.

4. Mobile Narratives for Battlefield Stress Management: A protocol

The preliminary trial showed the efficacy of mobile narratives in reducing the level of stress experienced during a commute. No effects were found in the other groups. These results suggest that 3G mobile handsets, even with their small screens and limited multimedia capabilities, may be used as a relaxation tool if backed by a specific therapeutic protocol and an engaging experience.

Given the positive outcome of the trial, we defined a specific protocol based on mobile narratives for the prevention and management of battlefield stress. Specifically, we developed the mobile narratives according to directed cognitive focus techniques (i.e., guided imagery, cognitive shifting, and controlled breathing). These techniques are employed not only to shift from negative to positive thoughts, but also to shift into a quiet state of relaxation.

The protocol is split in two parts:

o *Four Training Sessions* scheduled before leaving for the battlefield;
o *Booster Sessions* scheduled during the battlefield operations.

Both parts are based on four mobile narratives. Each one is about six minutes long and includes specific audio and video content: animated 3D computer-generated graphics of different mountain/lake environments narrated by a speaker.

For the development of the different 3D scenes we used the *3D CryENGINE Sandbox* developed by Crytek (http://www.crytek.com). Real time editing, bump mapping, dynamic lights, integrated physics system, shaders, and shadows are just some of the features allowed by this graphic engine:

o *Shaders*: A script system was used to combine textures in different ways to produce visual effects. It supports real time per-pixel lighting, bumpy reflections, refractions, volumetric glow effects, animated textures, transparent computer displays, windows, bullet holes, and shiny surfaces.

o *Terrain*: We used an advanced heightmap system and polygon reduction to create massive, realistic environments. The view distance can be up to 2km when converted from game units.

o *Lighting and Shadows*: We used a combination of pre-calculated, real time shadows, stencil shadows and lightmaps to produce a dynamic environment. We also included high-resolution, correct perspective, and volumetric smooth-shadow implementations for dramatic and realistic indoor shadowing.

4.1. Mobile Narrative 1

The camera strolls along the edge of the eastern flank of a green hill (Figure 3)

Figure 3. The visual content of the first Mobile Narrative

4.1.1. Text of the narrative: Introduction

There are only a few days until you leave for your mission.
The anxiety begins to grow and the usual questions begin to pop up in your mind.
Am I prepared enough?
What will it happen on the battlefield?
And what happens if I am shot?
You are going to be guided through a video in which you will learn some simple techniques to help you manage your anxiety.
You will not have to do anything other than relax, listening to the video, and abandoning your body and your mind.
You will see it will be an experience that we hope will help you.
[:44]

4.1.2. Text of the narrative: Stress Management Phase

You are on a mountain alone, calm.
The sky above you is blue.
You are walking slowly along a green path framed with majestic trees.
The large branches are full of green leaves.
The environment in which you find yourself gives you a sense of peace and of

calm.

The sun shines high in the sky.

You feel its heat on your face.

There are little white clouds surrounding the sun.

You continue to walk.

The landscape in front of you is wonderful.

The vegetation is thick and thriving.

The atmosphere around you is calm.

There's a light breeze grazing your face.

It's a pleasant feeling, to feel immersed in nature.

You are far away from all your thoughts, from all your problems.

Your mind is free from every worry.

You continue along the way.

You are walking towards a large white rock.

You slowly approach it and sit.

[1:45]

Free your mind completely.

Try to concentrate on you, on the feelings of your body, in order to revive yourself and cope with the emotion of anxiety experienced thinking about the mission.

The purpose of this journey is to put you in a position to manage your emotions independently from where you will be.

You are immersed in this incredible environment.

You are calm and relaxed.

Distant from all your worries, you feel protected.

Soon you will have to leave so let's prepare for the moments that will happen just before the leaving.

In the moments that precede the mission, you may feel agitated.

You may feel pain in your stomach that reminds you that you are alive, that you are here, that it is your turn to move next.

In these moments, it's important that you stay calm and remember that its absolutely normal to feel agitated, anxious, to feel your stomach churning, to feel like you remember nothing you have trained in before, even to feel like your mind is an empty book.

It seems paradoxical: you trained a lot, put in a lot of effort, and yet you feel as though you are not ready for this mission.

But don't worry.

These feelings are absolutely normal.

Listen to your heart beating fast when you approach the battlefield.

Your hands sweat while you wait in fear of what will happen.

But all these reactions are normal.

You may have the feeling of not knowing what to do, wondering if you will be ready to cope with the situation in an adequate way.

Or, you may find difficulty organizing what you have to do.

You may feel like you're not making sense.

But don't worry.

Relax as much as you can.

Concentrate and learn to monitor these negative thoughts that invade your mind.

Only let yourself think about the fact that you are ready and that you will be fine, you will be able to manage the situation.

Now, take a deep breath.
You feel only peace and tranquility.
Take these feelings with you.
[4:30]

4.2. Mobile Narrative 2

The camera strolls along a grassy path under a blue sky (Figure 4)

Figure 4. The visual content of the second Mobile Narrative

4.2.1. Introduction

You are going to begin the exploration of a new mountain path.
Through this journey you will learn the way to manage your anxiety.
Remember that the experience with this program will prepare you for the
    battlefield experience.
It will give you confidence in order to face the situation in the best way:
    without panic, without agitation.
You're now relaxed and prepared for a new journey.
[:31]

4.2.2. Stress Management Phase

You are now walking along a grassy path.
There are palms and giant trees surrounding your path.
It's a sunny day.
The sky is blue, and there are little clouds over you.
The colors around you are very beautiful.
A light breeze grazes your face, and you feel the fresh air that encircles you.
Your mind is free from all your worries, from all the problems that you've been
    dealing with.
Let your mind be free.
Try to relax in this paradise.
You are slowly walking under giant trees.
Now sit on the ground.

[1:14]

The panorama view around you is marvelous.

There's a thriving forest appearing in front of your eyes.

Majestic trees, high mountains rise up behind the trees, and a light breeze again touches your face.

You are immersed in a pleasant silence.

A great sense of peace surrounds you.

It leaves you with a deep calm inside.

Remember this sense of relaxation when you enter the battlefield.

It's normal that you feel worried about the situation, but you must be calm.

You must try not to be too anxious.

Reflect.

You are trained for this situation.

You are prepared for this mission.

It's perfectly normal to feel your heart beating at a fast pace.

It's perfectly normal for your hands to sweat or to have a dry mouth.

When these things happen, your mind may feel empty, too empty for having prepared so much.

But don't worry.

These things are absolutely normal.

The unease that you experience, it may show throughout your body.

Your heart pounding, you're shaking, you're sweating, your hands trembling, and your cheeks are flushing.

But you must remember to take your time when approaching the battlefield because all of these reactions in your body could happen there.

You must try to understand that all of these physiological reactions are absolutely normal.

You are anxious about this new experience and your body simply reacts in this way.

But you must learn to control your mind, to be as calm as you are now on the day of your test.

In the battlefield it's possible to have momentary lapses of memory, or moments of hesitation.

While you are deciding what to do, you might even become lost in the thread of what is happening, or lost in your thoughts so that it becomes difficult to understand what you are even doing, what you're even thinking.

But you should remember that all of these reactions are absolutely normal.

You have anxiety for this situation and your mind reacts in a manner that doesn't help you.

But you should trust in the potential of your mind.

Free your mind from your worries and open yourself to the feeling of peace and tranquility during your test.

[4:30]

4.3. Mobile Narrative 3

The camera strolls along a mountain path around a lake (Figure 5)

Figure 5. The visual content of the third Mobile Narrative

4.3.1. Introduction

Your deployment is coming up soon.
You've been training intensely.
Now you deserve a minute of distraction and rest in which you can concentrate on
    your body, on your mind.
You need to recharge and relax.
Remove yourself from your mind and all your thoughts.
Try to relax and prepare for a new journey.
Begin to free your mind and now take a deep breath.
[:35]

4.3.2. Stress Management Phase

Now you are walking along a mountain path.
Majestic trees surround you during this walk.
All around you it is very calm.
The vegetation is thick.
The age-old trees open themselves slowly in front of you, guiding you.
The sky above you is blue.
The sun heats your face with its beams.
Free your mind from the responsibilities of the day, from the intense studying that
    you have been doing lately.
Now relax in this rich atmosphere of peace and tranquility.
In front of you the path opens towards a clearing.
The ground opens up for a small lake.
The water moves slowly.
Its movement is nearly imperceptible.
You are sitting on the grass and observing the panorama view presented to your
    eyes.
[1:28]
Watch the small waves of the lake and concentrate now on your breath.
Try to control your breath.
When the waves enter the lake, breathe deeply so that you feel the fresh air as it
    enters your body.

Your lungs inflate themselves.

You feel your diaphragm as it is moving.

Now the waves stretch out at the shore.

Exhale slowly, letting out the air from your lungs gradually.

And again, inhale as the waves enter the lake.

Exhale as the waves return to the shore.

You have an extreme feeling of tranquility and well-being.

Your mind is empty.

You feel lighter. Still inhale. Exhale.

You're left with this feeling of pleasure.

You are in harmony with nature.

Remember this deep feeling of peace and tranquility when it's time to enter the battlefield. Remember this great sense of relaxation.

Remove the anxiety from your mind.

If you have trained a lot with determination to do well, if you know that you are ready, you do not need to worry about the outcome of your mission.

You will see that all will go well.

Reflect now on how much have trained.

If you are ready, there is no reason to worry.

Pay attention and use strategies that have worked well for you in the past.

Combine the information that you have read.

Try to memorize it.

And at the end think about the mission in its entirety in order to focus on any main objective.

You have everything you need in order to know if you in fact are ready.

If you know that you are ready there is no reason for you to feel too anxious.

Now take a slow breath, breathe in deeply, exhale at length, and admire the nature that encircles you, a feeling of peace and tranquility entering your mind.

Take with you this state of harmony when you have to leave.

[4:30]

4.4. Mobile Narrative 4

The camera strolls along a sunny path on the other side of the lake (Figure 6)

Figure 6. The visual content of the fourth Mobile Narrative

4.4.1. Introduction

Prepare for a visit to a new area of this environment.

Once again you will be able to free your mind from the activities of your day and you will be distracted by these wonderful mountains.

Now relax.

Learn to manage the anxiety that you could have during the exam with tranquility and peace.

Take a deep breath.

[:35]

4.4.2. Stress Management Phase

Now you are slowly walking along a short path.

Beside you there are giant trees with beautiful colors.

The sky is blue.

Not a cloud in the sky.

It's a wonderful day.

A small breeze grazes your face and the landscape in front of you is spectacular.

It gives a great feeling of peace, a deep feeling of tranquility.

Free your mind from everyday life and relax yourself.

Sit slowly on the white stone in front of you.

[1:14]

Enjoy the landscape that is open to your eyes.

Try to feel the warm sun all over you.

Now concentrate your attention on the upper part of your body.

Feel your shoulders, your arms.

Stretch your right arm out.

Slowly try to stretch it more than you think you can.

Try to control your breath as you stretch.

Inhale and exhale.

Now stretch the arm behind you.

Inhale exhale.

Again, increase the stretch.

Stretch your right arm in front of you more than you think you can now.

Feel the muscles of your shoulders and of your arm.

They're tense, but it's a satisfying feeling.

Feel your arm outstretched from your chest.

Feel it being relaxed, and light.

Now stretch your left arm.

Slowly bring it farther behind you than you feel possible.

Inhale. Exhale.

Now, stretch your left arm in front of you.

Take a deep breath.

Stretch the left arm and now bring it behind you more than you think possible.

Inhale slowly and exhale.

You feel the tension in your muscles.

You feel it as it changes your body.

Now, let your arm fall away from your chest.

Let it hang loosely and notice its new lightness.

Now the tension on your arms is gone.
Concentrate only on the feelings in your body.
You feel lighter, more relaxed.
A calm begins to surround you.
Now reflect on how much you did to prepare for this mission.
The time you have used to train.
Value your organization.
With good planning and focus, you should do well on this mission.
Don't allow anxiety to affect the outcome of your mission.
Focus on your preparation and on all the skills you have acquired to manage the
    mission before you.
Your body and your mind are light and far from every feeling of anxiety.
You must relax your mind before the beginning of the test and take with you the
    pleasant feeling you have right now in this moment.
Take this with you to the test.
[4:31]

4.5. Sessions

4.5.1. Prior the First Session

Right after the recruitment phase, the researcher will meet the sample, for about an hour, in groups of four or five subjects. The researcher will explain the rationale behind practicing coping skills (i.e., guided imagery, cognitive shifting and controlled breathing) and how to perform these techniques. The researcher will also give them written instructions to read prior to the first relaxation session, the following morning.

4.5.2. First to Fourth Session

For four bi-weekly mornings prior to starting their session of the day, the researcher will have the groups in one room and administer a battery of test (the same discussed before). The subjects will complete these tests before and after each relaxation session. The eventual control group will only take the battery once and will be dismissed from the experimental area.

- Immediately after the end of the tests, participants will install on their mobile phone the mobile narrative required for the session and eventually remove the previous one. During the session, subjects will sit in comfortable chairs in a quiet treatment room.
- To prepare for the mobile narrative experience the sample will follow for ten minutes two sample breathing techniques:
    o The subject will inhale slowly through the nose, while silently counting to three: he/she counts to three while holding the breath; then exhales slowly through the nose while counting to three.
    o The subject will breathe in through the nose until he/she can't hold in any more air. Next, through the mouth, he/she will take a quick extra gasp of air. Finally, exhale slowly and evenly through the mouth.
- After the breathing part, the sample will experience one of the four mobile narratives according to the order detailed before, either on a multimedia cellular phone (screen size: 240x320 pixel) or on an Ipod/Ipod Touch.

- After the session the researcher will conduct one focus group session with all participants. The purpose of these sessions is to discuss their impressions of the usefulness of the relaxation techniques and to address difficulties or problems.
- Every night, after these sessions, each subject will be expected to re-experience the mobile narrative on the cellular phone. No stress levels will be evaluated at this time. Therefore, they will also be asked to maintain a log on when they watched the video and their relaxation experience while practicing the techniques.

4.5.3. Booster Sessions

Daily booster sessions are designed to be used on the battlefield, in order to reinforce the skills gained in the original sessions. These sessions can be scheduled at least three days before active missions or other stressful duties.

- To prepare for the mobile narrative experience the soldier will follow the following breathing technique for five minutes:
  - The soldier will inhale slowly through the nose, while silently counting to three: he/she counts to three while holding the breath; then exhales slowly through the nose while counting to three.
- After the breathing part, the soldier will experience the third (first booster session) or the fourth (second booster session) mobile narratives, either on a multimedia cellular phone (screen size: 240x320 pixel) or on an Ipod/Ipod Touch.
- After the mobile narrative experience, the soldier will try to maintain the relaxation state for five minutes following the breathing technique below:
  - The soldier will breathe in through the nose until he/she can't hold in any more air. Next, through the mouth, he/she will take a quick extra gasp of air. Finally, exhale slowly and evenly through the mouth.

Conclusions

The "2006 Army Modernization Plan" is an operationally based report that describes the modernization and investment strategies for providing the best capabilities to the US Army today, supporting a sustained transformation process [14]. The document serves as a conceptual template for leveraging quality people and technology in order to achieve new levels of effectiveness.

A critical part of this report is related to the identification of emerging technologies that have the greatest promise for early incorporation into the Soldier as a System (SaaS) concept. The main goal of SaaS is to equip all soldiers with an integrated modular ensemble based on an open architecture that allows capabilities to be tailored to specific missions. The SaaS-related scientific and technological efforts also address technologies for the Mounted Soldier System (MSS), Air Soldier System (ASS), and Core Soldier System (CSS) ensemble. Specifically they pursue a wide range of technologies to enable Soldier systems. These include (p. 39):

- Technologies to provide individual Soldiers with platform-like lethality and survivability.
- Lightweight, long-endurance electric power generation and storage.
- Physiological status reporting and medical response technologies.

Also included within the SaaS concept is the development of new tools and methodologies for training and leader development (pp. 39-40):

- Training management tools to improve effectiveness of interactive distributed training systems.
- Methodologies utilizing realistic synthetic experience to accelerate the development of critical thinking and interpersonal communication skills.

Our suggestion is to include the development of a new generation of technology-supported stress coping techniques within this effort. This should allow the leverage of the different technologies and solutions included in the Future Combat Systems (pp. 41-42):

- Networked battle command systems to enable shared situational awareness and improved decision-making.
- Mobile-to-mobile wireless communications networks. The networks will provide large quantities of multimedia information (speech, data, graphics, and video) from point to point, and broadcast and multicast over distributed mobile wireless networks.

Specifically, we introduced the concept of mobile narratives: 3D audio-visual experiences, implemented on mobile devices, in which the narrative component is a critical aspect to induce a feeling of presence and engagement. In a preliminary research trial we showed the efficacy of mobile narratives in reducing the level of stress experienced during a commute. These results suggest that mobile multimedia devices, even with their small screens and limited multimedia capabilities, may be used as a relaxation tool if backed by a specific therapeutic protocol and an engaging experience. Specifically, through the link between the feeling of presence and the emotional state, mobile narratives may be used to improve the mood state in their users.

Given the positive outcome of the trial, we defined a specific protocol for the prevention and management of battlefield stress. In the protocol we developed the mobile narratives according to directed cognitive focus techniques (i.e., guided imagery, cognitive shifting and controlled breathing). These techniques are employed not only to shift from negative to positive thoughts, but also to shift into a quite state of relaxation.

We have planned a controlled trial to verify the efficacy of the developed protocol with a sample of active soldiers (US soldiers leaving for Iraq). The trial is scheduled for winter 2007.

Acknowledgments

The present work was supported by the Italian MIUR FIRB programme (Project "*Neurotiv - Managed care basata su telepresenza immersiva virtuale per l'assessment e riabilitazione in neuro-psicologia e psicologia clinica*" - RBNE01W8WH).

References

[1]   R.J. Hibler, Battlefield stress: management techniques. Mil Med, (1984), 149(1): p. 5-8.

[2]   W.S. Mullins and A.J. Glass, Neuropsychiatry in World War II, Volume 2, Overseas theatres. (1973).

[3]   C.A. Morgan, 3rd, A. Doran, G. Steffian, G. Hazlett, and S.M. Southwick, Stress-induced deficits in working memory and visuo-constructive abilities in special operations soldiers. Biol Psychiatry, (2006), 60(7): p. 722-9.

[4]   T.D.J. West, Army Health Promotion - Army Regulation 600-63. 1996, Washington, D.C.: Headquarters, Department of the Army.

[5]   U.S. Army, Management of Stress in Army Operations - Field Manual 26-2. 1983, Headquarters, Department of the Army: Washington, D.C.

[6]   S.M. Gerardi, The management of battle-fatigued soldiers: an occupational therapy model. Mil Med, (1996), 161(8): p. 483-8.

[7]   L. Ong, W. Linden, and S. Young, Stress management. What is it? Journal of Psychosomatic Research, (2004), 56: p. 133-137.

[8]   S.L. Robb, Music assisted progressive muscle relaxation, progressive muscle relaxation, music listening, and silence: A comparison on relaxation techniques. Journal of Music Therapy, (2000), 37(1): p. 2-21.

[9]   D. Villani, F. Riva, and G. Riva, New technologies for relaxation: The role of Presence. International Journal of Stress Management, (2007), 14(3): p. 260-274.

[10] C.D. Spielberger, R.L. Gorsuch, R. Lushene, P.R. Vagg, and G.A. Jacobs, Manual for the State-Trait Anxiety Inventor. 1983, Palo Alto, CA: Consulting Psychology Press.

[11] A. Gift, Visual Analog Scales: Measurement of subjective phenomenon. Nursing Research, (1989), 38(5): p. 286-288.

[12] D. Watson, L.A. Clark, and A. Tellegen, Development and validation of brief measures of positive and negative affect: The PANAS scales. Journal of Personality and Social Psychology, (1988), 54: p. 1063-1070.

[13] J. Lessiter, J. Freeman, E. Keogh, and J. Davidoff, A Cross-Media Presence Questionnaire: The ITC-Sense of Presence Inventory. Presence: Teleoperators, and Virtual Environments, (2001), 10(3): p. 282-297.

[14] U.S. Army, Army Modernization Plan. 2006, Headquarters, Department of the Army: Washington, D.C.

Section IV

Treatment

Lowering Suicide Risk in Returning Troops
B.K. Wiederhold (Ed.)
IOS Press, 2008
© 2008 IOS Press. All rights reserved.
doi:10.3233/978-1-58603-889-2-131

Pharmacotherapy of Suicidal PTSD Patients

Neven HENIGSBERG[1], Zrnka KOVACIC, Petra KALEMBER

*Department of Psychiatry, Croatian Institute for Brain
Research, School of Medicine, University of Zagreb, Šalata 12,
HR-10 000 Zagreb*

Abstract: The rate of co-morbidity is very high in posttraumatic stress disorder (PTSD) especially major depressive disorder and substance abuse. It is not clear if the suicidality in PTSD patients is predominantly caused by core PTSD symptoms or by co-morbid disorders. There is a lack of randomized controlled trials for treatment of suicidality in PTSD. Selective serotonin reuptake inhibitors (SSRIs) are widely used in PTSD treatment, but there is some evidence that they can increase risk of suicidality (self-harm behavior, suicidal thoughts, and suicide attempts) in younger age groups. Benzodiazepines have not been proven effective in the treatment of PTSD core symptoms. Benzodiazepines can even worsen clinical symptoms after acute traumatic experience, and they can induce consequent PTSD and depression, which may lead to increased suicidal risk.

Keywords: suicidality, suicide, self-harm, PTSD, pharmacotherapy, drug efficacy

Introduction

Posttraumatic stress disorder (PTSD) often occurs with different co-morbid psychiatric disorders like major depressive disorder, substance abuse, other anxiety disorders, personality disorders, etc. [1,2]. PTSD is also associated with a high risk of suicidality. The essential, previously unanswered question is as follows: Is the phenomenon of suicidality in PTSD patients related to PTSD per se, or is it related to the co-morbid disorders (especially major depressive disorder, alcoholism, or substance abuse)? The number of randomized controlled trials that primarily analyze suicidality in PTSD is very small. A review of literature adopted from Noyes [3], based on retrospective data from several studies, shows that the suicide rates for the patients with anxiety disorder ranged between 6-60%.

One more concerning fact needs to be mentioned. The new report from the FDA shows that there is an elevated risk for suicidality and suicidal behavior among adults younger then 25 years of age who are taking antidepressants in their therapy. The effect with adults between the age 25 and 64 who are on antidepressants therapy is neutral on

---

[1]Corresponding Author: Neven Henigsberg, Head, Department of Psychopharmacology, Croatian Institute for Brain Research, Medical School, University of Zagreb, Salata 12, HR-10000, Zagreb, Croatia; E-mail: neven.henigsberg@zg.t-com.hr

suicidal behavior and possibly protective for suicidality. In the subjects older then 65, antidepressants reduce the risk of both suicidality and suicidal behavior [4].

1. Meta-analyses of Suicide Risk in the Patients with PTSD and Other Anxiety Disorders

PTSD is an anxiety disorder that has a prevalence rate of around 9% in the general population [5]. Among other anxiety disorders, such as panic disorder, generalized anxiety disorder, obsessive-compulsive disorder, and social phobia, PTSD is known to have a high suicide risk; however, current literature does not display accurate prevalence risks. In the Epidemiological Catchment Area (ECA) survey, Weissman et al. [6] reported that 20 % of patients with panic attacks had a previous history of suicide attempts, while other authors pointed out that other co-morbid disorders increase the risk of suicidality in panic disorder patients [7,8]. Data for the risk of committing or attempting suicide in other anxiety disorders is even lower. For generalized anxiety disorder, there are no reports of considerably increased suicide risk [9]. In social phobia, some authors have reported a high suicide risk for these patients- around 5 % per year [10]- while other authors report that the risk of suicide is high only in patients that suffer from complicated social phobia [11]. Patients with obsessive-compulsive disorder are considered to have a low suicide risk [12]. As mentioned above, there are no epidemiological studies that reported the risk for suicide or suicide attempts in PTSD patients.

Khan et al. [9] reviewed available clinical data for incidence of suicides and suicides attempts in clinical trials submitted to the FDA. The patients were divided into five groups, depending on the diagnosis (panic disorder, social phobia, generalized anxiety disoder, obsessive-compulsive disorder, and PTSD). All of the patients were using different anti-anxiety medications. Authors evaluated the incidence of suicide and suicide attempts based on patient exposure years (PEY), which is the cumulative time that the patient is exposed to the investigational drug, active comparator, or placebo while in a study regimen. It should be emphasized that patients included in that meta-analysis had no or minimal co-morbid symptoms, and the diagnosis was established by using structured clinical interviews. The authors also restudied suicide attempt risk data from previous studies so they could compare the results. The results were unexpected considering the previous studies. It was expected that these patients would have a minimal risk for suicide. They found, however, that the suicide risk was higher in patients with anxiety disorders than in the general population by a factor of ten or more [13].

Patients with PTSD in clinical trails with sertraline had a crude suicide death rate 0.00% (0/757), and the PEY suicide incidence for PTSD was 0.00% (0/149.7). Incidence of suicide attempt had a crude rate of 0.13% (1/757), and the PEY suicide attempt rate was 0.67% (1/149.7). It is important to stress that it is difficult to generalize from clinical trial results because patients who have suicidal ideations are usually excluded from the trial, so the results do not exactly represent the population treated in regular clinical practice.

According to the Cochrane database, which analyzes psychosocial and pharmacological treatments for deliberate self-harm, both antipsychotic flupenthixol and dialectical behavior therapy result in decreased suicide risk when compared with standard after care. In both types of treatment, the number of participants was relatively small. Various pharmacological and psychotherapeutic approaches such as home-based family therapy (vs. standard after care), long-term therapy (vs. short-term therapy), antidepressants (vs. placebo), general hospital admission (vs. discharge), emergency card (vs. standard aftercare), intensive intervention plus outreach (vs. standard aftercare), and problem solving therapy (vs. standard aftercare) were not proven to decrease suicide risk [14].

2. Selective Serotonin Reuptake Inhibitors (SSRIs) in the Treatment of PTSD and Suicidality

Generally, selective serotonin reuptake inhibitors (SSRIs) are effective in the treatment of PTSD patients. However, double-blind placebo randomized controlled clinical trials are needed, considering the fact that most of the clinical trials were open labeled and the results of these studies can not be generalized [15].

Selective serotonin reuptake inhibitors (SSRIs) are drugs that are prescribed worldwide, not only by the psychiatrist but also by other physicians. These drugs are mostly described as safe and very effective in treating various psychiatric conditions [16]. However, recent reports raised some concerns in relation to suicidality. Baldwin et al. [17] showed in an early meta-analysis that SSRIs potentially decreased suicidal ideation as measured by a single question on the Hamilton depression score. A more recent study, which reviewed data from 77 trials submitted to the U.S. Food and Drug Administration (FDA), found a non-significant increase in suicide rates among patients taking SSRIs and those taking placebo or other antidepressants [18].

Fergusson et al. [19], as well as Gunnell et al. [20], performed a systematic review of data from controlled trials of antidepressants in adults. In the first study, they found a double increase in the rate of suicide attempts in the group of patients receiving SSRIs compared with the group of patients on placebo or other interventions. A difference was not seen in the group of patients using tricyclic antidepressants. There was also no difference in completed suicides across groups. The second study found a weak but not statistically significant odds ratio (SSRIs vs. placebo) for self-harm behavior but not a statistically significant influence of drug treatment on suicidal thoughts. Martinez et al. [21] investigated self-harm behavior and suicide in adult and pediatric patients who had depression who were treated with either SSRIs or tricyclic antidepressant (TCAs). They found increased risk of self-harm behavior in patients aged 18 and younger treated with SSRIs in comparison with the patients treated with TCAs.

3. Benzodiazepines in the Treatment of PTSD

As a class, benzodiazepines are among the most widely prescribed medications in PTSD patients.

A study with alprazolam did not show any improvement of PTSD core symptoms, and showed only a reduction of anxiety symptoms [22]. Furthermore, a preventive controlled trial with benzodiazepines in acutely traumatized persons did not show any efficacy [23]. The author found that with patients who received clonazepam or alprazolam during 1-6 months, after 6 months, 69% developed PTSD vs. 15% of patients in control group. Furthermore, depression was recorded in 54% of patients treated with benzodiazepines vs. 0% of persons in control group, similar to a finding by Mellman et al. [24]. They found that benzodiazepines did not protect patients after acute stress from developing PTSD. Due to a large number of PTSD patients who have co-morbid alcohol dependence, there is an increased risk of developing combined dependence with benzodiazepines [25].

Though benzodiazepines are not effective in the treatment of PTSD core symptoms, and are not recommended in the treatment of PTSD due to their dependence side effects [26,27] and the serious withdrawal symptoms that are related to their gradual removal [28], they are still a frequently prescribed treatment.

4. Conclusion

There is a current lack of scientific evidence on effective treatments in suicidal PTSD patients. More specific double-blind, randomized controlled clinical trials are necessary in the indication of PTSD and co-morbid disorders, and especially those with suicidality as the primary parameter of interest. As there are concerns that antidepressant treatment could increase, rather than decrease, suicidal ideation in younger age groups, there is a certain need to initiate larger scale research in order to determine the most effective treatment for younger suicidal patients suffering from PTSD.

5. References

[1]   Kessler RC; Borges G, Walters EE. Prevalence of and risk factors for lifetime suicide attempts in the National Comorbidity Survey. Arch Gen Psychiatry. 1999;56:617-26.
[2]   Kozaric-Kovacic D, Kocijan-Hercigonja D. Assessment of PTSD and comorbidity. Mil Med. 2001;41:78-83.
[3]   Noyes JrR. Suicide and panic disorders: a review. J Affect Dis. 1991;22:1-11.
[4] FDA. Clinical Review. Relationship between antidepressant drugs and suicidality in adults, 2006.
[5]   American Psychiatric Association. Diagnostic and Statistical Manual of Mental Disorders. IVth ed. Washington, DC: American Psychiatric Press; 1994.
[6]   Weissman MM, Klerman GL, Markowitz JS, Ouellette M. Suicidal ideation and suicide attempts in panic disorder and attacks. N Engl J Med. 1989;321:1209-14.
[7]   Friedman S, Jones JC, Chernen L, Barlow DH. Suicidal ideation and suicide attempts among patients with panic disorder: a survey of two outpatients clinics. Am J Psychiatry. 1992;149:680-5.
[8]   Johnson J, Weissman MM, Kerman GL. Panic disorder, comorbidity and suicide attempts. Arch Gen Psychiatry. 1990;47:805-8.
[9]   Khan A, Leventhal RM, Khan S, Brown WA. Suicide risk in patients with anxiety disorders: a meta analysis of the FDA database. J Affect Disord. 2002;68:183-90.
[10] Cox BJ, Direnfeld BA, Swinson MD, Norton GR. Suicidal ideation and suicide attempts in panic disorder and social phobia. Am J Psychiatry. 1994;151:882-7.
[11] Scheiner FR, Johnson J, Hornig CD, Liebowitz MR, Weissman MM. Comorbidity and morbidity in an epidemiologic sample. Arch Gen Psychiatry. 1992;49:282-8.
[12] Coryell W. Obsessive-compulsive disorder and primary unipolar depression. Comparisons of background, family history, course and mortality. J Nerv Ment Dis. 1981;169(4):220-4.
[13] Centre for Disease Control. 2000. CDC WONDERhttp://wonder.cdc.gov/wonder/usr/ananymous.
[14] Hawton K, Townsend E, Arensman E, Gunnell D, Hazell P, House A, et al. Psychosocial and pharmacological treatments for deliberate self harm (Review). Cochrane Database of Systematic Reviews 1999, Issue 4. Art. No:CD001764. DOI: 10.1002/14651858. CD001764.

[15] Crocket BA, Davidson JRT. Pharmacotherapy for posttraumatic stress disorder. In: Stein DJ, Hollander E, (eds.). Textbook of anxiety disorders. Washington DC: American Psychiatric Publishing, Inc.; 2002. pp. 387-402.

[16] Vandrhoff BT, Miller KE. Major depression: assessing the role of new antidepressants. Am Fam Physician. 1997;55; 249-54,259-60.

[17] Baldwin D, Bullock T, Montgomery D, Montgomery S. 5-HT reuptake inhibitors, tricyclic antidepressants and suicidal behaviour. Int Clin Psychopharmacol. 1991;6(suppl3):49-55.

[18] Khan A, Khan S, Kolts R, Brown WA. Suicide rates in clinical trials of SSRIs, other antidepressants, and placebo: analysis of FDA reports. Am J Psychiatry. 2003;160:790-2.

[19] Fergusson D, Doucette S, Cranley Glass K, Shapiro S, Healy D, Hebert P, et al. Association between suicide attempts and selective serotonin reuptake inhibitors: Systematic review of randomised controlled trials. BMJ. 2005;330:396-9.

[20] Gunnell D, Saperia J, Ashby D. Selective serotonin reuptake inhibitors (SSRIs) and suicide in adults: meta-analysis of drug company data from placebo-controlled, randomised controlled trials submitted to the MHRA's saftey review. BMJ. 2005;330;385-8.

[21] Martinez C, Rietbrock S, Wise L, et al. Antidepressant treatment and the risk of fatal and non fatal self harm in first episode depression: nested case controled study. BMJ. 2005;330;389-93.

[22] Braun P, Greenberg D, Dasberg H, Lerer B. Core symptoms of posttraumatic stress disorder unimproved by alprazolam treatment. J Clin Psychiatry. 1990;51:2368.

[23] Gelpin E, Bonne O, Peri T, Brandes D, Shalev AY. Treatment of recent trauma survivors with benzodiazepine: a perspective study. J Clin Psychiatry. 1996;57:390-4.

[24] Mellman TA, Bustamante V, David D, Fris AT. Hypnotic medication in the aftermath of trauma. J Clin Psychiatry. 2002;63:1183-4.

[25] Jacobsen LK, Southwick SM, Kosten TR. Substance use disorders in patients with post-traumatic stress disorder: a review of the literature. Am J Psychiatry. 2001;158:1184-90.

[26] Ballenger JC, Davidson JR, Lecrubier Y, Nutt DJ, Foa EB, Kessler RC et al. Consensus statement on posttraumatic stress disorder from the international consensus group on depression and anxiety. J Clin Psychiatry. 2000;61(5):60-6.

[27] Ballenger JC, Davidson JR, Lecrubier Y, Nutt DJ, Marshall RD, Nemeroff CB et al. sur. Consensus statement update on posttraumatic stress disorder from the international consensus group on depression and anxiety. J Clin Psychiatry. 2004;65(1):55-62.

[28] Risse SC, Whitters A, Burke J, Chen S, Scurfield RM, Raskind MA. Severe withdrawal symptoms after discontinuation of alprazolam in eight patients with combat-induced post-traumatic stress disorder. J Clin Psychiatry. 1990;51:206-9.

Lowering Suicide Risk in Returning Troops
B.K. Wiederhold (Ed.)
IOS Press, 2008
© 2008 IOS Press. All rights reserved.
doi:10.3233/978-1-58603-889-2-136

Wounds of War – Suicide of War-Veterans of Wars Waged on the Territory of Former Yugoslavia

Gordana DEDIC, Milivoje PANIC, Slavisa DJURDJEVIC.
*Department for Mental Health, Clinic of Psychiatry, Military Medical Academy,
Belgrade, Serbia*

Abstract. In the territory of former Yugoslavia, wars were waged within the period of 1991-1995 on the territory of Croatia and Bosnia and Herzegovina, and in 1999 in the territory of Kosovo and Metohia during NATO aggression, which resulted in mental consequences, or wounds of war, in some of the participants. The aim of our study was to describe the wounds of war, suicide of war-veterans, and professional staff, participating in these wars. Our second aim of this study was to suggest some preventive measures that could help in the further application of the Suicide Prevention Program in the modern Army of Serbia. On the basis of the data obtained by psychological autopsy of suicide, selected were 30 professional staff who committed suicide within the period of 1999-2007; 10 of them were war-veterans and 20 were the control group. War-veterans have positive psychiatric heredity, they more intensively practice bodybuilding, more often were punished due to problems at work, while within the scope of the presuicidal syndrome, they manifest isolation more often in comparison with the control group formed of the professional staff who committed suicide in the same period. It is concluded that the further application of the Suicide Prevention Program is focused on four risk factors of suicide in returning troops: the past enviromental factors (taking part in wars), egzogenic (punishments at work), endogenic (genetic) and behavioral (early recognition of the presuicidal syndrome).

KEY WORDS: suicide, war-veterans, military environment, psychological autopsy, prevention program, risk factors

Corresponding Author: professor Dedic Gordana, Department for Mental Health, Clinic of Psychiatry, Military Medical Academy, Belgrade, Serbia; E-mail: sdedic@sezampro.yu

Introduction

War is a social stress which intensifies when survival of the individual as well as of the social groups he or she belongs to is in extreme danger. However, war does not occur as an unexpected, violent and sudden life event, and the human race has developed capabilities for adaptation. On the other hand, considerable parts of society prepare appropriately and for a long time for war and for everything predictable in that situation; often, more often than in peace time, these situations are traumatic. War is a stress of wide range lasting for a relatively long period of time, full of individual and collective stresses and traumas. Danger preceding stress, and uncontrollability with helplessness in stressful situations, cause consequences, some of which can be very serious, such as posttraumatic stress disorder (PTSD).

War is an unusual experience, but when it happens, it happens to a large number of people and it unavoidably requires individuals to respond in an unusual way. In war, there is a discord between the requirements of the environment and individual capacities to solve this discord and overcome it by usual methods of solving problems in order to live as if nothing special happened. If the individual overcomes stress without the development of PTSD, this means the discord did not cause personality structure disorder. PTSD suggests that the individual who experienced trauma could not cope with stress (1,2).

The results of the wars waged on the territory of former Yugoslavia included numerous wounded victims and great damage to both private and state properties. Taking part in war conflicts unavoidably results not only in wounds and disability, but also in numerous psychophysical and psycho-social problems. Unfortunately, aside aggression toward themselves, a part of this population also has a problem of aggression toward their environment, most often upon the members of their families who try to "solve" the problems they are faced with by using violence and even arms.

Some responsibility for the increased number of suicides falls upon the unqualified media, which, not thinking of the consequences, writes about problems related to suicide. Texts are often illustrated with photos of victims and detailed descriptions of the suicide. This treatment of suicide is not useful for anyone, including the victim's family and the observer, in whom the photo most often produces unpleasant feelings.

In December 1999, the Department for Mental Health in the Military Medical Academy, Belgrade began to perform psychological autopsies to collect data on the suicides committed in the Army of Serbia. Our experiences, based on the studies of both epidemiological and risk factors determined during the psychological autopsy within the period of 1999-2003, were implemented in the Suicide Prevention Program in the Army of Serbia in 2003 (3, 4).

The aim of our study was to describe the wounds of war, suicide of war-veterans, professional staff and participants of wars waged on the territory of former Yugoslavia within the period of 1991-1995, during NATO aggression in 1999, as well as during the performance of their professional duties in the Land Security Zone.

Based on all of this, our second aim was to suggest some preventive measures that could help in the further application of the Suicide Prevention Program in the modern Army of Serbia.

1.   Materials and method

1.1. Subjects

Data for this study was obtained from findings of psychological autopsies after suicides of the professional staff (officers, professional soldiers) of the Army of Serbia who committed suicide within the period of 1999-2007. There were 30 cases of suicide from 1-12-1999 to 1-09-2007.

Examinees were divided into two groups. The first was called War-veterans, and it included ten people who had taken part in wars on the territory of former Yugoslavia, in Croatia, Bosnia, Herzegovina, Kosovo, and Metohia, and also during peaceful times in the Land Security Zone. The other control group included the remaining 20 professional military staff (PMS) who had committed suicide in the observed period.

1.2. Psychological autopsy

In 1999, the Department for Mental Health in the Military Medical Academy, Belgrade, began to perform psychological autopsies to collect data on the suicides committed in the Yugoslav Army. Psychological autopsies included professional military staff (officers, professional soldiers, conscripts, civilians, and students of military academies and schools), and regular soldiers in military service. To investigate motives and circumstances of the committed suicides, members of the suicide prevention expert team (a psychiatrist and psychologist) immediately, within the first three days after a suicide, went to the military unit where a suicide had been committed. They collected information from the colleagues, commanders, doctors, and the unit psychologist.

According to the data collected after suicide (a suicide questionnaire, heteroanamnesis data from the colleagues and parents, medical data, psychological data, and official data (personality opinion) given by the commander (opinion of the authorized court)), the psychiatrist and psychologist performed analysis of the suicide and gave a dynamic model of suicidal behavior.

They also performed a psychotherapeutic intervention in the unit for friends of the victim in order to decrease emotional tension within the unit and to clarify any additional moments that could elucidate the suicide. After that, the psychiatrist and psychologist visited the parents and family members of the person who had committed suicide and talked to them. Their goal was to support them through empathy and to help them to recognize their feelings of denial, self-doubt, anger, shame, and guilt.

1.3. Statistical analysis

In regards to descriptive statistical methods, measures of central tendency (arithmetic mean value) and measures of variability (standard deviation) were used. In regards to methods for testing statistical hypotheses, we used t-test. Statistical processing was performed on a PC using: Word, Excel 10 for data base and tables, and "SPSS" statistical software 9.0 (SPSS Inc, Chicago, IL, USA).

2.   Results

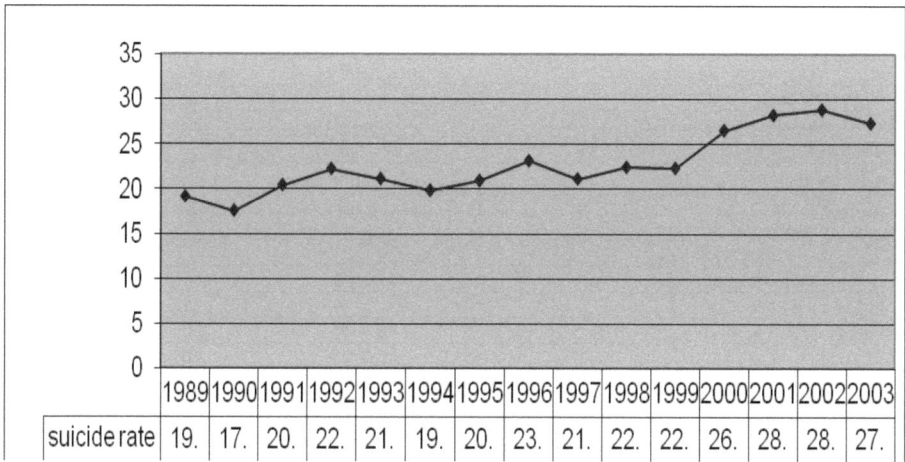

suicide rate	1989	1990	1991	1992	1993	1994	1995	1996	1997	1998	1999	2000	2001	2002	2003
	19.	17.	20.	22.	21.	19.	20.	23.	21.	22.	22.	26.	28.	28.	27.

Figure 1. Suicide rate in the civilian male population in republics of the former Yugoslavia

According to the National Police Agency statistics for the period of 1989-2003, suicide rates in the civilian male population in Republic of Serbia and Republic of Montenegro, republics of the former Yugoslavia, and later in Serbia and Montenegro went from 19.1 per 100,000 subjects in 1989, to 28.8 per 100,000 in 2002. An evident increase after the NATO bombings in 1999 (from 2000 on) can be observed. (Figure 1)

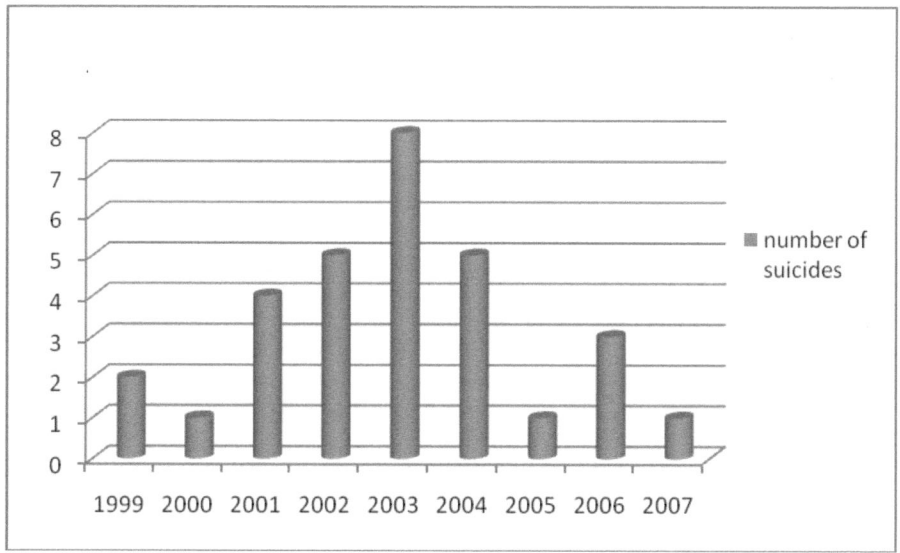

Figure 2. Number of committed suicides of professional staff in the Yugoslav Army / Army of Serbia and Montenegro and Army of Serbia (1999-2007)

Table 1. Sociodemographic data on professional miltary staff who committed suicide (1999-2007)

Variable	War-veterans	Controls	p
	%	%	
Rank			
Non-commissioned officer	80	50	
Officer	10	30	
Soldier under contract	10	20	
Combat actions	40		
Croatia	50	0	
Bosnia	30	0	0.001
Kosovo and Metohia	60	0	0.001
Land Security Zone	50	0	0.001
Completed military school	50	55	0.761
Problems with work	40	15	0.130
Punishment at work	40	20	0.060
Married	60	40	1.000
No children	60	60	0.150
Financial problems	40	10	0.169
Debts	30	10	0.012
Quarrels in marriage	20	30	0.477
Health problems	40	30	0.358
Alcohol consumption	20	25	0.546
Hospital treatment	10	15	0.455
Mental problems	70	25	0.590
Psychiatric heredity	50	20	0.030
Psychiatric treatment	20	10	0.157
Neurosis	60	50	0.385
Introversion	70	60	0.269
Gambling	10	20	0.157
Bodybuilding	30	10	0.012
Method of the suicide			0.724
fire-arm	80	90	
hanging	20	5	
drowning	0	5	
A suicide note	15,8	35	0.584
Presuicidal syndrome	100	65	0.001
Social isolation	20	65	0.074

3.   Discussion

After the war waged on the territory of former Yugoslavia from 1991 to 1995, various social and economic changes occurred. Yugoslavia was divided into six countries. The Yugoslav People's Army was not only renamed the Yugoslav Army in 1992, but it also changed structurally, nationally and fundamentally during the war and the post-war period. The cultural and historic context of those political events also gave rise to many changes in the cultural settings of the country. The Yugoslav Army changed its name again in 2004 to the Army of Serbia and Montenegro. Finally, in May 2006, after Montenegro had been separated, the Army changed its name to the Army of Serbia.

Until 1998, the military environment of the Yugoslav People's Army was characterized by a mean suicide rate of about 16 suicides per 100,000, a rate similar to military environments in many other countries (5-16).

By comparing the suicide rate in the Army of Serbia (former Yugoslav Army) with the rate in the general male population of the former Yugoslavia, that is, Serbia and Montenegro and today's Republic of Serbia, it can be noted that the suicide rate in the military environment is lower than the rate in the general male population (Graphic 1 and Graphic 2). There are several reasons for this, but the most important one is selection of military personnel at conscription (enlistment) and application for military schools (military high school, military academy, one-year specialized training). In this way, the presence of subjects with considerable mental problems is eliminated.

From 1999 to 2007 in the Yugoslav Army/Army of Serbia and Montenegro, 72 suicides were committed, out of which 30 were completed by professional staff.

We would like to stress that the highest number of suicides in the Yugoslav Army (n=36) were committed in 1999, before psychological autopsy was included. In that year, 17 suicides were committed among the conscripts in the army during the NATO bombing from March to June 1999, and that probably increased the total high incidence of the suicides committed by military staff within the aforementioned period.

Figure 2 shows that 1-8 professional staff committed suicide per year. Eight professional staff committed suicide in 2003, and 1 in 2000, with 2005 and 2007 being the highest and the lowest number of committed suicides within the observed eight-year period.

The high number of suicides in 2003 can be explained by previous political events and subsequent transformation of a military unit. Although we could not ignore a very poor financial situation and overburdened professional staff in that period, we found that high risk factors for suicides committed by professional military staff were: age of about 30, rank under lieutenant colonel, and activation to military service after attending public schools or after one-year of military specialized schooling.

Our experience from the Suicide Prevention Program in the Army of Serbia tells us that 3/4 of suicides committed by professional military staff occurred inside the military environment.

Two profiles of professional military staff who committed suicide can be distinguished:

a) Introvert, with poor social contacts, rigid, with high emotional control, with high accepted moral normative, professionally very effective, often in burnout, with silent (latent) depressive symptoms;

b) Extrovert, well adapted, with low level of emotional control, immature with impulsive reactions, inclined to hazardous games (gambling) or some criminative actions, under suspension or threatened with prison (3,4).

The low rate of suicide makes statistical analysis difficult.

On the basis of psychological autopsies of suicide performed since 1-12-1999, and for every suicide case of military personnel, it can be observed that the average age for war-veterans was 29.8± 4.37, and for the control group 30.90±7.08.

Both groups of the professional military staff had the rank of the noncommissioned officer, and only half of them had completed military school. Namely, many of the mobilized reservists, participants in wars on the territory of the former Yugoslavia, were good warriors, so when they were asked to enlist after the war, they accepted.

However, soldiers under contract, without military school and very successful in combat missions often had problems when accomplishing military duties in peace. Some of them were also activated into military service without a health examination. This was the reason for the proposal in the Suicide Prevention Program of the Army of Serbia that all candidates for military service must undergo physical examination.

Problems at work ($p < 0,5$) and punishment due to non-accomplished professional tasks ($p < 0.1$) were significantly more frequent in PMS from the group of war-veterans. War-veterans who experienced the combat zone of former Yugoslavia had difficulties with adaptation to the peace-time work conditions. The new principle of subordination did not fit them because they were subordinate to commanders without combat experience. Poor financial situations, which were the reality of the post-war period, got some of PMS into debt, then into gambling with the "possibility" to pay back out of military funds. Being involved in this way in some criminal activities, they were then found out by the financial control. Consequences of this were reprimands and fines, although none of the PMS from either group lost their job for this reason. This means that these debts were not so great that they could not be paid back by reducing their salaries. But, in a psychological sense, PMS from the group of warriors felt their penalties more as moral than financial ones.

PMS groups of warriors were more often married than those from the control group. In general, regardless of the marital status, PMS of both groups were in equal percentage childless. This finding must be accepted with doubt, because the number of PMS without children includes unmarried PMS of both groups. Problems in marriages, in relationship with their wives are less frequent in war-veterans than in those of the control group ($p < 0,5$). Therefore, we think that interpersonal problems (quarrels, disassociation) between spouses are not such great problems in the soldier's marriage as are financial ones in the family ($p < 0.1$). This situation caused them to go into debt, which, further on, created greater problems both in family and personal functioning in the family ($p < 0.05$).

Half of PMS of the war-veterans group were participants of war on the territory of Croatia, and a third of them were in the combat zone in Bosnia and Herzegovina, but more than a half were in the territory of Kosovo and Metohia during the NATO bombing. Two PMS of the war-veterans group took part in two combat zones in the territory of former Yugoslavia. The PMS of the control group did not take part in wars on the territory of former Yugoslavia, which was the basic criterion of forming groups. Taking part in two or more combat zones is characteristic for older PMS with higher military rank.

Accumulation of stressful events related to activities in the combat zones doubled and tripled in this way. We also emphasize that even today in peace-time, but also in times of struggle for the territory of Kosovo and Metohia, units of the Army of Serbia were engaged in the Land Security Zone (LSZ) bordering the territory of Kosovo and Metohia. Conditions of life and work in LSZ are similar to those in a combat zone. Soldiers of these units are separated from home and family and are exposed to permanent enemy fire for several weeks. This was the reason for including PMS from the LSZ into the group of war-veterans. PMS taking part in the field of operations of former Yugoslavia from 1991 to 1995 are also included in this group. The number of PMS suicides in the Land Security Zone from 2002 to 2007 is identical to the number of PMS suicides in those who took part in wars in the Croatian and Bosnian combat zones of former Yugoslavia within the period of 1991 to 1995. Heteroanamnestic data obtained from family members and friends show that the group of war-veterans is characterized by the presence of evident psychopathological changes in the presuicidal period.

Characteristics of this period include disorders in general everyday functioning, behavior, and alcohol consumption, which could suggest that mechanisms of facing stress before suicide were on average less efficient in comparison with most people. In the observed group of PMS, the most frequent health problems were alcoholism, depression, anxiety disorders, and behavior disorders, while somatic troubles were increased blood pressure, gastric ulcer, and ischialgia. These problems can very often be found in all PMS included in our study and is in accordance with the data from the literature (17,19,20).

Although alcohol is consumed in social situations more often in years before suicide, with occasional incidents of getting drunk and verbal conflicts, probably related to reduced tolerance to anxiety and frustration, occasional alcohol abuse was not the manifestation of more serious psychopathology in examinees from our study, except in one case of PMS from the war-veterans group who needed hospital treatment at the Clinic of Psychiatry of the Military Medical Academy. Alcohol abuse can be treated as an attempt at self-care in order to relieve suffering due to mental disorders, or it could be a symptomatic alcoholism. Alcoholism of the dipsomatic type does not occur independently, isolated from the mentioned disorders, and their common basis is non-efficient mechanisms of facing stress (17).

Gambling, also classified into dependence diseases, was observed in members of the PMS group. Faced with financial problems, some among both PMS groups tried to realize financial profit by gambling in order to get rid of debts. PMS from the control group were more often gamblers (p<0.5).

Mental disorders were noted in both PMS groups, and because of them, some subjects asked for a psychiatrist's help. There were more war-veterans among these people (p<0.5). In the social environment, there was noted neurosis, isolation, and disassociation more often in war-veterans' behavior (p<0.5). Psychiatric heredity is more often present in war-veterans in comparison with the control group (p<0.5).

A special oddity noted in the analysis of PMS' suicide is the practice of bodybuilding in both groups of PMS. However, we would still point out considerable obsession with the body in war-veterans when compared with PMS of the control group, who more often spent their time in the weightlifting room (p<0.05). Obsession with the body and the need to build their bodies with physical training suggests narcissism and a need to maintain the image of a strong and fearless man in their physical attributes.

The largest number of PMS committed suicide by fire-arm, which is typical in all armies of the world (4-16). However, PMS from the control group left a suicide note twice as often.

Presuicidal syndrome was noted in all war-veterans but in only 65% of PMS from the control group, which results in statistically highly significant differences between these two groups (p<001). The most conspicuous symptom and changed behavior noticed by family and friends is isolation, more often in the control group of PMS (p<0.l). By retrograde analysis, pre-suicidal syndrome was noted in all PMS from the group of war-veterans, but unfortunately this was not recognized in time. Findings obtained suggest that PMS from the group of war-veterans had considerable psychic disorders, particularly neurosis, even before occurrence of pre-suicidal syndrome in the period preceding suicide. But these disorders were not very noticeable in comparison with the same period in the control group in whom friends and members of the family noticed changes in their behavior. Unfortunately, all of these changes in behavior were not interpreted as a chance to intervene and/or to refer them for a psychiatric examination in order to prevent a completed suicide.

Criteria for PTSD characterized by symptoms of higher alertness, imposition, and avoidance were not so frequent and intense, which suggests that a serious problem did not occur in personal functioning and manifestations in the form of the clinical presentation of PTSD, nor did a disorder that would be diagnostically manifest with permanent personality disorders after such catastrophic experience (21). Unfortunately, aside from aggression upon themselves, a part of the population with PTSD suffers from the problem of aggression upon their surroundings, most often toward members of their families, because persons with PTSD often try to "solve" the problem they are faced with by using arms and violence.

The evident presence of pre-suicidal syndrome observed in the group of war-veterans, particularly the symptom of isolation, gives hope that by adequate education of the population this factor can be influenced. The ability to recognize early pre-suicidal syndrome is not only precious to military personnel and professionals (physicians and psychologists) for identifying a soldier or professional staff at risk of committing suicide, but is also helpful for further development of the Suicide Prevention Program (22-29).

3.1 Risk factors of suicide in returning troops

Groups of war-veterans differ from controls, firstly by the data on participation in the field of operation (Bosnian, Croatian, LSZ, K and M) as well as by problems at work, primarily punishment at work, present psychiatric heredity, bodybuilding, and manifestation of isolation within the scope of the pre-suicidal syndrome.

On the basis of the results obtained, we can separate four risk factors of suicide in returning troops:

1.　　Past environmental factors (taking part in war)
2.　　Exogenic (punishments at work)
3.　　Endogenic - genetic factors (heredity)
4.　　Behavioral (pre-suicidal syndrome)

1.　Basic risk factors for suicide in PMS were their military engagement in the combat zones during wars waged on the territory of former Yugoslavia from 1991 to 1995. Obtained results show that engagement of PMS in combat missions during the war on the territory of former Yugoslavia influenced development of psychic changes, some of which could be noticed both in family and professional functioning and which, associated with positive psychiatric heredity, influence the final outcome: suicide.

2.　The most important exogenic factor of suicide for PMS is punishment within the scope of professional problems. Punishments at work, however, are related to the problems of financial debt. Objective circumstances related to low incomes of PMS of the Army of Serbia during the last years forced them to "do fine" with additional jobs after regular working hours, but also to try to gain money easily by gambling, which opens new problems related to debt and the like. PMS and war-veterans of the fields of operation experience punishment as a narcissistic trauma, no matter to what degree, they are aware of the severity of breaking the law, which, in the system of influence of both systems of values, the part of personality that cannot accept this prevails, and this creates a risk factor of suicide.

3. The most important endogenic risk factor of suicide in war-veterans is psychiatric heredity to which attention should be paid at selection of candidates for military schools. Presence of mental diseases or suicide in the family is a risk factor of suicide in their professional career.

4. Behavioral manifestations are in the form of high degree of subjective suffering, which considerably influences disordered social and professional functioning. Personality of the PMS who commit suicide is characterized, according to the data from family and friends, by anxious-depressive symptomatology, suggesting serious disorganization of personality as a consequence of intensive emotional distress. Introversion is a typical characteristic of those who commit suicide.

3.2. Suicide Prevention Program in the Army of Serbia

In December 2003, we started to implement the Suicide Prevention Program in the Army of Serbia. The program is based on the USAF (US Air Force) strategy that proved to be effective (15,16). Suicide rates in other military services did not show a sustained decline over the same period. The Suicide Prevention Program is based on the studies of both epidemiological and risk factors determined during the psychological autopsy within the period of 1999-2003. The program also included a comprehensive suicide prevention strategy. A long-term objective of this program was to improve suicide prevention by identifying and modifying military-specific risk factors. The uniqueness of the program was its emphasis on early prevention by reacting to first signs of dysfunction or distress before the risk of suicide is imminent, as well as enhancing detection and treatment of those with an increased danger of committing suicide.

The Suicide Prevention Program was applied in three ways:

1. Selection (military, medical and psychological selection procedures to eliminate soldiers and cadets with serious medical, especially mental, problems).
2. Education (suicidal risk detection).
3. Motivation (social concern and mental health work with all employees in the Army of Serbia and with some of their family members).

We could say that the Suicide Prevention Program emphasized importance of the three preventive measures, namely, the rigorous psychological selection of professional staff for a specific military duty, education of officers and soldiers for better recognition and understanding of pre-suicidal syndrome and motivation for military duty. Within this program, there were many specific measures for suicide prevention, one of which was prevention of mobile phone usage during guard duty or the rule not to send to the guard soldiers under contract immediately after their coming back from holidays (3,4).

3.3. SOS telephone in military environment

From the middle of August, the Army of Serbia installed a special telephone line for persons in acute life crisis. The so-called SOS telephone enabled every member of the Army of Serbia to ask, if in crisis, for professional psychiatric or psychological help.

Psychological intervention by a psychiatrist or psychologist is done by phone, from talking to the person in crisis through the experience of containing the patient's sufferings, which the therapist analyzes and returns to the patient by way of rendering his understanding. Attention focused on the problem should help the patient to establish the capacity for thinking about the traumatic event and its meaning. Containing is hard work that includes reorganization of the real traumatic experience with all associated emotions, and complete guilt, fear, and hatred are released from the real event through the transfer with the therapist (30-36).

3.4. Further investigation plan

We plan to continue our investigation of suicide risk factors in the period of 2007-2010. Suggestions for further studies were made in order to improve the Suicide Prevention Program to identify eventual new risk factors of suicide in the military environment and to further apply the intervention program for reducing suicide rates.

The specific social status of the military staff in our country is even more emphasized by the fact that the Army of Serbia will be joining the Partnership for Peace. However, we hope to continue further investigation of suicide in the military environment, regarding both soldiers and officers, and to explore new risk factors of suicide as a means of preventing suicides.

The Suicide Prevention Program should focus on providing more knowledge about depression and detection of pre-suicidal syndrome and on making officers aware of their importance in the lives of their friends, their families, and themselves, particularly in times of despair and hopelessness.

We plan to further educate members of the military unit and their families through delivering lectures and organizing a program for continual education of physicians together with the military units in order to improve their knowledge of depression and pre-suicidal syndrome. We have also realized the application of an educational program for the military psychologists to improve their knowledge of depression and of intervention in crisis. Implementation of the Suicide Prevention Program within the regular curriculum of the Military Academy is also planned.

4.   Conclusion

War waged on the territory of former Yugoslavia had effects upon various changes in the social behavior of the individual. Unable to realize normal communication with their environment, a large number of persons with mental disorders including PTSD have problems in communication with the members of their families, friends or colleagues, which may cause other complications, including suicide, because they feel socially stigmatized and abandoned.

References

1. Koren D, Norman D, Cohen A, Berman J, Klein EM. Increased PTSD risk with combat-related injury: a matched comparison study of injured and uninjured soldiers experiencing the same combat events. Am J Psychiatry. 2005;162(2):276-82
2. Pereira A. Combat trauma and diagnosis of Posttraumatic stress disorder in female and male veterans. Mil Med 2002; 167(1): 23-27.
3. Dedic G. Panic M. Suicide prevention program in the Army of Serbia and Montenegro. Mil Med. 2007 May;172(5):551-5.
4. Dedic G. Milinkovic-Fajgelj O, Kolundzic D, Zivic B. Suicide prevention program in the Army of Serbia and Montenegro. Beograd: Vojnoizdavacki zavod; 2003 (Serbian)
5. Cabarkapa M, Panic M. Suicide in the military environment. Vojnosanit Pregl. 2004; 61(2):199-203. (Serbian)
6. Mancinelli I, Lazanio S, Comparelli A, Ceciarelli L, Di Marzo S, Pompili M, Girardi P, Tatarelli R. Suicide in the Italian military environment (1986-1998). Mil Med 2003; 168(2):146-52.
7. Stander VA, Hilton SM, Kennedy KR, Robbins DL. Surveillance of completed suicide in the Department of the Navy Mil Med. 2004;169(4):301-6.
8. Ritchie EC, Keppler WC, Rothberg JM. Suicidal admissions in the United States military. Mil Med. 2003;168(3):177-81.
9. Macfarlane GJ, Thomas E, Cherry N. Mortality among UK Gulf War veterans. Lancet. 2000 Jul 1;356(9223):17-21.
10. Rozanov VA, Mokhovikov AN, Stiliha R. Successful model of suicide prevention in the Ukraine military environment. Crisis. 2002;23(4):171-7.
11. Mollica R. Survivng torture. The New England Journal of Medicine 2004;351:5-7
12. Kaleveld L, English B. Evaluating a suicide prevention program: a question of impact. Health Promot J Austr. 2005;16(2):129-33.
13. Ramberg IL, Wasserman D. Suicide-preventive activities in psychiatric care: evaluation of an educational programme in suicide prevention. Nord J Psychiatry. 2004;58(5):389-94.
14. Hakanen J, Upanne M. Evaluation strategy for Finland's suicide prevention project. Crisis. 1996;17(4):167-74.
15. Knox K, Litts D, Talcott W, Feig C, Caine E, D Caine E, Romano J. Risk of suicide and related adverse outcomes after exposure to a suicide prevention programme in the US Air Force: cohort study. BMJ. 2003; 327 (7428): 1376
16. Staal A. The assessment and prevention of suicide for the 21st century: the Air Force's community awareness training model. MA. Mil Med. 2001;166(3):195-8.
17. Jacobsen L, Southwick S, Kosten T. Substance use disorders in patients with posttraumatic stress disorder: a rewie of the literature. Am J Psychiatry 2001;158:1184-1190
18. Dijanić Plasć I, Peraica T, Grubisić-Ilić M, Rak D, Jambrosić Sakoman A, Kozarić-Kovacić D. Psychiatric heredity and posttraumatic stress disorder: survey study of war veterans. Croat Med J. 2007 Apr;48(2):146-56.
19. Trlaja Ij, Kostić P, Dedić G. PTSD in war-wounded. Psihologija.1997;30(4): 425-436.
20. Hoge CW, Terhakopian A, Castro CA, Messer SC, Engel CC. Association of posttraumatic stress disorder with somatic symptoms, health care visits, and absenteeism among Iraq war veterans. Am J Psychiatry. 2007 Jan;164(1):150-3.
21. Hermansson AC, Timpka T, Thyberg M. The mental health of war-wounded refugees: an 8-year follow-up. J Nerv Ment Dis. 2002;190(6):374-80
22. Jurisic B, Marusic A. Self-concept, post-traumatic stress disorder symptoms and suicide ideation and behaviour in permanently physically disabled after a motor vehicle accident. Psychiatr Danub. 2006 Sep;18 Suppl 1:37.

23. Florkowski A, Gruszczynski W, Wawrzyniak Z. Evaluation of psychopathological factors and origins of suicides committed by soldiers, 1989 to 1998. Mil Med. 2001;166(1):44-7.
24. Giotakos O. Suicidal ideation, substance use, and sense of coherence in Greek male conscripts. Mil Med 2003;168(6):447-50.
25. Hansen-Schwartz J, Jessen G, Andersen K, Jorgensen HO. Suicide after deployment in UN peacekeeping missions--a Danish pilot study. Crisis 2002;23(2):55-8.
26. Hendin H, Haas AP. Am J Psychiatry. 1991 May;148(5):586-91 Suicide and guilt as manifestations of PTSD in Vietnam combat veterans.
27. Hyer L, McCranie EW, Woods MG, Boudewyns PA. Suicidal behavior among chronic Vietnam theatre veterans with PTSD. J Clin Psychol. 1990 Nov;46(6):713-21.
28. Kramer TL, Lindy JD, Green BL, Grace MC, Leonard AC. The comorbidity of post-traumatic stress disorder and suicidality in Vietnam veterans. Suicide Life Threat Behav. 1994 Spring;24(1):58-67.
29. Ritchie EC, Benedek D, Malone R, Carr-Malone R.Psychiatry and the military: an update. Psychiatr Clin North Am. 2006 Sep;29(3):695-707
30. Britvic D, Radelic N, Urlic I. Long-term dynamic-oriented group psychotherapy of posttraumatic stress disorder in war veterans: prospective study of five-year treatment. Croat Med J. 2006;47(1):76-84
31. Forbes D, Creamer MC, Phelps AJ, Couineau AL, Cooper JA, Bryant RA, McFarlane AC, Devilly GJ, Matthews LR, Raphael B. Treating adults with acute stress disorder and post-traumatic stress disorder in general practice: a clinical update. Med J Aust. 2007 Jul 16;187(2):120-3.
32. Kozaric-Kovacic D, Kocijan-Hercigonja D, Jambrosic A. Psychiatric help to psychotraumatized persons during and after war in Croatia. Croat Med J. 2002;43(2):221-8
33. Mohta M, Sethi AK, Tyagi A, Mohta A. Psychological care in trauma patients. Injury. 2003;34(1):17-25
34. McFall M, Malte C, Fontana A et al. Effects of an outreach intervention on use of mental health services by veterans with posttraumatic stress disorder. Psychiatr Serv 2000;51(3):369-74.
35. Klain E, Pavic L. Countertransference and empathic problems in therapists/helpers working with psychotraumatized persons. Croat Med J. 1999;40(4):466-72
36. Gregurek R, Pavic L, Vuger-Kovacic H, Potrebica S, Bitar Z, Kovacic D, Danic S, Klain E. Increase of frequency of post-traumatic stress disorder in disabled war veterans during prolonged stay in a rehabilitation hospital. Croat Med J. 2001;42(2):161-4.

Lowering Suicide Risk in Returning Troops
B.K. Wiederhold (Ed.)
IOS Press, 2008
© *2008 IOS Press. All rights reserved.*
doi:10.3233/978-1-58603-889-2-149

Suicide of a Service Member: How to Organize Support for the Bereaved Service Members in the Emotional Aftermath

Senior Captain John DEHEEGHER[1]
Clinical psychologist in the Centre for Mental Health (CMH)[2] in the Military Hospital of the Medical Component of Belgian Defence (Neder-Over-Heembeek, Brussels).

Introduction

Between 2001 and 2005, 66 members of Belgian Defence committed suicide. When a service member commits suicide, it not only affects his/her relatives and friends, but also affects the fellow service members of the unit. The Centre for Mental Health (CMH of the Military Hospital Queen Astrid, Brussels) of the Belgian Armed Forces has developed a structured crisis intervention program to help the military unit to better cope with the suicide of one of its members. The objective is preventive: enhancing support for the grief process of the bereaved colleagues and detecting those colleagues at risk for the development of psycho-social difficulties. The different aspects of the 'postvention trajectory of care' will be studied in this paper. First, we will go over the incidence of suicide in Belgian Defence. Next we will analyze the particular characteristics of bereavement after suicide in association with the needs of the victims. Further, the objectives and main components of the 'postvention trajectory of care' are explored. The structure of the psychosocial aid is explained, illustrated with several concise case illustrations. Attention is given to the pre-incident preventive actions, post-incident early psychological support for victims, as well as psychotherapeutic after care. The supportive advice for the key personnel in command of the unit is also reviewed. This paper aims at presenting a synthetic survey of the application of the concept of postvention by the Centre for Mental Health of the Medical Component of Belgian Defence.

---

1 John Deheegher , Clinical Psychologist - Senior Captain, Centre for Mental Health ,
Queen Astrid Military Hospital, Bruynstreet 1 B-1120 Neder-Over-Heembeek (Brussels) Belgium;
Telephone : 00 32 (0)2 / 264 44 53; e-mail : john.deheegher@mil.be

2 The CMH comprises a Service for Individual Assistance (SIA), a Service for Crisis Psychology (CCP) and a Service for Military Alcohology (CMilA). The activities of the three services are integrated in the different 'care trajectories' of the Centre for Mental Health. The author works in the domains of crisis psychology (CCP) and psychotherapy (SIA) in the Centre for Mental Health.[0]

1. The incidence of suicide in the Belgian Armed Forces

The World Health Organisation [1] identifies suicide as one of the three main causes of mortality worldwide. For young and middle-aged men in Europe, suicide is a leading cause of death. The statistics of suicide rates in Belgium of the World Health Organisation indicate that per 100.000 Belgian citizens, every year between 23 and 31 men or women between the ages of 25 and 54 commit suicide. This alarming rate has lead to the development of a regional action plan by the Flanders regional minister of wellness and public health, aimed at reducing the suicide mortality.

Belgian Defence makes a—sometimes irregular—registration of deaths by suicide. A parliamentary report [2] makes a provisional presentation of the statistics of suicide by military service members.

1.1. Global numbers of suicide mortality:

Belgian Defence employs approximately 40,000 service members. Between 2001 and 2005, 66 service members committed suicide. In the first half of 2003, a higher number of service members committed suicide without apparent causal relationship. The distribution of suicide in Belgian Defence by age groups and gender is less than the national statistics of civilian suicide rates in Belgium. Male service members between the age of 25 and 44 are especially at risk of committing suicide. Only 16 suicide attempts have officially been registered in Belgian Defence. Clinical practice in the Centre for Mental Health and the observations of suicide attempts by the WHO indicate however that attempts presumably are a multitude of registered suicides.

1.2. Particular rates of suicide

1.2.1. Distribution by Gender:

62 men and 4 women

1.2.2. Distribution by Age:

- Under 25: 5 suicides
- 25-34: 21 suicides
- 35-44: 44 suicides
- Older than 45: 12 suicides

1.2.3. Distribution by rank:

- 1st Corporal or Sr Corporal: 25
- Non Commissioned Officer (Sr Adjudant, 1st Sergeant-Major or Adjudant): 13

1.2.4. Distribution by Component:

- Land Component: 45
- Air Component: 23
- Naval Component: 8
- Medical Component: 3

1.2.5. Distribution by method of suicide:

- hanging: 20
- weapons: 12
- intoxication: 10
- The method of suicide was registered in only 42 cases

2. Grief after the suicide of a colleague: a particular bereavement

The loss of a significant person always entails emotional, cognitive, behavioral and physiological reactions of the persons close to the deceased. Suicide causes bereavement reactions that can be placed on a continuum which ranges from a general preoccupation with the sad memory of the deceased to overwhelming emotional and cognitive confusion and physical distress. This seems to indicate a grieving process similar to the bereavement reactions after natural death. A review of literature on suicide bereavement versus normal bereavement [3] however, shows that suicide entails bereavement that is weighed down by a specific dynamic.

2.1. Guilt feelings and feelings of blame

Not having been able to help a colleague in an emotionally problematic situation before suicide frequently creates feelings of guilt. Bereaved service members often feel guilty of ultimately not having been able to prevent the act of suicide. This can lead to self-blame and the fear (or perception) of blame in the social environment. Anecdotal information shows that bereaved service members are frequently preoccupied with the thought: "why didn't I see it coming, why didn't I listen to my colleague when I noticed that he was silent and isolated before the suicide?" The search for reasons or meaning in the act of suicide can be predominantly present in the colleagues. This can result in a feeling of failure, guilt feelings, and a fear of blame by the family or the military community.

Moreover, anecdotal observations show that bereavement is even more complicated in those cases where objective problematic factors in the work environment possibly contributed to the psychological or emotional pressure on the deceased. The global social support mostly crumbles. The military community often struggles to suppress emotions of guilt, anger and rejection. Often, emotional splitting divides the unit into an accused group and a victim group. Talking about bereavement after the suicide mostly brings latent anger to the surface. Open dialogue—important in the grief process—is therefore shunned as much as possible. Reconnaissance of the emotional aftermath of the suicide in these cases is often lacking in the commanding and key personnel of the unit.

An illustration:

A member of the Belgian military unit was under suspicion of having stolen petrol. The day after the interrogation, he committed suicide. His colleagues interpreted the suicide as a direct consequence of an overly severe interrogation. A deep split divided the unit. The general atmosphere was laden with repressed anger. The mourning in the unit was stifled.

2.2. Fear of social stigma and negative labeling

A suicide sets going a particular grief process. The bereaved service member can find himself burdened with the (perception of) ambivalent social appreciation of a death by suicide [3]. The (perception of) social stigma can lead to the avoidance of openly speaking about the heavy emotions of guilt, shame, anger or sadness.

The (perception of) negative attribution by society can undermine the necessary social support. The fear of social stigma can lead to the suppression of emotions associated with the deceased. The military 'stiff upper lip' culture can add to this malignant emotional coping behavior. The lack of emotional openness in bereaved colleagues can increase the risk of emotional isolation. The grieving colleagues bear the consequences of this lack of emotional openness: their psychological well-being is at risk. This fear of social stigma can moreover reinforce the reticence to seek help when assistance is required. Looking for psychological or psychiatric help is often avoided. Fear of being labeled as 'mad' can increase the threshold of seeking help.

The Flemish population of Belgium seems particularly reticent to talk about emotions [4]. Depressive feelings, feelings of helplessness, feelings of guilt or fear of negative public perception are not talked about openly. In addition to bereavement, a feeling of anger towards the deceased or a feeling of rejection by the deceased can also exist. These feelings are mostly perceived as taboo. Anecdotal evidence reveals that the fear of being labeled as weak is often present. This fear is omnipresent in a predominantly male military organization. The fantasy of male invulnerability is a leading principle in Defence, still a male bastion.

Bereavement after the suicide of a service member has a profound emotional impact on the colleagues. In comparison to the grief after natural death, the mourning after suicide can be weighed down by a feeling of guilt or blame, social stigma and shame, and finally the fear of negative labeling. Talking about the deceased can die down. This emotional muteness can delay the mourning. The supplementary pressure on the grief process justifies a proactive approach in the provision of assistance to help the stricken unit.

2.3. The service member's need for help

The number of bereaved after suicide should not be underestimated. It is not only the victim's family concerned. When a service member commits suicide, it also affects the fellow service members of the unit. His/her colleagues also go through the bereavement process. Research by Knieper [5] shows that each suicide deeply touches between 6 and 28 people. Applied to the military organization where 'everybody knows everybody' in and also outside the affected unit, this implies that the group of bereaved colleagues can be quite large in size.

The grieving process can be heavily influenced by the work environment. Social support can be conducive to working through the grief. At the same time, however, a (perceived) negative influence of the work environment can burden this process. Anecdotal observations show that clients in need of assistance nonetheless try to carry on alone. They sometimes suppress their emotions, recoil from seeking help with the appropriate psychosocial aid providers, and as a consequence find themselves confronted with the psychological turmoil of stagnated grief. Aid providers should therefore make allowance for the negative influences of the work environment and the possible harmful emotional coping strategies of a service member after the suicide of a colleague. They should distance themselves from a passive attitude—waiting for the client to come to the assistance organization for help—and adopt a proactive approach for the bereaved service members. Aid providers should actively involve themselves in the community. This enables them to enhance a positive recovery environment and decrease the threshold erected by fear of social stigma and apprehension of emotional openness.

The assistance should be standardized (i.e. the same structured approach for all victims in every incident) and multidisciplinary, to be able to answer the broad range of psychological complaints expressed by clients. This is the crux of the concept of 'postvention trajectory of care' that has been developed at the Centre for Mental Health (CMH) of the Military Hospital Queen Astrid of Belgian Defence.

The CMH works with psychiatrists, psychologists, psychiatric nurses and a social worker. The CMH is an umbrella organization which consists of three complementary services: the Service for Individual Aid (SIA), the Centre for Crisispsychology (CCP), and the Centre for Military Alcohology (CMilA). The integrated procedure in the case of psychosocial strategy of care after suicide necessitates an intense cooperation with the different psychosocial aid organizations of Belgian Defence, namely: the CMH, The Counsellors on Mental Operationality ('first line' psychologists who frequently pay visits to the units), the Social Services of Belgian Defence, and the Religious and Spiritual Service.

3. A structured postvention program: the 'postvention trajectory of care'

3.1. Objectives of the 'postvention trajectory of care'

- Pre-incident sensitization and education of key personnel on how to handle crisis situations in their unit.
- Advising the commanding officers and NCO's of the unit on how to cope with the grief after a suicide in the unit, how to enhance the grief process of the members of the unit and how to prevent secondary victimization (social stigma, rumors, etc.).
- Monitoring the psychological well-being in the unit after a suicide at different points in time.
- Crisis Intervention in the unit if individual service members or groups of colleagues are in need of 'on-scene' psychological assistance.
- Identification and referral of those service members in need of further psychotherapeutic aid.

The psychological aid of service members 'at risk' for psychological problems can help them cope with possible suicidal thoughts and in this way prevent suicidal 'acting out'.

The main objective of the 'postvention trajectory of care' is *preventive*. By means of the pre-incident education of key personnel, the post-incident advisory function for key personnel, the possible psychological crisis intervention for individual colleagues or groups of bereaved service members; and the referral and psychotherapeutic counseling for personnel 'at risk' of developing psychological difficulties, we try to decrease the number of service members who suffer psychosocially and limit the duration of psychological impairment after a suicide (e.g. pathological grief, posttraumatic symptoms, latent depressive symptoms with suicidal ideation, manifest depressive disorder etc.). To reach this objective, the chronology of postvention activities starts long before a suicide incident takes place and can cover a long period after the suicide of a service member. An 'on scene' psychological crisis intervention is punctual, not always indicated and only one of the instruments in the broad array of postvention activities over quite a long period.

3.2. Main Components of psychosocial aid after suicide

3.2.1. Pre-incident education

The CCP provides different modules of education for key personnel of Defence. These varied modules of education are aimed at education for the psychological impact of 'critical incidents' (with emphasis on bereavement after suicide in the work environment) and development of coping skills in the domain of victimology, psychotrauma and the management of psychosocial aid. These varied educational modules are based on the concept of 'Critical Incident Stress Management' developed by Mitchell & Everly [6] and the procedure of psychosocial aid as developed in the Canadian emergency plans [7].

3.2.2. Post-incident procedure of psychosocial care

   a) Proactive outreach after notification

The CCP is almost always informed about the occurrence of a suicide on the same day or the day after the incident by means of the 'serious event' message, distributed by the Operations Centre of the Belgian Defence Staff. This message contains basic information on the incident and the deceased. Our service contacts the commanding officer of the unit concerned as soon as possible. Sometimes the stricken unit contacts the CCP itself with a demand for assistance. In both cases, we inquire about the impact of the suicide in the unit and the need for psychosocial assistance. An immediate 'on scene' crisis intervention is not standard. Early 'on scene' interventions should not be intrusive but needed and accepted by the unit. In any case, the notification sets into motion a structured procedure for the management of psychosocial assistance (cfr 4.4).

   b) Analysis of the circumstances of the event and of the victim groups

The gist of the procedure is the collection of the relevant information necessary to make an analysis of the circumstances of the suicide and the composition of the victim groups. The analysis enables us to evaluate the psychological impact of the suicide on the service members of the unit. Based on the analysis of the psychological impact of the incident, the victim group is divided into:

   – Primary victims: those affected through their direct involvement, (e.g. witnesses of the act of suicide)

The primary victims are confronted with the potentially traumatogenic factors of the suicide. They may have been witnesses of the act of suicide, they may have been the first to come upon the victim and may even have provided first medical care or started resuscitation.

An illustration:

In an incident of suicide in a public place in the barracks, the victim's body was undressed in the course of the police investigation. During several hours, the colleagues were confronted with the undressed and uncovered remains of their deceased colleague. This disrespectful handling of the body by the police gave way to an intense anger in the service members of the unit.

The potentially traumatic factors described in criterion A of the diagnosis Post Traumatic Stress Disorder [8] can be applied to a service member (primary victim) confronted with a suicide event, namely:

The person concerned was confronted with one or more incidents which involved (threatening) death, a serious injury or a threat to the physical integrity of a fellow service member. The person concerned experienced reactions of intense anxiety, helplessness or horror.

Mitchell & Everly describe potentially traumatic Critical Incidents as "sudden, powerful events which are outside of the range of ordinary human experiences…they can have a strong emotional effect…have a stressful impact sufficient enough to overwhelm the usually effective coping skills of either an individual or a group." [6].

The Critical Incident can become traumatic and lead to latent or manifest post-traumatic suffering described in the criteria B, C and D of the diagnosis Posttraumatic Stress Disorder in the DSM IV. Different factors may contribute to the development of posttraumatic complaints after a Critical Incident. In a meta-analysis of risk factors for development of PTSD after trauma, Brewin et al. [9] concluded that factors such as education, previous trauma and childhood adversity predicted PTSD to a varying extent. Factors such as psychiatric history, reported childhood abuse and family psychiatric history had a modest but uniform predictive effect. But factors in the context of the trauma, such as trauma severity, lack of social support and additional life stress were more consistently predictive of PTSD. *These risk factors in the context of the trauma contribute to the vulnerability of some of the victims, which explains the need for the psychosocial care of the organization for its personnel after a suicide incident.*

The structured procedure for psychosocial aid can provide more information on the potentially traumatic risk factors in the context of the suicide. At the start of the procedure of psychosocial aid, the CCP of the CMH gathers the necessary information to make this 'risk factor' analysis and elaborate an intervention strategy. The objective is to help the key personnel of the unit in managing the suicide incident so that the circumstances are conducive for the process of mourning of the colleagues to run its course.

- Secondary victims: those emotionally involved with the deceased (e.g.: partner, children, service members who had a personal tie…)

Assistance is offered to the family and non-military significant others by the Social Services of Defence. When the suicide takes place at home and Defence is not directly involved in the circumstances of the suicide, the assistance of the family is often provided by the civilian 'victim aid' agency of the community. The military secondary victims may also experience and express a need for psychosocial assistance because of an emotional suffering. Range describes four main emotional experiences in bereavement after suicide: blame, stigma, a search for meaning, and the feeling of being misunderstood by the social environment [10].

An illustration:

In a team of guard personnel, a member unexpectedly committed suicide. They described him as always smiling, always ready with a joke. He left no sign whatsoever concerning the reasons for this act. There was no suicide letter. The contacts with his family were to no avail. His colleagues were taken aback and were left ignorant on the possible causes of the suicide.

Coping with suicide mourning is a difficult emotional experience. There may be supplementary negative effects, e.g.: crumbling social support and difficulty sharing feelings because of avoidance or denial of the cause of death; social support may even be avoided because of negative experiences ("After a suicide, others often say the wrong things.") [10]. The suicide may even cause manifest suicidal thoughts out of a latent depression (important to inquire about possible psychiatric vulnerability of the different victims). The emotional burden is severe especially in cases of violent suicide (weapons, hanging, and suicide by fire).

It is not only the (negative or positive) societal influence that affects the evolution of the grief process. Individual factors also play an important role. Mikulincer and Florian [11] concluded that people with an anxious-ambivalent attachment style reacted to real-life stressful situations with hypervigilance and brooding on the source of stress. Their need for social support and psychosocial assistance is often prominent. People with an avoidant attachment style used more distancing coping and less support seeking. They distance themselves from the social support in the work environment and their need for psychosocial aid can be avoiding or ambivalent. *The assessment of the victims (psychiatric history, previous trauma, coping style, etc.) and the information on the circumstances of the suicide can contribute to the identification of risk factors for individuals or groups of victims. The intervention strategy can next be adapted to this analysis.*

- Tertiary victims: personnel in coordinating and management functions, professional helpers (e.g.: Commanding Officer, Human Resources Officer, Platoon and Company Commanders, Regimental Sergeant-Major, Company Sergeant-Major, medical first aid providers, military police, psychosocial aid providers, etc.)

The functions of the tertiary victims are essential to keep things going in the unit in a time of crisis. The duties inherent in their functions essentially require task-oriented coping. They go through the same emotional experiences as the secondary victims, however. The organization of the funeral, the contacts with the family of the deceased, the continuing 'business as usual' of a military unit (e.g.: exercises, etc.) compel them—often unnoticed—to constrain the expression of their emotional experiences. This can eventually result in physical and emotional exhaustion in the weeks after the funeral. In the first weeks after the suicide, the pressure on the tertiary victims should not be underestimated. Their psychosocial well-being should be (informally) monitored on a regular basis.

c) Deliberation with and psychosocial advice for the commanding and key personnel

The hierarchy and key personnel (different ranks) of the unit have an important influence in shaping the interpersonal environment of the unit. A good, concerned interpersonal atmosphere in the unit is an important condition for the mourning process. A plan is made concerning the psychosocial assistance which will be provided for the unit. Considering their essential influence, the CCP of the CMH also advises the commanding and key personnel on coping with this critical incident. A brochure is distributed to the commanding and key personnel aimed at increasing their coping capacities in the management of the suicide. The brochure treats different subjects and explains:

– They can enhance an empathic attitude, stimulate social support and stress the importance of dialogue (active listening instead of taboo: avoiding conversation in relation to the deceased or the act of suicide). Blaming or tainting comments should at all cost be avoided. They should explicitly express their concern, sympathy and willingness to help their personnel. The responsibles of the unit should express their *recognition* of the primary, secondary and tertiairy victims for the strains they undergo in this emotionally demanding period.
– They should *prevent secondary traumatization*: avoid a supplementary direct confrontation of the victims with the circumstances of the suicide (shock of witnessing death) and avoid the victims enduring the overwhelming feelings of powerlessness, horror and anxiety.

An illustration:

Some years ago, a service member committed suicide with his pistol while on guard duty. Other personnel on guard received the order to clean up the gruesome consequences in the guard room after the police had finished their work. This order added to the overwhelming emotions of powerlessness, fear, horror and guilt the colleagues 'on guard' tried to cope with.

– They should implement the *principles of crisis communication*. The correct management of information can prevent or dispel rumors which thrive in times of unanswerable questions (question of blame and question of meaning of the suicide). There should be an open and honest communication on behalf of the hierarchy. The personnel should be aware that its leaders are taking the management of the crisis in hand. Crisis communication should be clear, trustworthy, transparent, quick, reliable, adapted to the public in view, coherent and proactive. Covering up information has to be avoided; it will otherwise inevitably result in rumors. The source of information should be centralized. The existence of a lack of correct information can also be communicated. Protect the victims from intrusive media. Keep the initiatives in their own hands concerning media information.

d) How to support the mourning process of the victims

To be able to address the broad array of possible psychosocial and religious needs of the victims, the *cooperation between the different aid services* is indispensable. In the 'postvention trajectory of care' the Centre for Mental Health, the Counsellors on Mental Operationality ('first line' psychologists who regularly pay visits to the different units of Belgian Defence), the Social Services of Belgian Defence and the Religious and Spiritual Service collaborate.

As soon as possible after the notification of the suicide and the deliberation with the hierarchy and the key personnel of the unit, a *brochure on suicide* is distributed to the personnel of the unit. The objective of the brochure is to suggest good coping techniques to work through the bereavement and to indicate maladaptive coping techniques to avoid. Also the names and coordinates of 'persons of contact' of the CMH are mentioned. This could lower the threshold for seeking help by the service members concerned.

Early 'on scene' psychological intervention is not standard. The 'Best practices consensus' by the workshop 'Mental Health and Mass Violence' points at ambivalent results of "single one on one recitals of events and emotions" [12]. Group discussions are only organized in the context of a severe risk of stagnation of the working-through process (e.g.: suppressed emotions because of objective guilt issues in the unit, when the suicide was violent and shocked colleagues, when secondary victimization is present, when internal conflicts split the unit, etc.). Usually the unit offers a supportive environment and adequate containment for the bereavement of its members. In spite of the severe and painful emotions of the victims, their coping is usually sufficient to make the mourning process possible. Early intervention is not a magic wand which makes painful emotions go away. If early psychological intervention is provided 'on scene' its aim is to support the victim's containment of overwhelming emotions.

An 'on scene' crisis intervention should be a manifest need of the victims, mostly expressed via the hierarchy of the unit. Psychological crisis intervention will only be provided when participation is voluntary and applied in a manner accepted by the victims. Early psychological intervention should only be applied when the basic needs of the victims (e.g.: safe environment, correct information, reconnaissance, rituals) have been answered. The term 'debriefing' is no longer used for psychosocial early interventions. The technique of 'psychological autopsy' is used in the Defence Forces of different countries and is useful to support the victims in their 'search for meaning' [13]. The use of the 'psychological autopsy' technique is still under consideration and has not yet been applied in the 'trajectory of care' in Belgian Defence.

The *funeral service* is an essential event in the grief process. It allows the bereaved service members to render their last respects to the deceased, give support to the family and comfort each other. The funeral is a final moment of separation which ends a period of disbelief and begins the return to reality. The participation in the funeral service should be made possible for all service members emotionally close to the deceased. If the family agrees to a funeral with 'military honors', the unit of the deceased will be involved officially in this ritual separation.

An illustration:

On the eve of a large military maneuver during three weeks, at great distance in Germany, a member of a participating unit committed suicide by fire. The emotional shock for most colleagues was significant. After deliberation with the representatives of the CMH – participating in the exercise, in the role 2 Field Hospital – the commanding officer gave the permission to temporarily leave the exercise for the personnel who wished to attend the funeral. This was appreciated by his personnel and contributed to the working-through of the mourning for their beloved colleague after his violent suicide. Several emotionally close colleagues consulted our operational module of the Role 2 Field Hospital for supportive counseling in the different weeks of the exercise.

e) Post-incident after care: Service for Individual Assistance (SIA) of the CMH

A benign atmosphere in the unit will support the working-through of the bereavement in most colleagues. A small group of survivors are at risk for the development of psychological difficulties which do not remit in the period of 4 to 8 weeks after the suicide. They may have pre-existing psychiatric conditions, may have been severely confronted 'at first hand' with the suicide or may have undergone secondary victimization. It is even possible that suicidal thoughts put individuals at risk of 'acting out'. The 'postvention trajectory of care' provides a continuity of care in the months after the event. Brief or long-term psychotherapeutic aid is provided for these victims. This psychotherapeutic aid can be cognitive-behavioral, client-centered, psycho-analytic or family system oriented. Psychiatric-pharmaceutical aid can also be provided.

3.3. Structure of the postvention crisis intervention procedure

A crisis intervention procedure developed well in advance of an incident is required to enable the aid providers to handle the crisis situation adequately. The procedure which is used for the 'postvention trajectory of care' in the CMH is based on the planification of psychosocial services in the Canadian emergency plans [7]

Step 1. Describe the incident
  – What happened and how did it happen?
  – Where did it happen and when did it happen?
  – Who was involved?

Step 2. Identification of the different target groups
  – How many people were involved?
  – Who are the victims and how were they involved?
    • Who were the primary victims (directly affected, cfr 4.3.2.b)?
    • Who were secondary victims (emotionally close to deceased, cfr 4.3.2.b)?
    • Who were the tertiary victims (personnel in coordinating, management and aid functions, cfr. 4.3.2.b)?

Step 3. Foresee the psychosocial impact on these target groups
  – Actual psychosocial impact, in the short, medium and in the long term
  – On a personal, familial and unit level as well as global society level

Step 4. Proactive evaluation of the psychosocial needs of the victims
  – Observe and listen for information on type, intensity and duration of reactions, ways of coping, degree of societal support, rumors and search for meaning.

- Collect factual information on the incident (+ reporting in press).
- Analyze and interpret the collective coping of the unit, the needs of the unit to be able to return to equilibrium.

Step 5.   Elaborate an intervention strategy
- Aimed at which target groups (primary, secondary, tertiary)?
- To address which psychosocial needs?
- When? How? By whom?
- In collaboration with which Unit Members (key personnel, Officers, NCO's, privates)?
- Where?
- When?

Step 6.   Evaluation of the capacity of the CMH to respond to the needs of the victims
- Which collaboration with other psycho-social aid providers is indicated?
  - Counsellors on Mental Operationality
  - Defence Social Services
  - Religious and Moral Services
  - Civilian Psychosocial aid providers
- Are the Human Resources of the aid providers sufficient?
- Are the Material Resources of the aid providers sufficient?

Step 7.   Evaluation of the intervention
Proactive but informal dialogue with key personnel and other service members of the unit, four to eight weeks after the suicide. Aim: to evaluate if the activities of the CMH helped the unit and its members to retrieve their pre-incident equilibrium. 'Face to face' or telephone dialogue is used to evaluate the efficacy of our postvention activities. Also a list of key words to evaluate our intervention and the psychological well-being in the unit can be used by the member of the CMH to ensure the standardization of our approach.

Step 8.   Re-evaluation of the psychosocial needs of the victims

4. Concluding remarks

Experience during preceding years indicated that service members confronted with the emotional demands of bereavement after the suicide of a colleague often did not attain the necessary provision of care. Boundaries between the different psycho-social aid providers, different procedures of care and an essentially passive approach hampered adequate psychosocial assistance.

The development of the 'postvention trajectory of care' has put forward a practice- and evidence-based, standardized and proactive approach in a climate of collaboration between the different psychosocial aid providers. A more effective, multi-disciplinary psychosocial assistance for service members after the suicide of a colleague is being provided. Professional continuity of care to prevent chronification of psychological difficulties after the suicide of a service member of the unit is put in place for the personnel of Belgian Defence.

References

[1] World Health Organisation (2007). Mental Health Programmes on Suicide Prevention. *Country Reports and Charts*. Retrieved September 15, 2007 , www.who.int/mental_health/prevention/suicide/coutry_reports/en/index.html.

[2] Parliamentary Questions,House of Representatives. (2006), Report on the incidence of suicide in Belgian Defence, *parliamentary questions and answers.* Retrieved September 15, 2007, www.dekamer.be/kvvcr/index.

[3] Cvinar, J.G. (2005). Do Suicide Survivors Suffer Social Stigma: A Review of the Literature, *Perspectives in Psychiatric Care,1, 14-21.*

[4] Van Heeringen .(2007). In Vlaanderen is er geen ruimte voor problemen. Alleen in Finland meer zelfdodingen dan bij ons. (There is no room for problems in Flanders. Only in Finland more suicides than in Flanders) *Journal 'Het Laatste Nieuws'.* Published on septembre 15-16 2007.

[5] Knieper, A. (1999). The survivor's grief and recovery. *Suicide and Life-Threatening Behavior, 29,* 353-364.

[6] Mitchell, J.T., Everly Jr, G.S. (1997). *Critical Incident Stress Debriefing, An Operations Manual for the Prevention of Traumatic Stress Among Emergency Services and Disaster Workers (2nd Ed.rev.).*Ellicott City, Maryland: Chevron Publishing Corporation.

[7] Gouvernement du Québec, Ministère de la Santé et des Services sociaux, Direction générale de la coordination régionale (1994). Planification des Services Psychosociaux dans le Cadre des Mesures d'Urgence. *Bibliothèque nationale du Québec.*

[8] American Psychiatric Association (2001). *Diagnostische Criteria van de DSM-IV-TR.* Lisse: Swets & Zeitlinger B.V.

[9] Brewin, C.R., Andrews, B., Valentine, J.D. (2000) Meta-Analysis of Risk Factors for Posttraumatic Stress Disorder in Trauma-Exposed Adults, *Journal of Consulting and Clinical Psychology, 68,* 748-766.

[10] Range, L.M. When a Loss is Due to Suicide : Unique Aspects of Bereavement. (1998). In Harvey J.H. (Ed.), *Perspectives on Loss, a Sourcebook* (pp. 213-220).Philadelphia: Brunner/Mazel.

[11] Miculinker, M., Florian, V. (1995).Appraisal of and Coping With a Real-Life Stressful Situation: The Contribution of Attachment Styles. *Personality and Social Psychology Bulletin, 21,* 406-413.

[12] National Institute of Mental Health (2002). *Mental Health and Mass Violence: Evidence-Based Early Psychological Intervention for Victims/Survivors of Mass Violence. A Workshop to Reach Consensus on Best Practices.* NIH Publication No. 02-5138, Washington, D.C.: US Government Printing Office.

[13] Dedic, G. (2007, 16 October). *Wounds of War: Lowering Suicide Risk in Returning Troops.* Presentation for NATO Advanced Research Workshop, Klopeiner See, Austria.

Lowering Suicide Risk in Returning Troops
B.K. Wiederhold (Ed.)
IOS Press, 2008
© 2008 IOS Press. All rights reserved.
doi:10.3233/978-1-58603-889-2-162

Understanding Combat Trauma – the Psychotherapeutic Meetings of Iraqi Veterans

Stanislaw ILNICKI [1], Sylwia DOBKOWSKA, Maciej ZBYSZEWSKI,
Radosław TWORUS, Piotr ILNICKI
*Department of Psychiatry and Combat Stress of the Military Institute
of the Medical Services, Warsaw, Poland*

Abstract. This article describes the process of the therapy in a group of Iraqi veterans, which took place in September, 2006. The psychotherapeutic meeting was organized by the Department of Psychiatry and Combat Stress in Warsaw. The group of veterans was composed of 16 male patients homogenous in age and ranking. During the meeting, the participants faced the opportunity to confront and to work through their traumatic experience.

The analysis of the interactions between participants showed an instant process of integration, creation of strong rules, and formation of three group leaders. Also, a change of attitude toward therapists (from disbelief to trust) occurred. The group rules were based on values such as loyalty and brotherhood transferred straight from the combat arena. Basic elements of group hierarchy were power of traumatic experience as well as range of damage.

The internal transformation of the participants took place during therapy. This resulted from death risk experience and working through the experienced trauma. Positive feedback and continuous contact with the clinic suggest that the veterans' problems call for psychotherapeutic treatment.

Keywords: combat trauma, PTSD, group therapy, veterans, Poland.

Introduction

The experience of combat trauma seemed to be quite a new question as there were not many studies describing problems of common soldiers in Poland [2-6]. The majority of the research concerning psychological issues amongst soldiers has focused on pre-deployment preparation as well as psychological support during the mission [4-8]. Relatively little research has been done on Posttraumatic Stress Disorder (PTSD) treatment post-deployment [5-9]. This situation called for intense investigation. The psychotherapeutic meeting, which took place September 5-15, 2006 in the Department of Psychiatry and Combat Stress (DPCS) of the Military Institute of the Medical Services in Warsaw, had been organized in order to give psychological support to Iraqi Polish Military Contingent (PMC) veterans. The veterans suffered different problems

---

[1] Corresponding Author: Stanisław Ilnicki, Department of Psychiatry and Combat Stress of the Military Institute of the Medical Services, ul. Szaserow 128, 00-909 Warszawa, Poland; E-mail: ilnickis@wim.mil.pl

after return from the mission. However, it was also the opportunity to learn what Polish troops think, feel and experience during a combat operation in Iraq.

The meeting lasted for 10 days. Sixteen of about 30 veterans, who primarily agreed to come for the meeting, took part in this enterprise. The group was homogenous in age, sex, ranking and trauma experience. Most of them were classified as injured by Military Medical Commissions. The others were waiting for the commission's verdict. See Figure 1.

Figure 1. The veterans of the Polish Military Contingent in Iraq – the participants of the psychotherapeutic meeting, September 5-15, 2006

1. Purposes

Organization of the meeting had two different purposes. The first dealt with diagnostic issues, while the second one was related to psychotherapy and psychological support. While pointing out diagnostic purposes, three questions should be mentioned. The first one is: what is the war experience of Polish troops taking part in military operations in Iraq who suffered from mental or physical combat damage? Next, we were interested in what kind of problems (aside from medical ones) actually bothered the veterans. We especially wanted to confront our conclusions with media information as this subject seems to be presented within the media context in a selective way. Finally we attempted to find out if any of the veterans suffered from any mental disorders, and if so, what were their character and range. Therapeutic purposes were focused on generating suitable psychological conditions which could enable veterans to cope with combat trauma symptoms. Moreover, we tried to check the efficacy of applying a group therapy model in combat trauma treatment.

2. Method and program

The staff included two psychologists, two psychiatrists, and two spectators. Therapeutic meeting contained different forms of psychological impact such as therapeutic community, integration meeting, projective art-therapy, and – having the key role – group therapy sessions. The program of therapy sessions was the authors' invention and was influenced by different theoretical models –both cognitive and psychodynamic [1]. Sessions were divided to different topical sections.   The psychologists were responsible for the psychotherapeutic process. The psychiatrists were engaged in psychoeducation and pharmacological support gaining much knowledge of PTSD during the experiments themselves [2,3]. The spectators were participating in therapy sessions and they were to record it by taking notes and using a voice recorder. However they did not sit within the group circle.

Introducing common breakfast to the every-day schedule was an additional factor which helps to integrate staff with participants. Aside from therapeutic meetings there were a few cultural events, like visiting a museum and the theater. Table 1 presents an exact schedule of the meeting. Meals and free time were skipped.

Table 1. The program of the meeting.

Day	Date	Subject
Tuesday	05.09	Opening of the meeting (Staff and participant presentation, discussing the program and Clinic regulations).
Wednesday	06.09	Integration meetings.
Thursday	07.09	Therapeutic community. Psycho-education meeting. Projective art therapy, integration meeting.
Friday	08.09	Therapeutic community, Therapy session, first topic: *Before mission.*
Saturday	09.09	Visiting Kings' Castle in Warsaw.
Sunday	10.09	Visiting the Polish Army Museum.
Monday	11.09.	Therapeutic community. Meeting with U.S.A. Ambassador and Minister of Defense. Therapy session, second topic: *Mission experiences.* Integration meetings: "Music, move, body".
Tuesday	12.09	Therapeutic community. Therapy session, second topic: *Mission experiences.* Integration meetings: "Music, move, body". Representative group of Polish Army performance.
Wednesday	13.09	Therapeutic community. Therapy session, third topic: *After comeback.* Integration meetings: "Music, move, body".
Thursday	14.09	Therapeutic community. Therapy session, third topic: *After comeback.* Projective art-therapy. Theatrical spectacle.
Friday	15.09	Summarizing meeting.

3. Therapeutic process

Most of the veterans suffered from many different symptoms typically related to combat stress. Some of these symptoms were declared by the participants just after arrival. The others could be observed during ten days of hospitalization. As they declared, they were bothered mostly by: irritability with uncontrolled aggression, sleep difficulties with nightmares, headaches, susceptibility to crying, alcohol or drug hunger and revenge fantasies with images of enemies' dead bodies. They also complained about the lack of hope of returning to normality and fear of social stigmatization and exclusion. In addition, we could observe strong dissociation symptoms; for instance, after sessions patients would smoke cigarettes together without speaking.

Most of the veterans had never had any experience with the psychiatric ward and psychotherapy before, so naturally they were expected to have a lot of fear. Indeed, when they came to the clinic, their lack of trust was evident. As they declared during the integration meeting, they were especially afraid of being treated like a guinea pig.

Equally, they worried about whether their problem would be accepted and appropriately understood. The following quote can describe this attitude: *Only a man who experienced a similar situation is able to understand it.* Finally, they were afraid that the meeting would not be used in order to help the following generations of veterans.

Aside from fears, the veterans had also a lot of hopes and expectations, which motivated them to take part in the meeting. What was very important is that they anticipated meeting their buddies from the same action. They also indicated openness, mutual regard and exchange of experience as significant factors of a successful meeting. The possibility of mutual help and working through the traumatic experience were their greatest hopes.

Patients' anxieties and expectations corresponded with the staff concerns. It was the first time we organized this kind of meeting. We were afraid that 16 male patients, restricted for 10 days, would not obey the regulations. Considering their mental state, the possibility of abusing alcohol would seem very probable. We also were concerned about lack of trust as the psychotherapists were civilians and one of them was a woman. Finally we were concerned the intensity of the trauma would disturb effective therapeutic work.

During the ten days of psychotherapeutic work we could observe phenomena which undoubtedly helped us to understand what had happened in Iraq. The most significant were the therapeutic process rate, creation of specific norms, and the structuralization of the group.

The group processes were surprisingly quick. The resistance period was very short, and the group was ready for real therapeutic work. At the same time the group started to integrate. Bonds between participants became really strong, and near the end of the meeting, one of the veterans even called them a family.

The group functioned in a very organized way. The norms created were obeyed with great respect. The norms were strong and specific. Mutual regard rapidly became an elementary rule. There was no disturbance when somebody was talking, all of the participants had time to tell about their experiences and express their feelings. There was almost no need for therapists to remind participants about the setting, because the group was so disciplined. The openness was one of the strongest rules. These patients, who were supposedly not telling all of the truth, were stigmatized.

However, the most impressive phenomenon referred to the transfer of values from the combat area to group functioning. Even the name "Brothers Company" (that was what the participants called themselves) showed the inherence of such values as loyalty, brotherhood and honor in the veterans' mentality. When observing group interactions one could see how the way of group functioning had resembled the way of functioning in the combat area. Openness in communicating difficult topics, courage in touching internal wounds and supporting weaker members were the best examples.

The crucial aspect of the group process was the leadership formation. What was interesting is that three different leaders had been formed. The first type of leader (we called him "the external leader") was responsible for communicating with the environment. He represented the group during meetings with people from the outside. The second type of leader (we called him "the internal leader") was a "norm guard". He was looking after whether the created norms were obeyed. He disciplined and consolidated the other participants and had a great influence on the whole group's attitude. Finally, the third type of leader (we called him "the emotional leader") was responsible for the atmosphere. He was supporting the others through letting them cry, and telling jokes and funny stories just to reduce the stress. The positions of all three leaders were very strong. Their impact on the group voice was indisputable.

The leadership formation was a part of group structuralization. It became quickly evident that every participant had a different group status. The position mostly depended on the injury range. Those who had been one step from death and suffered from serious wounds could expect much more respect. The leaders mentioned above experienced serious combat trauma which caused serious physical damage. During sessions they were often more active, especially in difficult situations from a life group perspective.

On the contrary, those participants who had not experienced physical wounds were marginalized and even excluded in one case. As was mentioned above, the rule of openness and telling the truth was strictly obeyed. After a few meetings it happened that one of the participants had broken both the openness and loyalty rules as he tried to show himself in a better light. The group noticed that. "The internal leader" summarized it: *There are some people who try to improve their status based on another's tragedy. I don't know how weak a person who is so shocked by a colleague's death despite not even being present during that must be. I think there is a great degree of falsity.* After these words the activity of the mentioned participant was systematically diminished and he soon became an outsider. We called this event a "deviant exclusion."

At the same time, the evolution in relationship between participants and therapists was occurring. At the beginning the participants came together with lack of trust and disbelief in therapy. It was followed by "a period of fight" when patients tried to change roles to occupy the therapist's place. However, as trust systematically grew, the veterans were finally able to talk about their painful and intimate matters. It even appeared like they were telling their secrets.

Therapeutic sessions developed with extreme tension and intensity as the veterans' stories were really emotionally appealing. The quotes below illustrate the intensity of the traumatic experiences:

Paul, 36 years old: *I raised my head and grabbed my gun. We were about to fight. I looked at my leg. I saw there was almost no leg, only some pieces of a man who was sitting in a puddle of blood. I couldn't feel any pain yet but I soon realized I was not okay. I saw my hand; all bones were on top. When I had recovered consciousness, I was thinking that I still had so many plans.*

Mark, 36 years old: *I felt a strong bang at my back. Before I realized what had happened to me I started to spin inertly. Then I realized I was under the wheels. Only one thought was occupying my head: hold your hands next to your body. In a moment I could hear some noise. Now I know there was a click of my broken bones, but then I did not know what it had been. (...) I realized that was my end (...) The thing I most regretted is I could not say goodbye to my family and friends because I was feeling my life was running out.*

This intensity could be easily observed in participants' behavior. During the ten days of the meeting the veterans were suffering from dissociation symptoms, sleep difficulties and increased frequency of nightmares. Moreover, there was one case of alcohol abuse, which could be identified as an acting out.

4. Discussion

The therapeutic work was supposed to help veterans react and work through the traumatic experience. Therapy sessions were divided into three topics so that the participants could organize their experience. As the sessions were emotionally touching, we met with strong reaction. Crying, swearing and leaving the meeting were the best examples. However, this effort was rewarded with sedation. The quote below pictures the process of reaction:

"I feel more comfortable, after I told about it, but it was hard, it is not easy. Especially because we are in a group where everybody is able to understand it. I feel some warmth within, despite that I am not calm inside".

Silencing the nerves seemed quite easy in comparison with the other symptom called "the survivor's sense of guilt". This symptom corresponded with experiencing strong trauma – losing a buddy. Telling about such events were always painful:

I am alive. The one who exchanged places with me was dead. He was young, inexperienced. Only young were dying over there (...) the face of the Buddy. The physician told me not to let him fall asleep. He held his head on my knees. He was looking all the time."

The survivor's sense of guilt must be treated as a chronic symptom. It surely requires long term therapy.

Perhaps the most impressive phenomenon was connected with working through the traumatic experience. There was a hard but fascinating way which began from a state of strong despair and depression and finished with the moment of transmitting the meaning of the trauma experienced. Either death's touch or physical disability originally caused the mental breakdown, but later, because of a perspective change, could lead even to recovering the meaning. Two quotes below illustrate working through the combat trauma:

Time cures the wounds. Once I valued my work the most, it was the most important thing, right before my family. Today it's the opposite: first family, afterwards long, long nothing, next - my work and the rest of the world. I'm even happy all these things happened - it made me realize many things. When a man has been given a second chance at life, he values it even more. We recognize real friends in real trouble. Those who I've been counting on let me down. Those who I didn't expect anything of helped me".

Many things in my life I can never do again. Those I can, I try to do very precisely and take as much pleasure as I can in it. Now I know how short and faint life is, I know that we should enjoy every day, because we never know if the next day ever comes. And sometimes, in order to appreciate life, we have to get a huge kick in our ass to realize, what in this life is really important."

During therapy it turned out that the ability to look at the problem through the group's perspective was a very important factor. Most of the participants at first were confident that their problems were the most upsetting and the most important. After listening to others' problems they often completely changed their attitude to their situation. It was evident that their situation needed to be appreciated.

In our opinion the therapeutic value of this meeting was considerable. Most of the participants came back home in much better form. Four of them were met with the proposal of long term hospitalization. When considering the structure of the meeting it seems that the homogenous group undoubtedly led to quick integration and strong attachments that encouraged the therapeutic success. On the other hand, this kind of a group was unlikely to take up the perspective of veterans' family members and especially the wives' perspective. This should be considered in the future.

When thinking about the meeting's value, the participants' opinions often converged with the authors' perspectives. First of all, they indicated the need of taking care of their families, but the most valuable thing was to building a family – like attachments.

Moreover, the possibility of seeing a buddy from the same action was a very important issue for them. They were satisfied that their effort can be useful in solving problems of other veterans. The appreciation of psychotherapy's impact should be mentioned too.

Figure 2. The participants of the psychotherapeutic meeting during planting of the memory tree

Conclusions

In summary, it must be admitted that the described meeting could be evaluated as a valuable initiative. Firstly, it showed what kind of problems the veterans have to cope with. When describing the range of their problems it must be emphasized that suicide risk is also included. Information obtained from such meetings could be very helpful both in academic work as well as in practical use in organizing aid for future veterans. Secondly, the meeting was helpful to understand what combat trauma really is. Taking the veterans perspective enabled us to help them diminish stress symptoms. What is more, it also turned out that the veterans were very gracious patients, with surprising openness to psychotherapy treatment. Finally, aside from the therapeutic value, the meeting had a great significance in diagnostic issues when considering combat stress assessment and treatment. Not only did it show the whole spectrum of combat trauma symptoms, but it also became evident that observed group phenomena, like the deviant exclusion, can also be helpful when assigning a diagnosis.

References

[1] J. Aleksandrowicz, Cz. Czabała, *Psychoterapia*. In: A. Bilikiewicz, S. Pużyński, J. Rybakowski, J. Wciórka (ed.), Psychiatria, vol. 3, Wydawnictwo Medyczne Urban & Partner, Wrocław 2003, 240.

[2] E.B Foa, T.M Keane, M.J. Friedman (ed.). (2000). *Effective Treatments for PTSD. Practice Guidelines from the International Society for Traumatic Stress Studies*. The Guilford Press, New York-London, 2000.

[3] Working Group VA/DoD, *Management of Post-Traumatic Stress. Clinical Practice Guideline*. Veterans Health Administration, Department of Veterans Affairs and Health Affairs, Department of Defense, Washington, DC, 2003.

[4] Glibowska, *Psychologiczne przygotowanie wojsk działających w warunkach trudnych i ekstremalnych*. In: O. Truszczyński et al. (ed.), *Służba żołnierzy i funkcjonariuszy służb państwowych wykonujących zadania w warunkach ekstremalnych*, Polskie Towarzystwo Naukowe Kultury Fizycznej, Warszawa, 2004, 85-93.

[5] S. Ilnicki, R. Tworus, M. Wiatr, *Problemy psychologiczne żołnierzy PKW w Iraku ewakuowanych przedterminowo z przyczyn zdrowotnych do kraju*. Ibidem, 167-171.

[6] L. Kosiorek, *Działalność psychoprofilaktyczna w I zmianie misji stabilizacyjnej Polskiego Kontyngentu Wojskowego w Republice Iraku. Doświadczenia i wnioski*. Ibidem, s. 34-40.

[7] J. Patoka, *Przygotowanie organizacyjne i merytoryczne wsparcia psychologicznego kolejnych polskich misji stabilizacyjnych*, Ibidem, s. 31-33.

[8] F. Potracki, *Przygotowanie organizacyjne i merytoryczne wsparcia psychologicznego kolejnych polskich zmian stabilizacyjnych*, Ibidem, 27-30.

[9] J. Wilk, A. Wiśniewski, *Przygotowanie i przebieg terapii żołnierzy dotkniętych zespołem stresu pola walki w Klinicznym Oddziale Psychiatrii 10 Wojskowego Szpitala Klinicznego w Bydgoszczy*, Ibidem, 110-115.

Section V

Increased Suicide with Co-Morbid Disorders

Lowering Suicide Risk in Returning Troops
B.K. Wiederhold (Ed.)
IOS Press, 2008
doi:10.3233/978-1-58603-889-2-173

Stress Events in a Month Before Suicide, Aggression and Impulsivity of Suicide Victims Relevant for Military Population

Peter PREGELJ[a,1], Martina TOMORI[a], Robert DOLNIČAR[b], Jože BALAŽIC[c], Tomaž ZUPANC[c]

[a]*University Psychiatric Hospital Ljubljana, Studenec 48, 1000 Ljubljana, Slovenia.*
[b]*Medical Center MORS, Štula b.š., 1000 Ljubljana, Slovenia*
[c]*Institute of Forensic medicine, Korytkova 2, 1000 Ljubljana, Slovenia.*

Abstract. Although military personnel are trained for combat and peacekeeping operations, accumulating evidence indicates that deployment-related exposure to stress events is associated with mental health problems and suicidal behaviour. Suicide accounted for substantial mortality among army personal and veterans. This data could be partially explained with observation that war-zone exposures may have considerable negative emotional or behaviour consequences. On the other hand, it is also well known that some personal characteristics as impulsivity and aggression could be connected with higher suicide risk. The extent to which violent and aggressive behaviour in the aftermath of deployment can be attributed to combat experience remains an area of debate and ongoing investigation. The aim of our study was to evaluate negative life events of suicide victims in a month before suicide. On the other hand, aggression and impulsivity of suicide victims was evaluated. In the three-year period, 90 suicide victims (28 women and 62 men) in the central region of Slovenia were examined using the method of psychological autopsy performed by specially designed questionnaire and from medical documentation. We compared a subgroup of suicide victims with previous aggressive behaviour and a subgroup of suicide victims without any previous reported aggressive behaviour. We observed that suicide victims with previous aggressive behaviour have higher a number of negative life events in the month before suicide and have higher impulsivity then others. We also observed that suicide victims with previous aggressive behaviour directed toward others have more often previous suicide attempts than suicide victims without previous aggressive behaviour. It could be concluded that negative life events of suicide victims with previous experience of aggressive behaviour may additionally contribute to increased suicide risk. In military environments, attention should be paid to such vulnerable individuals, especially during pre-deployment periods.

Keywords. Stress events, aggression, impulsivity, suicide victims, psychological autopsy, military personnel, deployment.

---
[1] To whom correspondence should be addressed; University Psychiatric Hospital, Studenec 48, 1260 Ljubljana, Slovenija, tel +38615872100, fax: +38615284618, e-mail: peter.pregelj@psih-klinika.si.

Introduction

Although military personnel are trained for combat and peacekeeping operations, accumulating evidence indicates that deployment-related exposure to stress events is associated with mental health problems and suicidal behaviour. The greatest challenge to the belief that social integration provides protection from suicide, however, comes from early observations such as Durkheim's data. It was officially reported that the highest rates of suicide were in the military, and it was concluded that the suicidal aptitude of soldiers is much higher than that of the civilian population of the same age [1]. Suicide accounted for substantial mortality among army personal and veterans [2, 3, 4, 5]. This data could be partially explained with observation that war-zone exposures may have considerable negative emotional or behaviour consequences. On the other hand, it is also well known that some personal characteristics such as impulsivity and aggression could be connected with higher suicide risk. The extent to which violent and aggressive behaviour in the aftermath of deployment can be attributed to combat experience remains an area of debate and ongoing investigation.

A better understanding of psychosocial characteristics of suicide victims and risk factors for suicide, as well as interconnections between known characteristics of suicide victims, is crucial for the design of suicide prevention programmes. Increasing amounts of data about suicidal behaviour indicate that suicide is familial [6]. The adoption study on suicide, performed in Denmark, compared the rates of suicide among biological and adoptive relatives of adoptees who committed suicide and in a matched living adoptee control group. The six-fold higher rate of suicide in the biological relatives of suicide adoptees and the absence of suicide among the adopted relatives of suicide versus control adoptees supports genetic rather than environmental effect [7].

Genetic associations between the death of a parent or a family member by suicide and increased suicide risk in their offspring were reported. Suicide rates have been shown to be twice as high in families with history of suicide as in families in which a suicide has not occurred [8]. It was determined by twin studies that up to 45% of the variance in suicidal ideation and behaviour may be attributable to genetic variables [9]. These data could be partially explained by hyporeactivity of the serotonergic system implicated in suicide and suicide attempts [10]. This decreased responsiveness of the serotonergic system has been hypothesized to implicate with impulsive and aggressive behaviour that in the coexistence with psychiatric illness and stressors, it makes an individual more prone to act on suicidal thoughts [11].

It was reported that a psychiatric disorder leading to hospitalization was the most prominent risk factor for suicide, and risk was extremely high for those recently discharged from the hospital [12]. Not only the family suicide history, but also the family psychiatric history, was reported to significantly increase the suicide risk [12]. However, it is also known that familial transmission of suicidal behaviour cannot be explained by the transmission of psychiatric disorder alone [6]. Several family studies of suicide and suicidal behaviour indicate transmission of suicidal behaviour even after controlling for the transmission of psychiatric disorder and for a proband diagnosis suggesting that familial transmission of suicidal behaviour may be mediated by the transmission of tendency to impulsive aggression [6]. High correlation between impulsivity and suicidality was reported [13, 14, 15]. Beside family history of suicide, presence of psychiatric disorders, and impulsive aggression, studies of suicide have identified a number of risk factors for suicide completion. These include previous suicide attempts, male sex, single marital status, unemployment, lower social class, substance abuse, physical illness, and family instability and abuse [16, 17, 18]. However, the relative importance and the magnitude of these effects, as well as differences in family history of suicide are poorly understood.

Standard method to assess psychopathology in suicide completers is the psychological autopsy [19]. The aim of our study was to compare main psychosocial characteristics in suicide victims with or without previous aggressive behaviour. Our special interest was to evaluate differences in the presence of psychiatric disorders, negative life events and impulsive aggression between subgroups of suicide victims with or without previous aggressive behaviour. The hypothesis is that suicide victims with previous aggressive behaviour have a higher number of negative life events before suicide and have expressed higher impulsivity and previous suicidal behaviour than others.

Methods

In the three-year period, 90 suicide victims in the central region of Slovenia were examined using the method of psychological autopsy performed by a specially designed questionnaire and from medical documentation. We compared a subgroup of suicide victims with previous aggressive behaviour and a subgroup of suicide victims without previous reported aggressive behaviour. All suicide cases were assessed on the basis of a notified consent from their relatives. By means of psychological autopsy, a specially designed questionnaire was carried out. Beside social demographic data, other information such as alcohol abuse, life events, previously suicidal, and aggressive behaviour was also gathered. In order to obtain the maximum amount of information and to decrease recall bias about the case and selective recall or selective forgetting, [19] we used one or two informants and evaluation of medical documentation when available. When data from the two sources did not match, the positive one (for dichotomous variable) or the higher value (in continuous variable) was selected and entered into the database. Altogether relatives of 212 suicide victims were asked to participate in the study. Relatives of the 90 suicide victims participated in the study. Twenty-seven female and 63 male suicide victims from the central part of Slovenia were included in the study during a three-year period (2004-2006). The study was approved by the Slovenian Ethical Committee. Data from the two sample subgroups (suicide victims with or without previous heteroaggressive behaviour) were compared. The subgroups did not differ significantly regarding gender or average age.

Statistical analyses

Demographic background of individuals in the sample was summarized by percentage, mean, and standard deviation. Statistical analyses were performed with SPSS for Windows (Chicago, USA). The two subgroups were compared (suicide victims with or without family history of suicide) non-parametrically by Chi-test and Fisher's exact test. T-test was employed for continuous variables. The level of statistical significance was set at $p=0.05$.

Results

Sample characteristics in general

The sample included 63 men and 27 women (90 altogether). The age range was 15-81 years, and the mean was 49.6 years (Figure 1). The majority, 81 (90%) victims were Slovenian nationality and were born in Slovenia, 9 (10%) victims were born in other parts of former Yugoslavia and were of other nationalities.

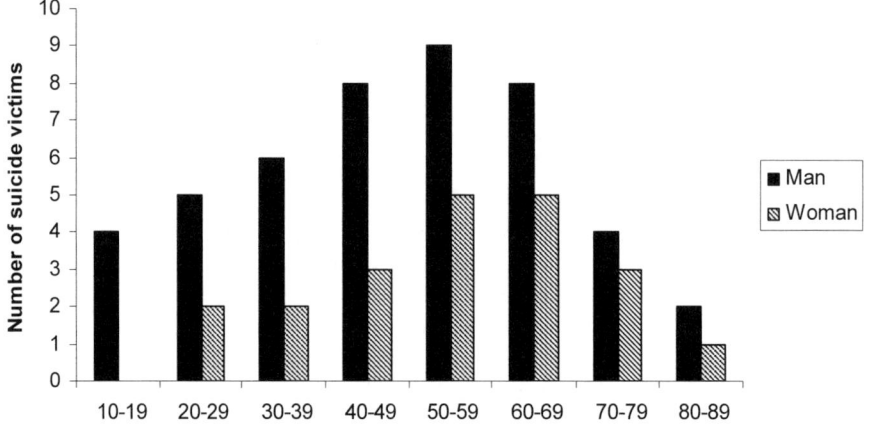

Figure 1. Sample characteristics in general – distribution by age and gender. Number of suicide victims in a separate age group is depicted for each gender. Black columns on the left hand side indicate data of male suicide victims. Lined columns on the right hand side indicate data of female suicide victims

Thirty (33%) were single, forty for (49%) married, fourteen (16%) divorced or widowed. Twenty two (24%) were employed, twenty (22%) unemployed, eight of them (9%) were students, thirty seven (41%) were retired and three victim were in the army. According to their religious believes the majority of victims (56) or (62%) belonged to the catholic religion, 24 or (27%) were not religious and 10 persons or (11%) belonged to other religions.

Table 1. General description of the sample of suicide victims.

		N	%
Gender	Male	63	70%
	Female	27	30%
Mean age		48,5	20,1
Marital status	Single	30	33%
	Married	44	49%
	Divorced or widowed	14	16%
Employment status	Employed	22	24%
	Unemployed	20	22%
	Student	8	9%
	Retired	37	41%
	Other	3	3%

Negative life events in a month before suicide

Private environment

Subgroups of suicide victims were significantly different in reported negative life events in a month before suicide ($p* < 0.05$). The share of suicide victims with reported negative life events connected with partnership was 52% for suicide victims with previous aggressive behaviour in comparison with 23% of suicide victims without previous aggressive behaviour. The difference was even higher regarding problems connected with the relationship with their children, 26% of suicide victims with previous aggressive behaviour have been reported to have problems with their children in comparison to 8% of the suicide victims without previous aggressive behaviour (Figure 2).

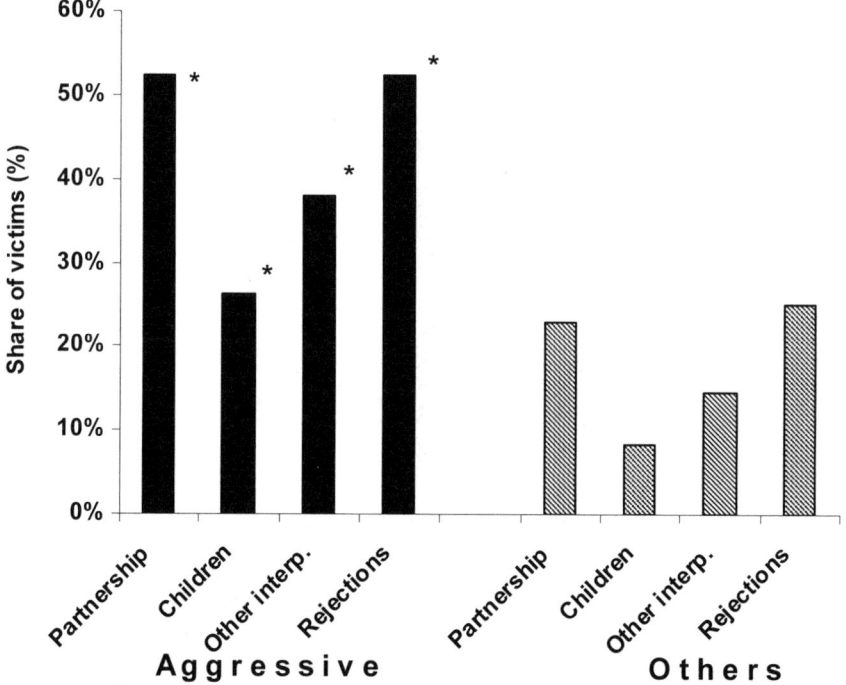

Figure 2. Reported negative life events connected with family or private environment in a month before suicide. Black columns on the left hand side indicate data of suicide victims with previous aggressive behaviour (N=42). Lined columns on the right hand side represent data of suicide victims without previous aggressive behaviour (N=48). Subgroups of suicide victims were significantly different in reported negative life events in a month before suicide ($p* < 0.05$). The share of suicide victims with reported negative life events connected with family or private environment was almost twice as high in the subgroup of suicide victims with previous aggressive behaviour (Aggressive) than in subgroup of suicide victims without previous aggressive behaviour (Other). Partnership – share of suicide victims in a subgroup with reported problems in partnership in a month before suicide, Children - share of suicide victims in a subgroup with reported problems with their children in a month before suicide, Other interp. - share of suicide victims in a subgroup with reported interpersonal problems not related with their working environment, Rejections - share of suicide victims in a subgroup with reported significant rejections by others in a month before suicide.

More than twice as often were reported negative life events regarding relationships with other persons in private life for suicide victims with aggressive behaviour (38% of them), in comparison to 15% of other suicide victims. The same was true for the reported significant rejections in relationships. Half of the suicide victims with previous aggressive behaviour have been reported to have significant rejections in relations with other persons in a month before suicide, and only one quarter of suicide victims in a subgroup without reported aggressive behaviour.

Working environment and finances

On the contrary to the negative life events connected to the private environment, we have not observed differences between subgroups of suicide victims with or without previous aggressive behaviour regarding negative life events connected with a working environment or with financial problems in the month before suicide (Figure 3).

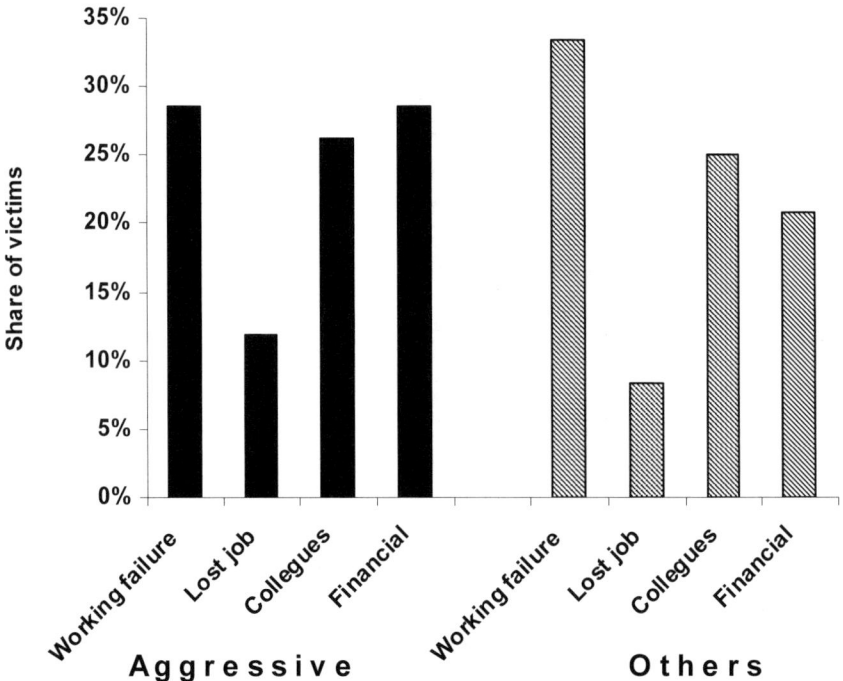

Figure 3. Reported negative life events connected with working environment and financial problems in a month before suicide. Black columns on the left hand side indicate data of suicide victims with previous aggressive behaviour (N=42). Lined columns on the right hand side represent data of suicide victims without previous aggressive behaviour (N=48). Subgroups of suicide victims were not significantly different in reported negative life events in a month before suicide. Aggressive - subgroup of suicide victims with previous aggressive behaviour, Other - subgroup of suicide victims without previous aggressive behaviour.

Previous suicidal behaviour

Suicide victims with or without previous aggressive behaviour were compared regarding previous reported suicidal behaviour. Subgroups of suicide victims differ significantly regarding share of suicide victims with previous reported suicide attempt. One third of suicide victims with previous aggressive behaviour have attempted suicide before suicide and 15% of those suicide victims without previous aggressive behaviour.

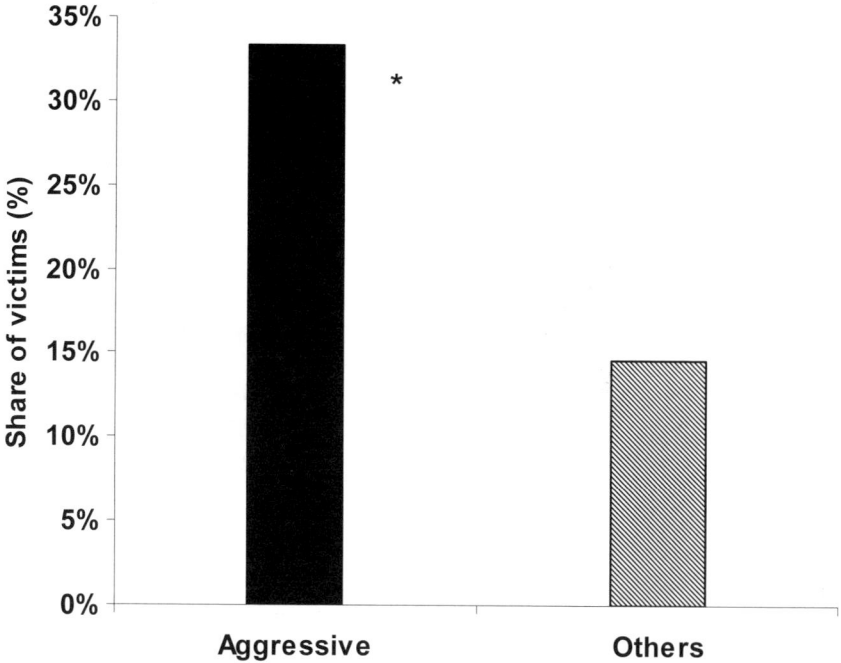

Figure 4. Previous suicidal behaviour of suicide victims. Black column on the left hand side indicates data of suicide victims with previous aggressive behaviour (N=42). Lined column on the right hand side represents data of suicide victims without previous aggressive behaviour (N=48). Subgroup of suicide victims with previous aggressive behaviour were reported to attempted suicide more often than suicide victims without previous aggressive behaviour (p*<0.05). Aggressive - subgroup of suicide victims with previous aggressive behaviour, Other - subgroup of suicide victims without previous aggressive behaviour.

Alcohol consumption and suicide methods

We have not observed the difference in alcohol consumption between subgroups of suicide victims with or without previous aggressive behaviour (p>0.05). Subgroups of suicide victims with or without previous aggressive behaviour were compared regarding used method of suicide. We have not observed differences between subgroups when separated violent from non-violent methods. The subgroups of suicide victims with or without previous aggressive behaviour also not differ regarding share of suicide victims in the subgroup with used firearms (Figure 5).

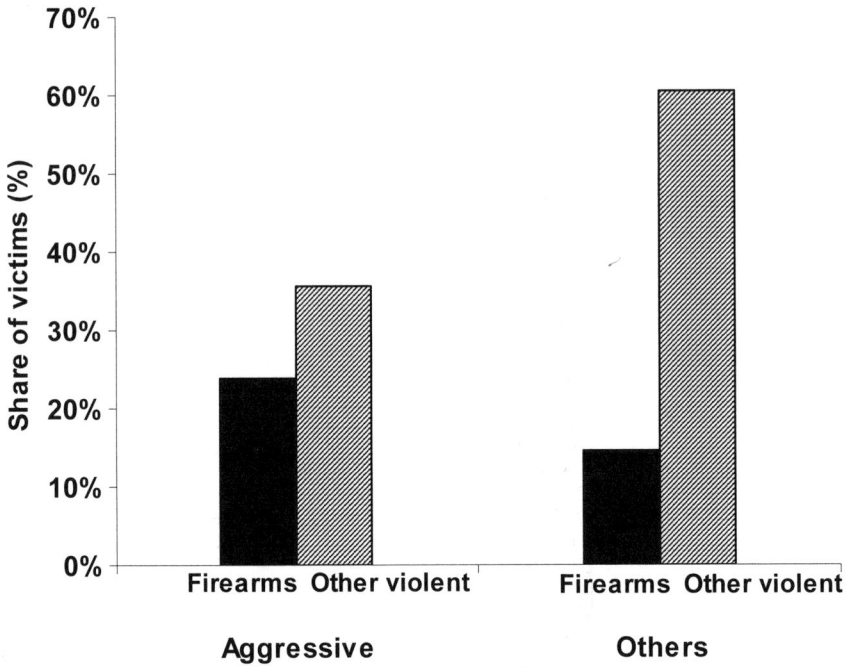

Figure 5. Violent suicide methods. The share of suicide victims regarding violent suicide methods and previous aggressive behaviour is depicted. Black columns on the left hand side indicate share of suicide victims used firearms as a method of suicide. Lined columns on the left hand side indicate share of suicide victims used other violent suicide methods. Differences in share of suicide victims used specific violent suicidal method were not observed between subgroups. Aggressive - subgroup of suicide victims with previous aggressive behaviour, Other - subgroup of suicide victims without previous aggressive behaviour. Firearms – firearms used as a suicide method, Other- violent – other violent suicide methods used.

Discussion

Research on suicide risk has suggested that aggression, hostility, and violence are important contributors to suicide risk [13, 14, 20]. Several studies have found a relationship between family loading for suicidal behaviour and aggression and anger in the proband or in the family of suicide victims [21, 22, 23, 24]. We observed that almost half of suicide victims had previous heteroagressive behaviour. On the other hand, stressful life events have a role in suicidal behaviour. It is known that stressful life events involving separation and rejection [25] and abusive relationships that may affect living conditions increase the risk of suicide [26, 27]. Clinical and non-clinical studies related to child maltreatment and its effects on psychopathology indicated that child abuse and neglect are correlated with suicidal behaviour in children, adolescents, and adults [28, 29]. Aggressive behaviour and stressful life events are relevant for military service, however, suicide risk could also be increased in the military because of access to weaponry, access to marksmanship training, and possible self-selection of more aggressive individuals [30]. In particular, it was reported that aggression is a possible suicide risk factor, particularly in young male subjects [22, 6]. On the contrary, it was also suggested in some research that military populations, despite consisting mainly of young men, are no more aggressive than the general population. [31] Others have suggested that military discipline or training may decrease expressed impulsivity [30]. However, lower suicide rates might be expected in the military, compared to individuals of similar age in the general population, because of the "healthy worker effect" [32], pre-enlistment selection or screening, and the structured, often supportive social environments in the military [32, 33]. To maintain battle fitness, military forces have well-developed medical services, which together with the cohesiveness of the organization, might be protective. However, we have not observed differences between subgroups of suicide victims with or without previous aggressive behaviour regarding negative life events connected with working environment or with financial problems in a month before suicide.

On the contrary, subgroups of suicide victims were significantly different in reported negative life events connected with a private life in a month before suicide (p*<0.05). The share of suicide victims with reported negative life events connected with partnership was two times higher for suicide victims with previous aggressive behaviour than in suicide victims without previous aggressive behaviour. The difference was even higher regarding problems connected with the relationship with their children. This data indicates that stressors in private life are often in suicide victims with previous aggressive behaviour in a period before suicide. These stressors are probably more difficult to control by the military authorities than stressors connected with a working environment.

Our data is in accordance with observations obtained when suicide victims were subdivided by the presence or absence of high levels of aggressive behaviour. They observed that the familial aggregation of suicidal behaviour was much greater in the first-degree relatives of aggressive versus non-aggressive suicide victims and nearly all the increased familial aggregation of suicidal behaviour was found in the relatives of aggressive suicide victims [22, 6]. It is important to account the alcohol misuse in investigations of the potential role of violence in suicide, as it is known that alcohol use disorders are strongly related to aggression [34] and suicide [35, 36]. Therefore, the apparent connection between violent behaviour and suicide may be misleading, attributable to high base rate of alcohol use disorders among suicide victims [27]. However, we have not observed the difference in alcohol consumption between subgroups of suicide victims with or without previous aggressive behaviour. Although subgroups differ regarding previous aggressive behaviour, we have not observed differences between subgroups regarding suicide methods either.

It was also reported that impulsivity correlated both with suicide and violence risk [37, 38]. Indeed, it was suggested that up to 45% of the variance in suicidal ideation and behaviour may be attributable to genetic variables [9] and decreased responsiveness of the serotonergic system could be implicated with impulsive, aggressive and suicidal behaviour [11]. We observed that subgroups of suicide victims with previous aggressive behaviour have more than two-times a higher share of suicide victims with a previous reported suicide attempt. One-third of suicide victims with previous aggressive behaviour have attempted suicide before suicide and 15% of those suicide victims without previous aggressive behaviour. This data indicates that heteroaggressive and autoaggressive behaviour could be observed in the same group of suicide victims. This data is in accordance with previous observations that suicidal behaviour has been found to cluster in families, since the rate of suicide is elevated in the families of attempters and the rate of attempted suicide is elevated in the families of suicide completers [39, 6]. However, it remains unclear as to what extent this can be explained by the familial clustering of other factors.

Limitations and Strengths of the study

One limitation of the study is that proxy interviews were used for suicide cases, which involves inherent risk for false negative attributable to memory effects, guilt feelings and the stigma of mental illness [40]. Both the interviewer and the informant were aware of the suicide outcome and certain associations might be anticipated that could lead to over reporting of some psychiatric symptoms. Second, there was no formal test of measurement reliability; however, only two interviewers made all interviews and there were no statistical differences in observed variables between subgroups of cases interviewed by each interviewer. The use of data from multiple sources, including psychiatric records, rendered our results less vulnerable to recall bias. A third limitation is that no adjustment was made for multiple comparisons. Fourth, some subgroups in our study were small. There was a risk of false negative findings attributable to low statistical power. Finally, we chose suicide victims without previous aggressive behaviour as a comparison group without population comparison subgroup. This data should be considered as preliminary. However, this is to our knowledge the first psychological autopsy study focusing specially on subgroup of suicide victims with previous aggressive behaviour of suicide in Slovenia.

Conclusions

The data indicates that stressors in private life are often in suicide victims with previous aggressive behaviour in a period before suicide. These stressors are probably more difficult to control by military authorities than stressors connected with a working environment, however, those in charge for leadership, supported by medical service, could address this issue.

References

[1]   E. Durkheim, Suicide: A Study in Sociology. Spaulding J, Simpson G, trans. Glencoe, Ill: The Free Press, 1951.
[2]   E.C. Ritchie, W.C. Keppler, J.M. Rothberg, Suicidal admissions in the United States military. Mil Med **168** (2003), 177–181.
[3]   N. Krupenik, Russian Army's suicide toll 22.7% of all casualties. Itar-Tass, 1999
[4]   Spooner MH: Suicide claiming more British Falkland veterans than fighting did. CMAJ **166** (2002), 1453.
[5]   R. Nelson, Suicide rates rise among soldiers in Iraq. Lancet **363** (2004), 300.
[6]   D.A. Brent, J.J. Mann, Family genetic studies, suicide, and suicide behavior. American Journal of Medical Genetics Part C **133C** (2005), 12-24.
[7]   F. Schulsinger, Biological psychopathology. Annual Review of Psychology **31** (1980), 583-606.
[8]   B. Runeson, M. Asberg, Family history of suicide among suicide victims. American Journal of Psychiatry **160** (2003), 1525-1526.
[9]   D.J. Statham, A.C. Health, P.A. Madden, et al., Suicidal behaviour an epidemiological and genetic study. Psychological Medicine **28** (1998), 839–855.

[10] J.J. Mann, D.A. Brent, V. Arango, The neurobiology and genetics of suicide and attempted suicide: a focus on the serotonergic system. Neuropsychopharmacology **24** (2001), 467-477.

[11] M. Kamali, M.A. Oquendo, J.J. Mann, Understanding the neurobiology of suicidal behaviour. Depression and Anxiety **14** (2001), 164–176.

[12] P. Qin, E. Agerbo, P.B. Mortensen, Suicide risk in relation to socioeconomic, demographic, psychiatric, and familial factors: a national register-based study of all suicides in Denmark, 1981-1997. American Journal of Psychiatry **160** (2003), 765-772.

[13] R. Plutchnik, H.M. Van Praag, H.R. Conte, et al., Correlates of suicide and violence risk 1: the suicide risk measure. Comprehensive Psychiatry **30** (1989a), 296-302.

[14] R. Plutchnik, H.M. Van Praag, H.R. Conte, Correlates of suicide and violence risk: III. A two-stage model of countervailing forces. Psychiatry Research **28** (1989b), 215-225.

[15] A. Apter, M. Kotler, S. Sevy, et al., Correlates of risk of suicide in violent and nonviolent psychiatric patients. American Journal of Psychiatry **148** (1991), 883-887.

[16] R.F. Diekstra, W. Gulbinat, The epidemiology of suicidal behaviour: a review of three continents. World Health Statistics Quarterly **46** (1993), 52-68.

[17] G. Turecki, Suicidal behavior: is there a genetic predisposition?. Bipolar Disorders **3** (2001), 335-349.

[18] F. Angst, H.H. Stassen, P.J Clayton, et al., Mortality of patients with mood disorders: follow-up over 34-38 years. Journal of Affective Disorders **68** (2002), 167-181.

[19] K. Hawton, L. Appleby, S. Platt, et al., The psychological autopsy approach to studying suicide: a review of methodological issues. Journal of Affective Disorders **50** (1998), 269-276.

[20] M. Kotler, G. Finkelstein, A. Molcho, et al., Correlates of suicide and violence risk in an inpatient population: coping styles and social support. Psychiatry Research **47** (1993), 281-290.

[21] P.H. Wender, S.S. Kety, D. Rosenthal, et al., Psychiatric disorders in the biological and adoptive families of adopted individuals with affective disorders. Archives of General Psychiatry **43** (1986), 923-929.

[22] D.A. Brent, J. Bridge, B.A. Johnson, et al., Suicidal behavior runs in families. A controlled family study of adolescent suicide victims. Archives of General Psychiatry **53** (1996), 1145-1152.

[23] B.A. Johnson, D.A. Brent, J. Bridge et al., The familial aggregation of adolescent suicide attempts. Acta Psychiatrica Scandinavica **97** (1998), 18-24.

[24] K. Hawton, C. Haw, K. Houston, et al., Family history of suicidal behaviour: prevalence and significance in deliberate self-harm patients. Acta Psychiatrica Scandinavica **106** (2002), 387-393.

[25] C.L. Rich, G.M. Warstadt, R.A. Nemiroff, et al., Suicide, stressors, and the life cycle. American Journal of Psychiatry **148** (1991), 524-527.

[26] J.E. Bailey, A.L. Kellermann, G.W. Somes, et al., Risk factors for violent death of women in the home. Archives of Internal Medicine **157** (1997), 777-782.

[27] K.R. Conner, C. Cox, P.R. Duberstein, et al., Violence, alcohol, and completed suicide: a case-control study. American Journal of Psychiatry **158** (2001), 1701-1705.

[28] J. Brown, P. Cohen, J.G. Johnson, et al., Childhood abuse and neglect: specificity of effects on adolescent and young adult depression and suicidality. Journal of American Academic Child and Adolescent Psychiatry **38** (1999), 1490-1496.

[29] A. Roy, Childhood trauma and suicidal behavior in male cocaine dependent patients. Suicide & life-threatening behavior **31** (2001), 194-196.

[30] M.A. Turner, L.A. Neal, Military forensic psychiatry (editorial). Br J Psychiatry **183** (2003), 10–11.

[31] J. McPherson, Forensic aspects of the armed forces, in Principles and Practice of Forensic Psychiatry. Edited by Bluglass R, Bowden P. London, Churchill Livingstone (1990), 13–96.

[32] L.M. Carpenter, Some observations on the healthy worker effect. Br J Indust Med **44** (1987), 289–291.

[33] J.M. Rothberg, P.T. Bartone, H.C. Holloway, D.H. Marlowe, Life and death in the US Army: in corpore sano. JAMA **264** (1990), 2241–2244.

[34] K. Graham, K.E. Leonard, R. Room, et al., Current directions in research on understanding and preventing intoxicated aggression. Addiction **93** (1998), 659-676.

[35] H.M. Inskip, E.C. Harris, B. Barraclough, Lifetime risk of suicide for affective disorder, alcoholism and schizophrenia. British Journal Psychiatry **172** (1998), 35-37.

[36] G.E. Murphy, R.D. Wetzel, The lifetime risk of suicide in alcoholism. Archives of General Psychiatry **47** (1990), 383-392.

[37] A. Apter, R. Plutchnik, H.M. Van Praag, Anxiety, impulsivity and depressed mood in relation to suicidal and violent behavior. Acta Psychiatrica Scandinavica **87** (1993), 1-5.

[38] N. Horesh, T. Rolnick, I. Iancu, et al., Anger, impulsivity and suicide risk. Psychotherapy and Psychosomatics **66** (1997), 92-96.

[39] D.A. Brent, J.A. Perper, G. Moritz, et al., Familial risk factors for adolescent suicide: a case-control study. Acta Psychiatrica Scandinavica **89** (1994), 52-58.

[40] B. Barraclough, J. Bunch, B. Nelson, et al., A hundred cases of suicide: clinical aspects. The British Journal of Psychiatry **125** (1974), 355-373.

Lowering Suicide Risk in Returning Troops
B.K. Wiederhold (Ed.)
IOS Press, 2008
doi:10.3233/978-1-58603-889-2-184

Virtual Reality as an Adjunct for Training and Treatment

Brenda K. Wiederhold, Ph.D., MBA, BCIA[1,2]
Mark D. Wiederhold, M.D., Ph.D., FACP[2]
[1] *Virtual Reality Medical Center, San Diego, CA, United States*
[2] *Virtual Reality Medical Institute, Brussels, Belgium*

Abstract. For more than a decade, virtual reality (VR) has had a significant impact on behavioral healthcare, permeating the field with its multiple effective uses. One area in which VR shines is providing a continuum of care for the military to treat wounded warfighters. The Interactive Media Institute and its affiliate the Virtual Reality Medical Center are funded to provide VR as an adjunct to traditional training and therapeutic applications.

Pre-deployment, VR-enhanced Stress Inoculation Training (SIT) can be used to provide troops (e.g. combat medics, flight medics, tactical forces) with skill sets to accomplish their tasks. The immersive nature of VR allows soldiers to experience a near real-life combat situation and the precise control VR enables users to practice their tasks repetitively in identical or varied situations, whichever the individual trainee requires. Stressors can be increased systematically so that the skills learned can be performed under increasingly anxiety-provoking situations.

This creates soldiers who are better able to perform under the most demanding conditions. In addition, these virtual combat situations evoke physiological responses, creating the opportunity for troops to practice managing their stress reactions to high pressure or dangerous situations. It is hoped that this repetition and practice will produce soldiers who are more competent and resilient. Post-deployment, VR exposure can augment traditional cognitive-behavioral therapy protocols for treating Posttraumatic Stress Disorder (PTSD). While working with both active duty and veteran populations, it appears that VR exposure may be more effective in providing the individual with an environment in which he/she can stop the avoidance- often a hallmark of PTSD. In a VR environment, the individual is transported back into a wartime setting and can slowly and systematically begin to consolidate the fragmented memories in order to allow emotional processing to occur and desensitization to be achieved.

Finally, VR is being successfully used as an adjunct to traditional treatments for those with both chronic and acute pain, and for help in rehabilitating those who have sustained physical, cognitive or neurological injuries.

Keywords: Virtual Reality, Stress Inoculation Training, Posttraumatic Stress Disorder, Pain, Rehabilitation, Military

Corresponding Author: Brenda K. Wiederhold, Ph.D., MBA, BCIA; Virtual Reality Medical Center, 6155 Cornerstone Court East, Suite 210; San Diego, CA 92121; (858) 642-0267; Virtual Reality Medical Institute, 28/7 Rue de la Loi, 1040 Brussels, Belgium, +32 2 286 8505, bwiederhold@vrphobia.com

Background

Untreated depression is the number one cause of suicide. Many service members returning from Iraq have experienced depression or more severe Post Traumatic Stress Disorder (PTSD). It is estimated that 1 out of every 6 returning American service members will develop some form of depression. This is a treatable condition.

The Virtual Reality Medical Center (VRMC) and its partner organizations have been working for the past decade to apply our clinical virtual reality (VR) expertise to a full range of military troop support. We are currently conducting Stress Inoculation Training (SIT), Posttraumatic Stress Disorder (PTSD) treatment, rehabilitation therapy, and pain distraction techniques for the United States military, resulting in a program that provides a *continuum of care* for troops. The aim of this program is to treat and prevent the psychological and physical wounds of war that often lead to severe reactions such as severe depression and even suicide in veterans. Because of initial successes and promising results, these programs are now being extended to help address the needs of coalition forces in both NATO and partner countries.

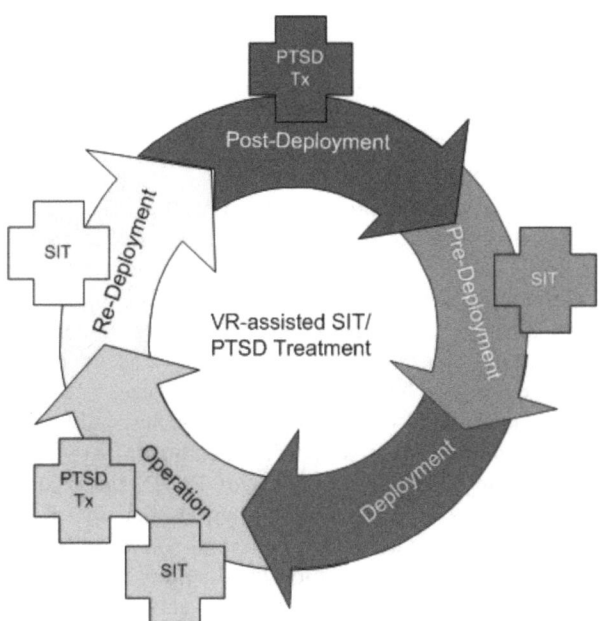

Figure 1. VRMC's continuum of care model for troops

According to the National Institutes of Health, PTSD affects an estimated 5.2 million Americans in any given year, often resulting in a diminished quality of life and considerable emotional suffering. The current rate of PTSD among Army and Marine Corps troops returning from duty in Iraq is approximately 19%. Military experts believe the rate is still increasing. A continuing upward trend seems especially likely given the unique nature of the terrain and combat situations in the Iraq theater. According to recent reports, the number of Iraq War soldiers who will experience PTSD is higher than the Gulf War due to such factors as ground combat and extended deployments [1]. The distress caused by PTSD symptoms, especially if left untreated, can lead to anxiety, depression, and even suicide. Clearly, PTSD is a significant health threat for military personnel. Learning to treat, or even prevent, this disorder is crucial to maintaining healthy troops and military families. At the VRMC we employ VR with the goal of providing effective tools for both pre- and post-deployment.

As pre-deployment tools, we have developed VR-enhanced SIT and virtual environment tactical training to:

1.   Effectively teach military personnel tactical and trauma care skills.
2.   To enable them to practice stress management techniques with the intent to improve performance during real-life combat situations.

In a simulated environment, situations with an extremely high stress level and a cognitive load not often encountered in real life can be created. These scenarios, combined with physiological monitoring and expert instruction, give military personnel the tools they need to learn to better handle stress through techniques such as breathing retraining and relaxation. In this way, simulation can help them achieve both job specific skills proficiency training and more general stress hardening skills, which develops more proficient and resilient troops.

For those soldiers who do not have access to VR SIT pre-deployment or for whom pre-deployment training was not sufficient to prevent PTSD, we have developed and tested VR therapy environments for post-deployment use. By placing a patient with combat-related PTSD in a virtual war setting, having him or her carefully experience that situation in a controlled way, the patient is able to begin habituation to his or her specific PTSD symptoms, reappraising the instigating situation. This graded and targeted exposure allows emotional processing to fully occur, in turn reducing PTSD symptoms and the distress and hopelessness that they cause.

Several years ago Shipherd, Beck, Hamblen, Lackner, and Freeman [2] discovered that Cognitive Behavioral Therapy (CBT) treatments targeted solely at PTSD symptoms not only improved the symptoms of PTSD, but also improved patients' functioning in regard to pain. This finding suggests that the treatment of PTSD in general may extend to alleviate other symptoms (such as depression and pain), eliminating the need for direct intervention to solve those problems, thereby reducing the likelihood that a veteran would commit a drastic act (e.g. suicide, bodily harm).

The VRMC has developed VR systems to help distract patients from the acute pain of medical procedures and the chronic pain of longer-term injuries such as amputations. The immersive and interactive nature of VR engages the full attention of users, leaving little attention left to focus on sensing pain. As pain has been found to be a largely attentional sensation, VR has proven to be effective at reducing pain in both acute and chronic situations.

Finally, aside from pain, many war-related injuries may require physical, cognitive and neurorehabilitation. Here, again, VR can play a major role. Researchers at VRMC are testing the possibilities VR offers to make rehabilitation processes more effective and efficient. The interactivity of VR alleviates the monotony and unpleasantness of traditional rehabilitation regimens. In addition, the ability to purposefully add and subtract stimuli from virtual environments allows therapists to customize VR treatments to each patient's specific cognitive needs and abilities, reducing the time, and in turn the cost, of rehabilitation therapy.

By using VR to enhance training, treatment, pain distraction, and rehabilitation, VR works to alleviate and treat symptoms of many wounds of war, both physical and mental. Through these pre- and post-deployment VR interventions, we hope to help prevent severe reactions to combat stress, such as suicide.

1. Virtual Reality for Training

Stress Inoculation Training (SIT) is a type of training used to prepare individuals for anxiety-provoking situations, diminishing the potential for a negative psychological reaction. In CBT, SIT is accomplished through gradual, controlled, and repeated exposure to a stressor. The goal behind this exposure is to desensitize or "inoculate" the person against the stimuli that would otherwise cause panic or a "fight or flight" response. This repeated exposure allows the individual to calmly and accurately accomplish the tasks at hand while in a stressful environment. Developed in the late 1970s by Donald Meichenbaum, SIT was originally designed for use with multiple populations. Since SIT is a technique to help harden individuals to future potentially traumatizing events, it also makes intuitive sense to use this method to help train those in the military.

Deployed personnel must often perform in extremely stressful environments, and optimum performance under such conditions requires effective management of physiological, psychological, and emotional responses to stressful stimuli. An acute stress reaction (ASR) or combat and operational stress reaction (COSR) can occur during exposure to exceptionally stressful events like those encountered in combat, resulting in extreme sympathetic nervous system arousal and impaired performance. Longer term reactions to these situations can include acute stress disorder and PTSD. During VR-enhanced preventative SIT, military personnel "experience" highly stressful situations in a virtual environment. Repeated exposure enables performers to gradually become desensitized to stimuli that may initially elicit such strong physiological arousal that performance is impeded (i.e., "freezing in the line of fire"), and therefore psychological trauma should be less likely.

SIT is intended both to create more effective troops and to help prevent or reduce rates of PTSD in returning troops. There is existing evidence that SIT can reduce PTSD. In a 2000 study by Deahl et al., a group of 106 male British soldiers preparing for a 6-month tour of duty in Bosnia received a combination of pre-deployment stress training and post-deployment psychological debriefing. After deployment, participants demonstrated a drastically reduced incidence of PTSD and other psychopathology as compared to controls, approximately one-tenth that of figures reported from other military samples. In fact, the level was so low that it precluded any possible debriefing effect.

In 2005, VRMC completed a three-year study sponsored by the Defense Advanced Research Projects Agency (DARPA), which proved the effectiveness of a low-fidelity laptop simulator to train military personnel. Phase I results (n=8) indicated that those trained in a VR simulation while having stressors added (being shot at while tending to the wounded) were able to perform skills more effectively in the test phase of the study when compared to those trained in a "sterile" VR environment (no one shooting at them while tending to the wounded). Participants who trained under stress scored significantly higher in the test phase while those who trained in the sterile environment were pulled off task, which caused mistakes to be made ("patients died"). In addition, physiological monitoring showed that those who trained under stress remained relatively calm and relaxed in the test phase while the stress indicators of those who trained in a sterile environment rebounded to near-initial levels. Physiological indices indicated that individuals were unaware when they were becoming too physiologically aroused and perhaps not in the optimum training or performance state. Investigators were also able to see changes in heart rate, brain wave activity, and skin conductance that correlated with peak performance [3].

In Phase II of the DARPA study, 970 participants were drawn from a combination of elite units of the U.S. Navy, Marine Corps, and Coast Guard. The objectives of the investigation were to examine the effectiveness of VR training simulators to teach military personnel tactical and trauma care skills, enable personnel to practice stress management techniques, and to improve troop performance during real-life combat situations. The test group first received training in a virtual combat scenario while their stress and arousal levels were measured with non-invasive physiological monitoring. The control group did not receive virtual training. Afterward, all participants were tested in a real-world version of this same combat scenario to determine the effectiveness of training in a virtual environment.

Significant transfer of skills from virtual to real world exercises was demonstrated through standard, objective performance measures and after-action analysis of video by subject matter experts. The study proved VR training to be an extremely effective and efficient method of preparing military personnel for combat situations.

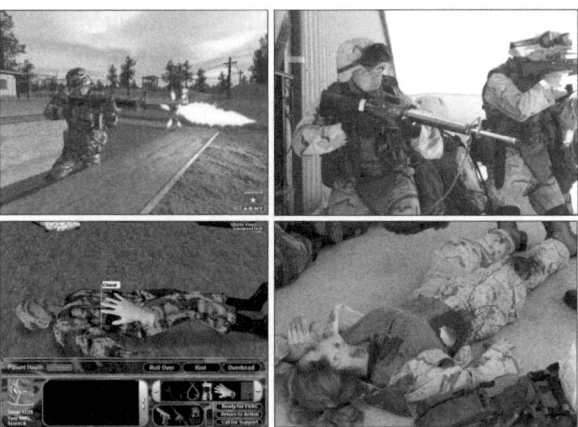

Figure 2. Participants practice in VR and then transfer of skills is tested in a realistic setting prior to deployment.

VRMC has also provided VR SIT training systems for the U.S. Army's Aeromedical personnel at Fort Rucker, Alabama. Data was collected during training (n = 63-75), and trainees will now be tracked once they return from deployment. Preliminary findings with a sample of 25 medics suggest that those who learned coping techniques during the VR training exhibited lower levels of stress than the control group [4]. Uses for the data may include:

1. Studying the relationship between physiological arousal and performance outcomes;
2. Evaluating adjunctive training techniques (such as relaxation training) to manage physiological arousal and enhance performance;
3. Longitudinal tracking of physiological levels during training to determine the fidelity of the relationship between blood pressure/heart rate and combat operational stress reactions (COSRs) and PTSD, which could eventually act as a predictive tool for screening troops before they are deployed [5-7].

In addition to decreasing stress, SIT for military personnel is designed to improve performance. Training under stressful conditions pre-deployment improves performance by first teaching personnel to recognize signs of physiological and emotional arousal and secondly, educating them on how to control their stress levels. In our ongoing SIT studies, we train military personnel in virtual environments such as an Iraqi village, a shoot house, or a ship. These simulations can be viewed on desktops, laptops, through a head-mounted display (HMD), or as a 3-wall CAVE (computer automatic virtual environment) projection system, depending on the needs of the specific population to be trained. This training is then transferred to real-world exercises in structures designed specifically for tactical training. This ensures a transfer of training from virtual to real world, with remediation if skills have not been learned sufficiently.

The VRMC is currently conducting a study funded by the U.S. Army's Telemedicine and Advanced Technology Research Center (TATRC), to test the efficacy of virtual reality video game (VRVG) training in preparing combat medics for real-life combative medical scenarios. The purpose of the VRVG is to provide an inexpensive training tool that will allow medics to experience situations outside of their everyday training. The game tests the medics' knowledge of medicine, combat training skills, and ability to function under the pressure of a battlefield situation. The VRVG contains virtual scenarios of terrain that the medics are not able to experience in their current real-world training. The game also allows medics to learn from their mistakes and repeat scenarios until they successfully complete a task, building confidence and skill mastery.

In summary, as studies indicate, aside from SIT for general skill education and hardening, VR can also be used for tactical training in elite populations such as combat medics, flight medics, law enforcement, and the coast guard. VR allows stimuli to be presented in a systematic, controlled fashion, and data from physiological monitoring provides objective evidence of instances when stimuli are eliciting appropriate stress responses from the trainee. This knowledge enables training to be individualized to each user, focusing on those specific parts of the experience with which the individual needs the most improvement. By understanding how each user is reacting during training, the simulation can then be modified to add or subtract stressors as would be appropriate to the situation [8]. For example, quick mastery of a scenario can be followed-up with a more challenging mission, and physiological indicators that the participant is too overwhelmed to learn can be adjusted by reducing stressors until the trainee is again prepared to move forward. Combining subjective ratings, physiological data, personality type, and self-report questionnaire scores with expert clinical observations makes it possible to further refine and improve clinical and research-based protocols.

2. Virtual Reality for Stress Management

Virtual reality and other advanced technologies are increasingly being used as tools for stress management. The portability of high-tech gadgets enables people to carry treatment programs with them into potentially stressful situations. For example, soldiers may carry specially programmed PDAs into battle, enabling them to assess their stress levels while deployed and obtain advice and reminders about how to manage their stress as they fulfill their duties. Civilians, too, are able to carry assessment and treatment programs on their cell phones or Palm Pilots to help them manage their stress. Whether people encounter stressful situations at work, or find themselves facing a feared situation elsewhere in their lives, they can turn to these programs for distraction, or more importantly, for help remembering their coping skills [9].

3. Virtual Reality for Treatment

As previously discussed, deployment stress is a serious (and growing) problem. The long-term form of combat stress, PTSD, has a negative impact upon return-to- duty rates and health care costs. It is a disabling, often chronic problem, which frequently results in poor treatment outcomes and disability payments to PTSD-diagnosed veterans that may continue for years, if not decades. It also may reduce quality of life, not only for the veteran, but his family and extended community as well. In short, PTSD can result in negative ramifications for society as a whole.

The Diagnostic and Statistical Manual IV-TR (DMS-IV TR) classifies PTSD as a heterogeneous disorder that develops following exposure to traumatic events (e.g. seriously injury, threat of injury, death). Symptoms of PTSD, which persist for at least one month, include increased anxiety or arousal, dissociation, avoidance of stimuli associated with the trauma, numbing of general responsiveness, and flashbacks to the traumatic experience [10]. Both anxiety-reducing medication as well as CBT can help in recovery.

However, these types of traditional therapies do not have acceptable recovery rates. Front-line antidepressant medications for the disorder—such as selective serotonin reuptake inhibitors—rarely yield better than a 40% reduction in Clinician Administered PTSD Scale (CAPS) scores, and most patients will still meet criteria for PTSD at the end of an adequate treatment trial [11]. Regarding traditional psychotherapy, based on a meta-analysis published in 2005, only 44% of all those who enter treatment will be classified as improved at the end of the treatment period [12].

Prior to the availability of VR therapy applications, the existing standard of care for PTSD was imaginal exposure therapy, in which patients "relive" the traumatic event in a graded and repeated process [13]. Exposure therapy is based on emotional processing theory (EPT). Applying EPT to PTSD, fear memories are stored as a "fear structure" and include psychological and physiological information concerning those stimuli, their meaning, and the patient's previous responses (Foa & Kozak, 1986) [14]. Once accessed and emotionally engaged, the structure is open to modification through CBT and, over time, will result in extinction of the fear response.

Although exposure therapy has been shown to be effective [15, 16], one hallmark of PTSD is avoiding reminders of the trauma [13]. Because of this, many patients are unable or unwilling to effectively visualize the traumatic event during imaginal therapy. In studies that address treatment non-responders, failure to engage emotionally or visualize well enough to elicit an emotional response are cited as most predictive of non-response to treatment, since the fear structure is not accessed during therapy and is therefore not open to change [17 -19].

This is where VR can step in to enhance treatment. In recent years, VR has been shown to improve treatment efficacy for PTSD in survivors of many types of trauma, including victims of motor vehicle accidents, war veterans, and those involved in the 9/11 World Trade Center attacks [13, 16, 20-22]. By placing people with PTSD in an environment where a trauma has occurred (in veterans it could be a virtual combat setting), and then having them slowly experience that situation in a controlled way, the patient may begin to habituate to their PTSD symptoms and come to reappraise the instigating situation. This allows emotional processing to occur, and thus frees PTSD sufferers from their intrusive memories and disturbing symptoms.

With its inherent immersive nature, VR overcomes many of the shortcomings of imaginal exposure. VR provides external visual and auditory stimuli for the patient, thus eliminating the need for intense imagination skills. And, unlike in vivo therapy, which takes the patient into real-world scenarios (which is not practical or even possible with war veterans), VR permits the patient to interact with anxiety-inducing scenarios in the safety and confidentiality of the therapy room. The patient's ability to exert initial control over the situation (e.g. deciding to go to therapy, controlling the level of anxiety they are willing to experience) also seems a safer, more tolerable starting point for many. In VR exposure therapy the therapist and patient, in their therapeutic alliance, create a hierarchy of anxiety-inducing situations. These situations can then be recreated in VR under the therapist's control. Audio and visual stimuli can be added and subtracted to create the exact "dosage" required for treatment. In addition, both the patient and therapist can determine the duration and intensity of treatment, creating a safe environment in which the patient can re-process his/her fear. Moreover, multiple exposures can be completed during a single therapy session, making for more efficient time usage and reduction of costs [16].

In research funded by the Office of Naval Research (ONR), we have begun to explore whether exposure therapy for PTSD-diagnosed troops using a CBT approach is more effective when enhanced with VR. VRMC graphic designers and software developers created a Virtual Baghdad environment as a clinical therapy aid for military personnel with PTSD. The Virtual Baghdad environment is an immersive, highly realistic environment in which users can freely navigate the terrain and interact with virtual people. The virtual world, which can be viewed on a laptop computer or with a head-mounted display (HMD), features a market, a battlefield (with a car, helicopter, humvee, and explosions), a battalion aid station, and houses. The environment is comprised of sights and sounds, such as Arabic prayer from a temple, helicopters thundering overhead, distant explosions, vehicles burning, terrorists running while firing guns, and the voices of Iraqi civilians. Based on interviews with a population of Marine and Navy personnel recently diagnosed with combat-related PTSD and receiving treatment, we found that these were some of the most salient memories they associate with recurring, intrusive thoughts [23]. This information enabled us to make a VR environment based on end-user input.

Figure 3. One computer allows the therapist to control stimuli with the touch of a button to increase or decrease arousal experienced by the participant. A second computer shows exactly what the participant is seeing inside the head-mounted display. A third computer allows the therapist to see in real-time the physiological indices of the participant.

Project completion participants will include 136 US Navy Seabees and medical personnel who have acute PTSD stemming from combat exposure. Outcome measures focus on the general symptom categories targeted by exposure therapy, such as re-experiencing traumatic memories, avoidance of these memories, and physiological arousal. Due to the intense nature of the VR treatment, troops' mental status is monitored closely by the lead psychologist as well as a staff psychiatrist and assessed during every visit for suicide risk. In addition, an on-call person is available 24 hours a day to address any problems troops experience during treatment, and all patients are given a "survival plan" at the onset of treatment.

Under this research grant, the system is being tested at Balboa Naval Hospital and Camp Pendleton in California. Initial pilot testing of the system indicates that VR therapy produces both subjective (self-report) and objective (physiological) arousal in individuals suffering from PTSD. In our previously reported first case study of a soldier undergoing VR-enhanced cognitive behavioral therapy with this system positive results were obtained. At the end of 10 treatment sessions, the patient scored below the PCL-

M "strict" criteria for a PTSD diagnosis [24]. Data from the first six treatment completers is also promising [25].

In a second study funded by ONR, we are using this same Virtual Baghdad environment during Stress Inoculation Training (SIT) protocols to determine if providing stress-hardening skills prior to deployment can decrease incidence of PTSD in returning troops.

In a prior project, funded by the Telemedicine and Technology Research Center (TATRC), VRMC shipped a VR system to Iraq. There, the system was tested and valuable user feedback was obtained for further system development and improvement. Feedback indicates that in-country clinicians would appreciate the ability to use a VR PTSD tool as part of an early intervention protocol. Having the end user as a participant in the development loop has always been an essential part of system development at VRMC and a part of patient success in overcoming their disorders.

Current SIT and PTSD U.S. customers include the U.S. Army, U.S. Navy, and Department of Veterans Affairs which has systems currently in place in 8 facilities around the U.S. VRMC does not, however, limit its training and treatment systems to use in the United States. Our first overseas customer was the Military Institute of the Health Services in Krakow, Poland. Currently, Poland has the second largest number of troops in Iraq of all of the strategic allies. Research suggests that the rate of PTSD among Polish troops may be similar to or even higher than that of U.S. troops. It is our hope that the VR training program we recently established in Poland will allow the medical providers in Poland to more effectively help their soldiers by incorporating this tool into their established treatment program. We also hope this will further lend itself to the clinical investigation of the system's cross-cultural effectiveness. A second system is being installed in Zagreb, Croatia in early 2008. Negotiations to install VRMC's PTSD treatment systems are currently under way with a number of other NATO and Partner countries.

4. VR for Physical, Cognitive, and Neurorehabilitation

The rehabilitation process is designed to restore a patient's physical, sensory, and/or mental capabilities which have been lost due to injury, illness, or disease. *Physical* rehabilitation is the process of restoring a patient's lost function through hands-on treatment, exercise, and patient education. *Cognitive* rehabilitation is a structured set of therapeutic activities designed to retrain an individual's ability to think, use judgment, and make decisions. *Neuro*rehabilitation is working to re-establish a person's ability to function following a disabling injury or illness that has affected the brain and/or spinal cord.

War veterans with combat injuries often require significant treatment and rehabilitation, and this can be a strain on both economic and health care resources. Rehabilitation is among the largest sectors of healthcare costs in the United States. Total treatment expenditures are growing rapidly due to the aging of the United States population, as well as to higher rates of battle-related injury. As of August 2005, it was estimated that over 12,500 U.S. troops had been wounded in Iraq, and because of advances in protective armor and battlefield medical care, more of these military personnel are surviving their wounds. While saving the lives of wounded troops is certainly top priority, it does mean that more people with amputated limbs, traumatic brain injury, and other physical and cognitive injuries are returning to the U.S. for rehabilitation and treatment. The long term care of thousands of wounded veterans promises to be a huge expense [26].

This tremendous cost to the healthcare system generates an immediate need for new clinical approaches to both improve the efficacy and efficiency of rehabilitation techniques and reduce the total cost of such treatment. Recent improvements in technology now make it possible to develop portable home rehabilitation systems that have the potential to dramatically improve rehabilitation outcomes for neurological and musculoskeletal injuries, while reducing overall rehabilitation costs by decreasing the need for in-person treatment [27, 28].

Nonetheless, even when the hurdle of expense is removed, rehabilitation treatments are often less effective because they are painful or tedious. Frustration with ineffective rehabilitation, loss of daily functioning ability, and continuing pain and other symptoms due to combat injuries can also cause depression and more severe psychological and behavioral reactions, such as suicide. However, there are ways to improve motivation and treatment efficacy in rehabilitation in hopes of preventing these drastic actions.

In order to make rehabilitation regimens less monotonous and more engaging, we have begun to use VR to enhance traditional rehabilitation methods. There are many reasons why VR applications are effective for rehabilitation. First, VR is an interactive, experiential medium. VR users become directly engaged with the virtual experience. If a patient is being asked to kick his leg to block a virtual soccer ball, this is much more engaging than simply extending the leg over and over again. Case by case reactions even indicate that VR can make rehabilitation "fun." By increasing the motivation and enthusiasm for a patient's compliance with rehabilitation therapy, VR becomes an advantageous addition to traditional therapy for patients. Due to its immersive and interactive qualities, VR has the potential to help achieve the compliance necessary for effective rehabilitation.

Beyond this, VR creates a safe setting where patients can explore and act without feeling threatened [29]. Patients can make mistakes without fear of dangerous, real, or humiliating consequences [30]. Moreover, unlike human trainers, computers are infinitely patient and consistent [30]. In this way, VR and other advanced technologies can serve as a method for objectively tracking performance improvements over the course of rehabilitation therapy.

4.1. Physical Rehabilitation

As of June 30, 2007, the U.S. Department of Defense reported 1,005 individuals deployed to Iraq or Afghanistan who are amputees, of whom 708 suffered major limb amputations (Congressional Research Service Reports). Many more veterans have suffered less severe injuries that will require physical rehabilitation for recovery of important daily functions. In motor rehabilitation, VR offers significant advantages over traditional therapy alone. First, VR creates a safe, controlled environment for repetitive practice, and repetitive practice is crucial when learning motor tasks. Second, VR provides immediate, real-time feedback about performance.

For example, several studies have demonstrated that rehabilitation gains can be achieved using VR and other advanced technologies. In one study, seven post-stroke elderly patients undergoing physical rehabilitation therapy for a weak arm interacted with a virtual environment using a Sony PlayStation II EyeToy™. Researchers encouraged patients to use their weak arms when interacting with the games in the VE.

By the end of the experiment, two chronic stroke patients had succeeded in using their weak arm to clean the left side of a virtual window. All of the patients reported that they had enjoyed the experience [31].

VR in this context consists of off-the-shelf kinesthetic video games, such as Sony's Eyetoy™, Dance Dance Revolution and Taiko Drum Master. Kinesthetic video games focus on the player's body movements for input and control instead of a traditional joystick or controller. For example, Sony's EyeToy™ contains soccer, window washing, and dancing scenarios that require the user to use arm and body movements to block balls, eliminate spots on a window, or complete specific dance moves. Dance Dance Revolution utilizes a game pad and asks users to step on specific areas of the pad at certain times in a type of choreographed dance that engages both the body and the mind. Taiko Drum Master is played by hitting the drum peripheral in time with notes traveling across the screen. Tasks increase in difficulty from single notes, to drum rolls, to different rhythms and speeds.

The body and arm movements required to play these games encourage improvement in balance, strength and range of motion. Due to the nature of kinesthetic video games, it is conceivable to use them for physical therapy in order to make treatment sessions more comfortable and entertaining, in turn making them less tedious and improving patient compliance.

Our preliminary research results based on subjective questionnaires and functional capacity indicate that the experimental condition may elicit increased heart rate and respiration, insinuating that this group is working harder during treatment sessions than the control [32]. Participants in the experimental group also seem to enjoy the music and interaction made possible through VR. These results suggest that VR may enhance the rehabilitation process, creating a more effective form of treatment. Long-term benefits of this form of treatment may include improved treatment time and reduced dropout rates, therefore reducing the economic costs of rehabilitation. Side benefits may include a reduction in depression, often found at increased levels in troops who have suffered physical injuries or amputations.

The successful history of using simulation technology for rehabilitation of injuries has created a significant opportunity to apply these new treatment paradigms to those injured in the Iraq War and other conflicts worldwide. While these technologies will have immediate benefit for injured military personnel, their development will also serve to catalyze improvement and change within clinical rehabilitation at large. VR may indeed help create a more enjoyable and effective method of rehabilitating patients with war-induced injuries than the current paradigm.

4.2. Cognitive Rehabilitation

Advanced technologies and VR can provide important advantages in cognitive rehabilitation as well. VR can be manipulated in ways that the real world cannot. For example, VR can be used with patients with little or no language capabilities. It can convey rules and abstract concepts with images and sound. The near real-world environments provided through VR can be used for vocational training and as a way to train cognitive tasks in brain damaged patients [30]. Studies have even shown VR to be effective in patients with Alzheimer's disease. A study by Hofmann et al. [33] asked ten patients suffering from mild to moderate Alzheimer's disease to move through a virtual environment that simulated pictures of the patient's typical surroundings, home or usual shopping route, and photographs of the patient at an earlier age. Results indicated that after three weeks of training, patients could perform the task more quickly and needed less help navigating the environment. In addition, eight out of the ten patients made fewer mistakes.

VRMC is developing advanced computer-assisted rehabilitation systems specifically designed to improve the treatment of the physical and cognitive injuries resulting from battle-related trauma. By employing recent advances in simulation and measurement technology, as well as improved rehabilitation paradigms that leverage the brain's ability to relearn after an injury (neuroplasticity), it is possible to bring next-generation rehabilitation technology to bear upon the immediate needs of injured military personnel. The long-term benefit of this project will be the development and deployment of advanced rehabilitation technologies and strategies. While these technologies will have immediate benefit for injured military personnel, their development will also serve to catalyze improvement and change within clinical rehabilitation at large.

4.3. Neurorehabilitation

Along with PTSD, Traumatic Brain Injury (TBI) is being called one of the signature wounds of the Iraq War. A recent study found that 88% of military personnel treated at an echelon II medical unit in Iraq had been injured by IEDs or mortar [34]. Most are caused by the pressure wave from blasts from Improvised Explosive Devises or other explosives. While penetrating head injuries are easily diagnosed, TBI (especially mild TBI) is invisible, and much harder to diagnose and treat. Symptoms may be vague and can mimic other disorders. However, the impairment experienced by TBI sufferers can affect memory, speech, and activities of daily living. Once diagnosed with TBI, rehabilitation exercises are essential for recovery.

To improve the diagnosis process VRMC has been funded to develop and test a portable VR system that can assess cognitive ability at baseline and after exposure to a blast. VRMC will develop VR-based tests of cognitive ability which will ultimately be administered to troops at the beginning of their deployment, establishing individual baseline data that can be compared with data collected from the same person should he/she experience a blast injury. These VR assessments are not only convenient in their portability, but they can be completed in less than 10 minutes (compared with up to two hours for a pen and pencil test) and reliably detect symptoms of TBI.

The same system, in a second phase of development, provides "serious video games" that will restore cognitive function in troops diagnosed with mild to moderate TBI. Working with the University of Central Florida (UCF), VRMC has begun the development of a haptics-enhanced true 3D stereo mixed reality system designed to stimulate and improve cognitive functions in troops who suffer from TBI. The ultimate goal is to provide a cost-effective mixed reality tool that is rugged and portable enough to be used in the field. Using this product, troops suffering from TBI caused by blasts can be immediately diagnosed and undergo effective and inexpensive cognitive rehabilitation with the goal of allowing them to return to service.

5. Virtual Reality for Pain Distraction and Reduction

Due to combat injuries and fatigue, veterans are often saddled with chronic pain, which can result in disability. In fact, these veterans are much more likely (15%-35%) to experience PTSD than those without chronic pain (2%). Outside of the military, a 1992 study found that 50% of patients with chronic pain after a motor vehicle accident developed PTSD [35], and a more recent study found that 51% of patients with chronic lower back pain had PTSD [36]. The same combination of pain and stress occurs in deployed personnel. It is thought that the pain may serve as a constant reminder of the traumatic event, exacerbating PTSD symptoms. In addition, studies show that up to 100% of patients with chronic pain tend to be clinically depressed. Therefore, it is necessary to treat both physical and mental wounds of war to prevent severe reactions such as suicide. Moreover, due to the possible link between pain and the development of PTSD, the efficacy of pain reduction treatments during medical procedures and recovery should be considered.

In the past, medication has been the conventional solution to alleviating pain during medical procedures; however, in many instances, utilizing solely medications does not provide optimal results. Once again, this is where VR can help.

Many studies have found VR to be effective as a technique to distract patients from experiencing pain [37]. The immersive nature of VR allows virtual reality environments to distract patients undergoing various medical procedures in ways that go above and beyond other techniques. To start, the 360 degree field of view in a HMD effectively blocks out any visual or auditory stimuli related to a medical setting. In addition, the interaction inherent in VR engages the patient's mind, leaving him little, if any, attention to dedicate to sensing pain.

VR has been found to be effective in reducing reported pain and distress in patients undergoing burn wound care, chemotherapy, dental procedures, venipuncture, ambulatory surgery and many other painful procedures by drawing attention away from the patients' mental processing, thereby decreasing the amount of pain they consciously experienced.

At VRMC, we have developed several interventions for pain distraction. The first was a National Institute on Drug Abuse funded study to create a system to distract patients from pain during dental procedures, including replacement of crowns, fillings, root canals, and cosmetic dental work. Overall, dental patients using the VR system reported a reduction in the level of discomfort and pain while exploring the interactive virtual worlds. Another significant finding was that seven out of ten patients estimated their time in the virtual environment while undergoing the procedure to be significantly less than the actual time spent under procedure. This indicates that time perception is altered during VR distraction, reducing the amount of time patients experience pain [37].

A second study conducted by VRMC at the pain clinic at Balboa Naval Hospital involved six patients with both acute and chronic pain. Each participant experienced two sessions: a pain focus session and a VR session in a virtual environment called Icy Cool World. Both physiological measurements and subjective pain ratings were recorded. The results showed that the participants' peripheral skin temperature was significantly higher during the VR session (indicating physiological relaxation), and pain ratings were significantly lower during the VR session (indicating a 75% reduction in perceived pain). These findings support the idea that VR distraction works to reduce both chronic and acute pain [37].

In addition, VRMC is working with several public health hospitals in Mexico City to decrease pain during and after invasive surgical procedures [38]. Displaying a variety of virtual environments in head-mounted displays, researchers were able to test pain reduction effects in more than 300 participants ranging from 2 days to 70 years of age, male and female. Invasive procedures addressed have included upper gastrointestinal endoscope, infectious surgery, colonoscopy, labor and delivery, caesarean surgery, neonatology critical care unit (CCU), post surgical care, CCU of heart, kidney transplant CCU, epidural block, and ambulatory surgery.

Patient distress was found to be different with each procedure, but the three groups who benefited most from VR exposure were patients in post surgical critical care unit of the heart, colonoscopy, and ambulatory surgery. The degree of pain relief depends on disease, sex, age, and anatomical region manipulated during the procedure. VR was found to work best for patients who accept and can concentrate during hospitalization or manipulation in medical or surgical procedures. One impressive benefit of VR is that the necessary dosage of medication was greatly reduced in patients who used VR. Patients did not have to be put under general anesthesia, which allows a significant decrease in the risk and costs of the procedure.

In ongoing studies at University of Wuerzburg, Germany, we are collaborating with researchers to understand what impact, if any, the content of the virtual world has on pain perception. This will, again, allow more effective worlds to be developed for patient care (Mühlberger et al, 2007) [39].

Though it is unlikely that troops will be using VR for dental work any time soon, the principles of this and other studies on using VR for pain distraction can be applied to a military population. For example, patients with phantom limb pain, a frequently debilitating symptom among amputees, have responded to the application of VR technology. Professor Jonathan Cole of the Poole Hospital, University of Bournesmouth, and the University of Southampton in the United Kingdom, reported on the use of virtual environments for the alleviation of phantom limb pain [40]. The enhancement of missing-limb perception through the use of VR technology has been effective in alleviating phantom limb pain, while at the same time permitting a much greater perceptual range of absent limb motion.

This is merely the start of what VR can do to decrease pain in the military population. It is hoped that by developing these systems to alleviate pain in military personnel, we may be able to avoid or attenuate the frustration, depression, and anxiety symptoms associated with acute and chronic pain, therefore preventing troops from committing acts of desperation, such as ending their lives.

Conclusion

Decades after the first simulators were used to train fighter pilots, advanced technologies and simulations are impacting military medicine. It has been shown that VR and other advanced technologies can play a significant role in increasing the efficacy and efficiency of medical treatment for military personnel. It is our goal to develop and continually improve systems that can be integrated into a continuum of care for troops. Pre-deployment, this can involve SIT and stress management education. During deployment, these applications can be used to assess mental health disorders and alleviate physical and emotional suffering in wounded troops. Post-deployment, VR can help veterans return to normal life, whether that involves treatment for stress reactions like PTSD, physical rehabilitation for injuries such as amputation or soft tissue damage, cognitive and neurorehabilitation for brain injuries, or pain management. It is our hope that this continuum of care will help prevent suffering in veterans and their families, and will ultimately help reduce the suicide rate in returning troops.

References

[1] Litz, B.T. (2004) (Ed). Early Intervention for Trauma and Traumatic Loss. New York: Guilford Publications.

[2] Shipherd, J.C., Beck, J.G., Hamblen, J.L., Lackner, J.M., and Freeman, J.B. (2003). "A preliminary examination of treatment for posttraumatic stress disorder in chronic pain patients: a case study." J Trauma Stress. 16(5): 451-7.

[3] Wiederhold, M.D., & Wiederhold, B.K. (2004b). Training Combat Medics Using VR. CyberTherapy 2004. January 10-12, 2004, San Diego, CA.

[4] Stetz, M. C., Long, C. P., Schober, W. V., Cardillo, C. G., & Wildzunas, R. M. (2007). Stress Assessment and Management while Medics Take Care of the VR Wounded. In B.K. Wiederhold, S. Bouchard & G. Riva (Eds.), Annual Review of CyberTherapy and Telemedicine (pp. 165-172). San Diego: Interactive Media Institute.

[5] Stetz, M. C., Wildzunas, R. M., Wiederhold, B. K., Stetz, T. A., & Hunt, M.P. (2006a). The Usefulness of Virtual Reality Stress Inoculation Training for Military Medical Females: A Pilot Study. In B.K. Wiederhold, S. Bouchard & G. Riva (Eds.), Annual Review of CyberTherapy and Telemedicine (pp. 51-58). San Diego: Interactive Media Institute.

[6] Stetz, M. C. (2007). Flight Medics' Virtual Reality Training to Enhance Performance under Combat Stress. Presented at Medicine Meets Virtual Reality 15, Long Beach, California.

[7] Stetz, M.C., Thomas, M.L., Russo, M.B., Stetz, T.A., Wildzunas, R.M., McDonald, J.J., Wiederhold, B.K., & Romano, J.A. Jr. (2007). Stress, mental health, and cognition: a brief review of relationships and countermeasures. Aviation, Space, and Environmental Medicine, 78(5 Suppl), B252-260.

[8] Wiederhold, B.K., Bullinger, A.H., Wiederhold, M.D. (2006). "Advanced technologies in military medicine." In J.J. Roy (Ed.), Novel Approaches to the Diagnosis and Treatment of Posttraumatic Stress Disorder. Amsterdam: IOS Press, 148-160.

[9] Riva, G., Grassi, A., Villani, D., Gaggioi, A., & Preziosa, A. (2007), Managing exam stress using UMTS phones: the advantage of portable audio/video support. Stud Health Technol Inform., 125: 406-8.

[10] American Psychiatric Association 2000. *(DSM-IV-TR) Diagnostic and statistical manual of mental disorders*, 4th edition, text revision. Washington, DC: American Psychiatric Press, Inc.

[11] Hamner MB, Robert S, Frueh BC. (2004). "Treatment resistant posttraumatic stress disorder: Strategies for intervention. CNS Spectrums, 9(10):740-752.

[12] Bradley, R., Greene, J., Russ, E., Dutra, L., and Westen, D. (2005). "A multidimensional meta-analysis of psychotherapy for PTSD." Am J Psychiatry, 162(2): 214-27.

[13] Difede, J., and Hoffman, H.G. (2002). "Virtual reality exposure therapy for World Trade Center Post-traumatic Stress Disorder: a case report." CyberPsychology & Behavior, 5(6): 529-35.

[14] Foa, E.B., & Kozak, M.J. (1986). Emotional processing of fear: Exposure to corrective information. *Psychological Bulletin*, 99, 20-35.

[15] Laor, N., Wolmer, L., Wiener, Z., Reiss, A., Muller, U., Weizman, R. & Ron, S. (1998). "The function of image control in the psychophysiology of posttraumatic stress disorder." Journal of Traumatic Stress, 11, 679-696.

[16] Wiederhold, B.K. & Wiederhold, M.D. (2004). "Virtual Reality Therapy for Anxiety Disorders." American Psychological Association Press.

[17] Jaycox, L.H., Foa, E.B., Morral, A.R. "Influence of emotional engagement and habituation on exposure therapy for PTSD." J Consult Clin Psychol, 66(1): 185-92.

[18] Kosslyn, S.M., Brunn, J., Cave, K.R., and Wallach, R.W. (1984). "Individual differences in mental imagery ability: a computational analysis." Cognition, 18(1-3):195-243.

[19] Van Etten, M.L., and Taylor, S. (1998). "Comparative efficacy of treatments for post-traumatic stress disorder: a meta-analysis" Clinical Psychology & Psychotherapy, 5(3): 126-144.

[20] Rothbaum, B.O., Hodges, L., Alarcon, R., Ready, D., et al. (1999). "Virtual reality exposure therapy for PTSD Vietnam Veterans: a case study. J Trauma Stress, 12(2): 263-71.

[21] Walshe, D.G., Lewis, E.J., Kim, S.I., O'Sullivan, K., and Wiederhold, B.K. (2003). "Exploring the use of computer games and virtual reality in exposure therapy for fear of driving following a motor vehicle accident." CyberPsychology & Behavior, 6(3):329-34.

[22] Wiederhold B.K. & Wiederhold M.D. (2000). "Lessons learned from 600 Virtual Reality Sessions." CyberPsychology & Behavior, 3(3): 393-400.

[23] Spira, J.L., Pyne, J.M., Wiederhold, B.K. (2006). Experiential methods in the treatment of combat PTSD. In C.R. Figley & W.P. Nash (Eds), For Those Who Bore the Battle: Combat Stress Injury Theory, Research, and Management. New York: Routledge.

[24] Wood, D.P., Murphy, J., Center, K., McLay, R., Reeves, D., Pyne, J., Shilling, R., & Wiederhold, B.K. (2007). "Combat related posttraumatic stress disorder: A case report using virtual reality exposure therapy with physiological monitoring." CyberPsychology & Behavior, 10(2), 309-315.

[25] Wood, D.P., Murphy, J.A., Center, K.B., Russ, C., McLay, R.N., Reeves, D., Pyne, J., Shilling, R., Hagan J., & Wiederhold, B.K. (2008). Combat Related Post Traumatic Stress Disorder: A Multiple Case Report Using Virtual Reality Graded Exposure Therapy with Physiological Monitoring. In Medicine Meets Virtual Reality 16 (pp. 556-561). Amsterdam: IOS Press.

[26] Glasser, R.J. (2005), A ware of disabilities: Iraq's hidden costs are coming home, Harper's Magazine, http://uslaboragainstwar.org/article.php?id=8862.

[27] Hoenig, H., Sanford, J.A., Butterfield, T., Griffiths, P.C., et al. (2006). "Development of a teletechnology protocol for in-home rehabilitation." J Rehabil Res Dev, 43(2):287-98.

[28] Sugarman, H., Dayan, E., Weisel-Eichler, A., Tiran, J. (2006). "The Jerusalem TeleRehabilitation System, a new low-cost, haptic rehabilitation approach." CyberPsychology and Behavior, 9(2), pp. 178-182.

[29] Riva, G. (2005), "Virtual Reality in Psychotherapy: Review." CyberPsychology & Behavior, 8(3): 220-230.

[30] Standen, P.J., & Brown, D.J. (2005). "Virtual Reality in the Rehabilitation of People with Intellectual Disabilities: Review." CyberPsychology & Behavior, 8(3): 272-282.

[31] Rand, D., Kizony, R., & Weiss, P.L. (2004). "Virtual reality rehabilitation for all: Vivid GX versus Sony PlayStation II EyeToy." "Proceedings of the 5th International Conference on Disabilities, Virtual Reality, & Associated Technologies, Oxford, UK, Sept. 18-20, 2004, pp. 87–94.

[32] Wiederhold, B.K., & Wiederhold, M.D. (2006). "Evaluation of Virtual Reality Therapy in Augmenting the Physical and Cognitive Rehabilitation of War Veterans." International Journal on Disability and Human Development. 5(3), 211-215.

[33] Hofmann, M., Rosler, A., Schwarz, W., Müller-Spahn, F., Kräuchi, K. Hock, C., et al. (2003). "Interactive computer training as a therapeutic tool in Alzheimer's disease, Comprehensive Psychiatry, 44, 213-219.

[34] Murray, C.K., Reynolds, J.C., Schroeder, J.M., et al. 2005. Spectrum of care provided at an Echelon II medical unit during Operation Iraqi Freedom. Military Medicine. 2005, 170: 516-520.

[35] Hickling, E.J., & Blanchard, E.B. (1997). "The private practice psychologist and manual-based treatments: post-traumatic stress disorder secondary to motor vehicle accidents." Behav Res Ther, 35(3): 191-203.

[36] DeCarvalho, L.T. (2003). "Predictors of posttraumatic stress disorder symptom severity level in chronic low back pain patients." Dissertation Abstracts International- B, 64/08, p. 4030.

[37] Wiederhold, M.D., & Wiederhold, B.K. (2007). Virtual reality and interactive simulation for pain distraction. Pain Medicine, 8(S3), S182–S188.

[38] Mosso, J.L., Rizzo, S., Wiederhold, B., Lara, V., et al. (2007). "Cybertherapy—new applications for discomfort reductions. Surgical care unit of heart, neonatology care unit, transplant kidney care unit, delivery room-cesarean surgery and ambulatory surgery, 27 case reports." Stud Health Technol Inform, 125:334-6.

[39] Mühlberger, A., Wieser, M. J., Kenntner-Mabiala, R., Pauli, P. & Wiederhold, B. K. (2007). Pain modulation during drives through cold and hot virtual environments. CyberPsychology & Behavior, 10(4), 516-522.

[40] Gallagher, S. (2004). "Nailing the lie: An interview with Jonathan Cole." Journal of Consciousness Studies, 11(2), pp. 3-21.

Subject Index

Lowering Suicide Risk in Returning Troops
B.K. Wiederhold (Ed.)
IOS Press, 2008

Author Index